for Young Actors

DATE DUE

FEB 14 2004			
GAYLORD			PRINTED IN U.S.A

For
Zoa Jensen
and
Larry Capo
and
Gordon Ostrowski

Great Scenes
for Young Actors

· · ·

V O L U M E   I I

Edited by
Craig Slaight and Jack Sharrar

YOUNG ACTORS SERIES

A Smith and Kraus Book

808.82
GRE
Cop. 1 – V. II
 # 15.00
1/00

A Smith and Kraus Book
Published by Smith and Kraus, Inc.
PO Box 127, Lyme, NH 03768

Copyright ©1998 by Smith and Kraus
All rights reserved
Manufactured in the United States of America
Cover and Book Design by Julia Hill

First Edition: September 1998
10 9 8 7 6 5 4 3 2

The Library of Congress Cataloging-In-Publication Data

Prepared by Quality Books Inc.

Great Scenes for Young Actors Volume II /

Craig Slaight, Jack Sharrar, editors. —

p.   cm.   — (Young actors series)

Includes bibliographical references.

ISBN 1-57525-107-8

1. Drama—Collections. 2. Acting.

I. Slaight, Craig, 1951– II. Sharrar, Jack, 1949–

PN2080   808.82

91-60869

Contents

. . .

Scenes for One Female and One Male

Scenes for Two Females

Scenes for Two Males

Scenes for Groups

Introduction

•   •   •

In this second volume of scenes for young actors, we are happy to present an exciting collection of material—much of it from contemporary plays—which we believe will provide you with worthy challenges for continuing actor training.

As with our previous volumes, we have selected material that is representative of the broad spectrum of life experience—material that will take you out of yourself and propel you into the lives of characters that you, perhaps, would never have encountered except through the artistry of a playwright. And, in keeping with our philosophy, the material we have included all looks at life from the perspective of young people.

In this collection you will find scenes from plays that are grounded in realism, scenes that move beyond the boundaries of realism into myth and ritual, and scenes that are absurdist. We have set each scene in context and provided a glimpse of what the play explores. You must always read the entire play from which a scene has been drawn, however; otherwise you will have cheated yourself and the character. In addition to scenes from professional playwrights, we have included a series of "dramatic études"—original open-ended scenes for practice—to help warm you up and fine-tune your creative imagination.

We hope that you find this volume helpful to you in your ongoing quest to further develop your acting instrument—your vocal, emotional, and physical self.

Craig Slaight
Jack Sharrar
San Francisco, Calif., 1998

Dramatic Études

• • •

é.tude (ā'to͞od') n. 1. A piece of music used for practice in developing a given point of technique.

Before diving into this collection of scenes taken from plays, we offer you an exercise that explores character choices, dialogue, given circumstances, time and place, and objectives, without the specifics of a given story. We call these "Dramatic Études": a piece of dramatic dialogue created specifically for practice in developing character techniques.

Our experience working with young actors has led us to the conclusion that stretching techniques in short beats is great preparation for character work from a longer play. Here is an opportunity to apply your imagination to an open text and discover the wide range of choices that are possible within a given line of dialogue.

No matter the role, the actor must make certain decisions about the life of a character in order to play the real "want." Frequently what a character says isn't necessarily what the character wants—rather it is the vehicle through which the character attempts to get what they want. Furthermore, it is only *one* vehicle (or tactic, or instrument, or ploy) in the attempt to reach the ultimate objective. Consider the following dramatic étude:

John, Burt, and Cindy were inseparable friends all through high school. They did everything together. John has been away now for a year in an overseas study program in England. Just back in town, he's eager to reconnect with his best friends. John encounters Burt in the local music store. The following exchange takes place:

BURT: Well, John, how are things.

JOHN: Perfect.

BURT: Perfect, huh?

JOHN: Perfect. Especially after seeing you.

BURT: Have you seen Cindy?

JOHN: No I haven't, have you?

BURT: As a matter of fact, I've been seeing quite a lot of Cindy lately.

JOHN: You are a lucky man, Burt.

BURT: I think so, too.

JOHN: Maybe I'll see you two together sometime soon.

BURT: I think we would both like that.

JOHN: Me too. Well, I gotta run. I'll be in touch. *(John exits.)*

Having supplied John's circumstance and his want, the reading of the scene seems fairly clear. Let's look at the same set of dialogue with a new circumstance and a new want. John despises Burt because he stole his girlfriend, Cindy, from him. It was an extremely painful and cruel affair for John because Burt and Cindy did nothing to hide their glee at dropping John. In fact, he has been made the fool—especially by Burt, who contends that John wasn't man enough for Cindy. John will stop at nothing to get back at Burt. Now let's read the lines again, considering the circumstance, the relationship and our newly identified "want" from John. The addition of stage directions helps enhance the scene, taking the want beyond words to include behavior as well:

(Same music store.)

BURT: *(In a loud voice so everyone can hear.)* Well, John, how are things?

JOHN: *(Starts to leave.)* Perfect.

BURT: *(Stopping him.)* Perfect, huh?

JOHN: *(Pushing him.)* Perfect. *(Takes a step toward Burt.)* Especially after seeing you. *(He grabs Burt.)*

BURT: *(Calm resolve.)* Have you seen Cindy?

JOHN: *(Tightens his grip.)* No I haven't, have you?

BURT: As matter of fact, I've been seeing quite a lot of Cindy lately.

JOHN: *(Knocks Burt down.)* You are a lucky man, Burt.

BURT: *(Gets up and starts to leave.)* I think so too.

JOHN: *(Grabs Burt from behind—speaks softly into his ear so no one else can hear.)* Maybe I'll see you two together sometime soon.

BURT: *(A threat.)* I think we would both like that.

JOHN: Me too.

(A beautiful young lady joins John and takes his hand.)

JOHN: Well, I gotta run. I'll be in touch. *(John exits.)*

• • •

Without altering the words, this exchange of dialogue can reveal very different intentions and meaning. What is behind the dialogue becomes the thing that is "played," while what is said helps accomplish the objective, the goal, the want, the intention.

What follows are other dramatic études not from plays and without the specifics of the circumstance, the relationship, or the objective. The characters are identified only as "A" and "B." The goal in the exercise is to create who the people are, their relationships, the given circumstances, and the individual wants of the two characters. These scenes can take many forms. They can be comedies, tragedies, serious drama. The specifics you apply will determine whether the work is cliché or vividly compelling and unique, so search for what is fresh and alive. The more you commit to the specifics you choose, and the deeper the work between you and your partner, the greater the gain in expanding your technique.

We hope these dramatic études will help deepen your acting choices and provide a place to explore. Afterwards, we challenge you to dig into the scenes from the plays that follow, and to apply your new awareness of character choices to the given circumstances, relationships, and objectives that these plays explore—to make a commitment to playing vivid and specific objectives that live deep beneath the lines.

• • •

Étude #1

A : Is it hot, or what?

B : *(A look.)*

A : Troubled?

B : *(Takes a step away.)*

A : You know, that's what I love about you.

B : *(Concentrates on something in the distance.)*

A : What is it?

B : *(Gestures "quiet.")*

A : I can't believe it!

B : *(Starts searching for paper and pen.)*

A : Calm down. This is so like you!

B : *(Stops searching—looks at "A.")*

A : What?

B : *(Hugs "A.")*

A : See ya. *(Exits.)*

B : *(A knowing smile.)*

Étude #2

A : Not another step.

B : Don't fight it.

A : No, it's been too long.

B : What do you need?

A : *(A look.)* As if you could give.

B : Frankly, I expected this.

A : Sure you did.

B : No...Really.

A : No...Really.

B : Why does it always lead us here.

A : Where?

B : Here.

A : Does it?

B : Yes.

Étude #3

A : So...

B : So...

A : It's up to you.

B : Never again.

A : O.K.

B : That's it?

A : That's it.

B : From now on?

A : As you say.

B : Reconsider.

A : Not this time.

B : Ever?

A : *(A look—then walks off.)*

Étude #4

A : Finally!

B : What?

A : Let's not pretend.

B : Who's pretending?

A : It's always the same.

B : Only when you insist.

A : Is it that bad?

B : *(No answer—pause—a look.)*

A : Really. Well that certainly says it.

B : Says what?

A : Don't make me say it in front of you.

B : Let's start over.

A : If you're sure.

B : Finally!

Étude #5

A : We can't stay here.

B : Why not?

A : It's not safe.

B : You keep saying that.

A : Because it's true.

B : You're overreacting.

A : Not this time.

B : It seems quiet enough.

A : Don't kid yourself.

B : When do you think it will happen?

A : Could be any moment.

B : Or maybe never.

A : I doubt that.

B : Are you afraid?

A : Even more than yesterday.

B : At least we're together.

A : But for how long?

B : Does anyone know we're here?

A : I'm sure of it.

B : Did you just hear something?

Étude #6

A: Where have you been?

B: Didn't you get my message?

A: What did it say?

B: Does it matter now?

A: Why shouldn't it?

B: How good are you at keeping a secret?

A: Have I ever let you down before?

B: How would I know if you did?

A: Are you going to tell me?

B: Do you swear not to tell anyone else?

A: What are you getting at?

B: Can I trust you?

A: Who can you trust?

B: What does that mean?

A: You can't figure it out?

B: Are you insulting me?

A: Why would I do that?

B: Can we talk about this later?

A: Why not right now?

B: Why are you pressuring me?

Étude #7

A : I hate you.

B : You don't mean that.

A : More than you'll ever know.

B : Why are you telling me now?

A : Because I think you need to know.

B : That really hurts.

A : You've changed so much.

B : Not by choice.

A : I can't understand you.

B : I'm not asking you to.

A : It's her fault, you know.

B : Don't blame her.

A : She changed you.

B : Maybe.

A : I thought you were stronger than that.

B : So did I.

A : I don't think we should see each other again.

B : That sounds so final.

A : It's the only way.

B : I feel lost.

Étude #8

A : You've been gone an hour.

B : Has it been that long?

A : Where did you go?

B : Out.

A : Can't you be more specific?

B : Not really.

A : Did you miss me?

B : What do you think?

A : I'm not sure.

B : That's your problem.

A : You should have called.

B : You were waiting for that?

A : The entire time.

B : Maybe I should have.

A : But you didn't.

B : Too late now.

A : Are you still mad?

B : Not like I was.

A : I wish you would have stayed.

B : Well, I'm back now.

Étude #9

A : Now, you can't tell.

B : I wish you wouldn't do this.

A : It's already done.

B : Oh God.

A : I'm counting on you.

B : This changes everything.

A : Why?

B : As if you didn't know.

A : Aw, c'mon.

B : I'm not sure.

A : I'm still me.

B : Great.

A : *(Goes to slap "B.")*

B : *(Parries the blow.)* Uh-uh-uh. You need me now.

A : You're right. It does change things.

B : You bet.

Étude #10

A : What was that?

B : Don't look.

A : I'm only human.

B : Maybe that's not enough.

A : I don't understand.

B : It makes me sick.

A : Perhaps I could help.

B : Don't get involved.

A : Don't you care?

B : Yes, I do.

A : So?

B : Look—there's another one. No don't look.

A : What do you want?

B : World peace.

Great Scenes
for Young Actors

. . .

VOLUME II

Scenes
for One Female
and One Male

. . .

Abraham Lincoln Dies at Versailles

by James Prideaux

The Play: A girl meets a sixteen-year-old boy in the gardens at Versailles and discovers that he is the grandson of the late President Lincoln. Ironically, the little girl's mother had witnessed Lincoln's address at Gettysburg and she relates her story of that memorable event.

Time and Place: Versailles, France, September, 1889.

The Scene: *In this opening scene, Susan, a charming sixteen-year-old girl, discovers an equally charming boy sitting on a bench in the garden at Versailles reading a guidebook.*

• • •

GIRL: Do you mind if I sit next to you? I'm absolutely exhausted and the next bench is miles off.

BOY: *(Politely, closes book, half rises.)* Of course.

GIRL: Thank you. *(Sits, after a moment.)* Aren't the gardens vast! And so intricately designed. I don't see how the ancients managed to rendezvous in them. I should think they'd get lost every time they set out.

BOY: Well, I expect they knew them better than we do.

GIRL: I expect. And, of course, the French can always manage to rendezvous, can't they? No matter how difficult the conditions.

BOY: So I've been told.

GIRL: Well, I've only been told.
(Boy smiles.)

GIRL: What are you smiling at?

BOY: Actually, at the word "ancients." It sounds so…archaic. As if Versailles were the pyramids.

GIRL: Well, after all, it has been over a hundred years, hasn't it? Poor Marie Antoinette! I hate sad stories, don't you?

BOY: Yes, I do.

GIRL: I refuse to believe a sad story. I simply refuse.

BOY: On so beautiful a day, it would be sacrilege.

GIRL: Exactly.

BOY: *(After a moment.)* Are you alone?

GIRL: Of course not! *(Amused.)* What are you suggesting! My mother's right over there in that bevy of English tourists. Are you?

BOY: Yes. At the moment. But I'm in France with friends.

GIRL: In France with friends. It sounds so pleasant, doesn't it?

BOY: It is.

GIRL: Older friends?

BOY: No. A couple of school chums. But they're not as interested in history as I am so we've separated for the day.

GIRL: How lucky you are not to be in a bevy of tourists! You're an American?

BOY: *(Nods.)* Could you tell by my accent?

GIRL: Instantly.

BOY: But I live in London at the moment.

GIRL: So do I! What fun! What's your name?

BOY: They call me Jack.

GIRL: What do you mean, they call you Jack?

BOY: Everybody calls me Jack. It's easier.

GIRL: Easier than what?

BOY: Oh, just… (Shrugs.) …easier than my real name.

GIRL: Why? Are you very rich?

BOY: Of course not.

GIRL: I am. We are. Very rich. They call me Susan.

BOY: How do you do?

GIRL: How do you do? Because that's my real name.

BOY: Very nice.

GIRL: My mother's an American…I mean, she was before she married my father. So I suppose I'm half American. Why are you living in London?

BOY: Oh, well, it's because of my father's work.
(Girl looks questioningly.)

BOY: He's…

GIRL: *(After a moment.)* He's what?

BOY: He's the American Ambassador to Great Britain.

GIRL: *(Lightly.)* I'm not impressed by that.

BOY: Well, I certainly didn't mean—

GIRL: Is that why you're so hedgy?

BOY: Hedgy?

GIRL: You hedge. Withhold. They call you Jack…it's easier. My family, you know, moves in diplomatic circles quite easily.

BOY: I should think you'd move in any circles quite easily.

GIRL: Is that a compliment?

BOY: If you'll accept it as such.

GIRL: I should be delighted. How old are you?

BOY: I'm sixteen.

GIRL: *(Crestfallen.)* Oh.

BOY: You can't be older.

GIRL: Of course I'm not older…but I prefer men who are.

BOY: Sorry.

GIRL: I suppose it doesn't really matter.

BOY: I don't think it matters at all.

GIRL: It depends on what we have in mind.

BOY: Well, for the moment, we might stroll.

GIRL: How can I? I'm with those awful bores! I can't just walk off with a strange man. But we could sit a bit. If we look intent in conversation I'm sure they'll think we're having a literary discussion. Or, better still, history. What is the book?

BOY: A guidebook.

GIRL: Perfect. Tell me…I can't wait to hear…what was the precise year of the building of the palace of Versailles?

BOY: *(Leafs through book.)* The precise year? Well, I'm not sure they say the precise year. I think it may have covered a number of years…but to say precisely…

GIRL: Never mind. That's quite enough. What are your secret thoughts?

BOY: I beg your pardon?

GIRL: Your secret thoughts. When you have them, what are they?

BOY: *(After a moment.)* Are you prepared for my answer?

GIRL: Aren't I?

BOY: I don't wish to shock you.

GIRL: I don't mind being shocked...a little.

BOY: They have to do with sports.

GIRL: Sports?

BOY: To be specific—baseball.

GIRL: I'm shocked.

BOY: I warned you.

GIRL: I had hoped for something more...

BOY: ...intellectual?

GIRL: ...unusual.

BOY: I'm afraid I'm very usual. I have no distinction whatsoever, well, except for the fact that...

GIRL: ...except for the fact that your father is the American Ambassador to Great Britain. Oh, dear.

BOY: Except for the fact that I have an all-consuming interest in the American Civil War.

GIRL: The American Civil War? Why?

BOY: Because of my family, who played a part in it. I know every battle...every advance...every retreat. And what else? I'm very fond of boating and the sea, if that helps.

GIRL: Not a great deal.

BOY: I've been a frequent guest on President Arthur's yacht. Does that do anything for me?

GIRL: You see, you keep trying to impress me. Well then, do, if you feel you must. What else?

BOY: Nothing. Nothing at all. I would like it very much if you would like me for myself alone. I'm really very glad you sat down here. I was feeling quite sorry for myself and somewhat lonely and you came along and now I feel as if my entire stay in France is suddenly a success.

GIRL: That's much better...Jack.

BOY: *(Smiles.)* Susan.

(They are silent for a moment.)

GIRL: They'll come and take me away in a moment.

BOY: Could we have supper?

GIRL: Who? You and I?

BOY: Yes.

GIRL: The two of us? Unescorted?

BOY: Of course not. With anybody...I suppose my friends wouldn't do, but anybody you like...your mother...

GIRL: She wouldn't let me. She wouldn't come. Not with a stranger...even if your father is the American Ambassador. Although she's a great snob...I mean, I love her dearly, she's a lovely person...but a simply great snob, which amuses my father enormously considering that she comes from America...oh, I didn't mean...

BOY: I don't mind what you mean. Susan, we must manage somehow to have supper together!

GIRL: Yes! What shall we do?

BOY: We'll have to convince her somehow that— *(In his excitement, he drops the book. He instinctively reaches down to pick it up with his arm and winces in pain. He retrieves it with the other hand.)*

GIRL: What's wrong with your arm?

BOY: It's nothing.

GIRL: You're not in pain, are you?

BOY: It's nothing, really.

GIRL: How could you play baseball?

BOY: It happened here...just recently...in Paris. It's a kind of blood poisoning, apparently. It isn't serious. Please forget about it.

GIRL: Have you been to a doctor?

BOY: Yes.

GIRL: What did he say?

BOY: He said I'd live. At least, I think that's what he said. My French is a bit shaky. Please forget it.

All My Sons

by Arthur Miller

The Play: During WWII, Joe Keller and Herbert Deever ran a machine shop that provided airplane parts. When it was discovered that many of the parts sold had been defective and had caused the needless death of many pilots, Deever was convicted and sent to prison; Keller managed to escape the charge. Keller's son Chris has returned home to make a life for himself; his other son, Larry, is missing in action. Chris soon expresses his love for his brother's former girlfriend, Ann, Deever's daughter. The dark discoveries that are uncovered when Deever's son *(Ann's brother),* George, pays a visit, lead the play to a tragic conclusion.

Time and Place: The backyard of the Keller home in the outskirts of an American town, August, 1947.

The Scene: *Chris (early twenties) professes his love for Ann (early twenties) and talks about the difficulty of resuming his life after the war.*

• • •

CHRIS: *(Calling after him.)* Drink your tea, Casanova. *(He turns to Ann.)* Isn't he a great guy?

ANN: You're the only one I know who loves his parents!

CHRIS: I know. It went out of style, didn't it?

ANN: *(With a sudden touch of sadness.)* It's all right. It's a good thing. *(She looks about.)* You know? It's lovely here. The air is sweet.

CHRIS: *(Hopefully.)* You're not sorry you came?

ANN: Not sorry, no. But I'm…not going to stay…

CHRIS: Why?

ANN: In the first place, your mother as much as told me to go.

CHRIS: Well…

ANN: You saw that...and then you...you've been kind of...

CHRIS: What?

ANN: Well...kind of embarrassed ever since I got here.

CHRIS: The trouble is I planned on kind of sneaking up on you over a period of a week or so. But they take it for granted that we're all set.

ANN: I knew they would. Your mother anyway.

CHRIS: How did you know?

ANN: From *her* point of view, why else would I come?

CHRIS: Well...would you want to?

(Ann studies him.)

CHRIS: I guess you know this is why I asked you to come.

ANN: I guess this is why I came.

CHRIS: Ann, I love you. I love you a great deal. *(Finally.)* I love you.

(Pause. She waits.)

CHRIS: I have no imagination...that's all I know to tell you.

(Ann, waiting ready.)

CHRIS: I'm embarrassing you. I didn't want to tell it to you here. I wanted some place we'd never been; a place where we'd be brand new to each other...You feel it's wrong here, don't you? This yard, this chair? I want you to be ready for me. I don't want to win you away from anything.

ANN: *(Putting her arms around him.)* Oh, Chris, I've been ready a long, long time!

CHRIS: Then he's gone forever. You're sure.

ANN: I almost got married two years ago.

CHRIS: ...why didn't you?

ANN: You started to write to me...

(Slight pause.)

CHRIS: You felt something that far back?

ANN: Every day since!

CHRIS: Ann, why didn't you let me know?

ANN: I was waiting for you, Chris. Till then you never wrote.

And when you did, what did you say? You sure can be ambiguous, you know.

CHRIS: *(He looks toward house, then at her, trembling.)* Give me a kiss, Ann. Give me a...
(They kiss.)

CHRIS: God, I kissed you, Annie, I kissed Annie. How long, how long I've been waiting to kiss you!

ANN: I'll never forgive you. Why did you wait all these years? All I've done is sit and wonder if I was crazy for thinking of you.

CHRIS: Annie, we're going to live now! I'm going to make you so happy. *(He kisses her, but without their bodies touching.)*

ANN: *(A little embarrassed.)* Not like that you're not.

CHRIS: I kissed you...

ANN: Like Larry's brother. Do it like you, Chris.
(He breaks away from her abruptly.)

ANN: What is it, Chris?

CHRIS: Let's drive some place...I want to be alone with you.

ANN: No...what is it, Chris, your mother?

CHRIS: No...nothing like that...

ANN: Then what's wrong?...Even in your letters, there was something ashamed.

CHRIS: Yes. I suppose I have been. But it's going from me.

ANN: You've got to tell me—

CHRIS: I don't know how to start. *(He takes her hand. He speaks quietly, factually at first.)*

ANN: It wouldn't work this way.
(Slight pause.)

CHRIS: It's all mixed up with so many other things...You remember, overseas, I was in command of a company?

ANN: Yeah, sure.

CHRIS: Well, I lost them.

ANN: How many?

CHRIS: Just about all.

ANN: Oh, gee!

CHRIS: It takes a little time to toss that off. Because they weren't just men. For instance, one time it'd been raining several days and this kid came to me, and gave me his last pair of dry socks. Put them in my pocket. That's only a little thing...but...that's the kind of guys I had. They didn't die; they killed themselves for each other. I mean that exactly; a little more selfish and they'd 've been here today. And I got an idea—watching them go down. Everything was being destroyed, see, but it seemed to me that one new thing was made. A kind of...responsibility. Man for man. You understand me?—To show that, to bring that on to the earth again like some kind of a monument and everyone would feel it standing there, behind him, and it would make a difference to him. *(Pause.)* And then I came home and it was incredible. I...there was no meaning in it here; the whole thing to them was a kind of a—bus accident. I went to work with Dad, and that rat-race again. I felt...what you said...ashamed somehow. Because nobody was changed at all. It seemed to make suckers out of a lot of guys. I felt wrong to be alive, to open the bankbook, to drive the new car, to see the new refrigerator. I mean you can take those things out of a war, but when you drive that car you've got to know that it came out of the love a man can have for a man, you've got to be a little better because of that. Otherwise what you have is really loot, and there's blood on it. I didn't want to take any of it. And I guess that included you.

ANN: And you still feel that way?

CHRIS: I want you now, Annie.

ANN: Because you musn't feel that way any more. Because you have a right to whatever you have. Everything, Chris, understand that? To me, too...And the money, there's nothing wrong in your money. Your father put hundreds of planes in the air, you should be proud. A man should be paid for that...

CHRIS: Oh Annie, Annie...I'm going to make a fortune for you!

Arcadia

by Tom Stoppard

The Play: Moving back and forth between the nineteenth and twentieth centuries, *Arcadia*, examines the nature of truth and time and the contrast between Classical and Romantic sensibilities, among other issues.

Time and Place: A room on the garden front of a large country estate in Derbyshire, England, April, 1809.

The Scene: *In scene one, Thomasina Coverly (thirteen) is taking a lesson in mathematics from her tutor, the twenty-two-year old Septimus Hodge. Thomasina, however, has questions about a very different subject—or is it?*

• • •

THOMASINA: Septimus, what is carnal embrace?

SEPTIMUS: Carnal embrace is the practice of throwing one's arms around a side of beef.

THOMASINA: Is that all?

SEPTIMUS: No…a shoulder of mutton, a haunch of venison well hugged, an embrace of grouse…*caro, carnis;* feminine; flesh.

THOMASINA: Is it a sin?

SEPTIMUS: Not necessarily, my lady, but when carnal embrace is sinful it is a sin of the flesh, QED. We had *caro* in our Gallic Wars—"The Britons live on milk and meat"—*"lacte et carne vivunt."* I am sorry that the seed fell on stony ground.

THOMASINA: That was the sin of Onan, wasn't it, Septimus?

SEPTIMUS: Yes. He was giving his brother's wife a Latin lesson and she was hardly the wiser after it than before. I thought you were finding a proof for Fermat's last theorem.

THOMASINA: It is very difficult, Septimus. You will have to show me how.

SEPTIMUS: If I knew how, there would be no need to ask *you*. Fermat's last theorem has kept people busy for a hundred and fifty years, and I hoped it would keep *you* busy long enough for me to read Mr. Chater's poem in praise of love with only the distraction of its own absurdities.

THOMASINA: Our Mr. Chater has written a poem?

SEPTIMUS: He believes he has written a poem, yes. I can see that there might be more carnality in your algebra than in Mr. Chater's "Couch of Eros."

THOMASINA: Oh, it was not my algebra. I heard Jellaby telling cook that Mrs. Chater was discovered in carnal embrace in the gazebo.

SEPTIMUS: *(Pause.)* Really? With whom, did Jellaby happen to say? *(Thomasina considers this with a puzzled frown.)*

THOMASINA: What do you mean, with whom?

SEPTIMUS: With what? Exactly so. The idea is absurd. Where did this story come from?

THOMASINA: Mr. Noakes.

SEPTIMUS: Mr. Noakes!

THOMASINA: Papa's landskip architect. He was taking bearings in the garden when he saw—through his spyglass—Mrs. Chater in the gazebo in carnal embrace.

SEPTIMUS: And do you mean to tell me that Mr. Noakes told the butler?

THOMASINA: No. Mr. Noakes told Mr. Chater. *Jellaby* was told by the groom, who overheard Mr. Noakes telling Mr. Chater, in the stable yard.

SEPTIMUS: Mr. Chater being engaged in closing the stable door.

THOMASINA: What do you mean, Septimus?

SEPTIMUS: So, thus far, the only people who know about this are Mr. Noakes the landskip architect, the groom, the butler, the cook and, of course, Mrs. Chater's husband, the poet.

THOMASINA: And Arthur who was cleaning the silver, and the bootboy. And now you.

SEPTIMUS: Of course. What else did he say?

THOMASINA: Mr. Noakes?

SEPTIMUS: No, not Mr. Noakes. Jellaby. You heard Jellaby telling the cook.

THOMASINA: Cook hushed him almost as soon as he started. Jellaby did not see that I was being allowed to finish yesterday's upstairs' rabbit pie before I came to my lesson. I think you have not been candid with me, Septimus. A gazebo is not, after all, a meat larder.

SEPTIMUS: I never said my definition was complete.

THOMASINA: Is carnal embrace kissing?

SEPTIMUS: Yes.

THOMASINA: And throwing one's arms around Mrs. Chater?

SEPTIMUS: Yes. Now, Fermat's last theorem—

THOMASINA: I thought as much. I hope you are ashamed.

SEPTIMUS: I, my lady?

THOMASINA: If *you* do not teach me the true meaning of things, who will?

SEPTIMUS: Ah. Yes, I am ashamed. Carnal embrace is sexual congress, which is the insertion of the male genital organ into the female genital organ for purposes of procreation and pleasure. Fermat's last theorem, by contrast, asserts that when x, y and z are whole numbers each raised to power of n, the sum of the first two can never equal the third when n is greater than 2.

(Pause.)

THOMASINA: Eurghhh!

SEPTIMUS: Nevertheless, that is the theorem.

THOMASINA: It is disgusting and incomprehensible. Now when I am grown to practise it myself I shall never do so without thinking of you.

SEPTIMUS: Thank you very much, my lady. Was Mrs. Chater down this morning?

THOMASINA: No. Tell me more about sexual congress.

SEPTIMUS: There is nothing more to be said about sexual congress.

THOMASINA: Is it the same as love?

SEPTIMUS: Oh no, it is much nicer than that.

(One of the side doors leads to the music room. It is the other side door which now opens to admit Jellaby, the butler.)

SEPTIMUS: I am teaching, Jellaby.

JELLABY: Beg your pardon, Mr. Hodge, Mr. Chater said it was urgent you receive his letter.

SEPTIMUS: Oh, very well. *(Septimus takes the letter.)* Thank you. *(And to dismiss Jellaby.)* Thank you.

JELLABY: *(Holding his ground.)* Mr. Chater asked me to bring him your answer.

SEPTIMUS: My answer? *(He opens the letter. There is no envelope as such, but there is a 'cover' which, folded and sealed, does the same service. Septimus tosses the cover negligently aside and reads.)* Well, my answer is that as is my custom and my duty to his lordship I am engaged until a quarter to twelve in the education of his daughter. When I am done, and if Mr. Chater is still there, I will be happy to wait upon him in— *(He checks the letter.)* —in the gunroom.

JELLABY: I will tell him so, thank you, sir.

(Septimus folds the letter and places it between the pages of "The Couch of Eros.")

THOMASINA: What is for dinner, Jellaby?

JELLABY: Boiled ham and cabbages, my lady, and a rice pudding.

THOMASINA: Oh, goody.

(Jellaby leaves.)

SEPTIMUS: Well, so much for Mr. Noakes. He puts himself forward as a gentleman, a philosopher of the picturesque, a visionary who can move mountains and cause lakes, but in the scheme of the garden he is as the serpent.

THOMASINA: When you stir your rice pudding, Septimus, the spoonful of jam spreads itself round making red trails like the picture of a meteor in my astronomical atlas. But if you stir backward, the jam will not come together again. Indeed, the pudding does not notice and continues to turn pink just as before. Do you think this is odd?

SEPTIMUS: No.

THOMASINA: Well, I do. You cannot stir things apart.

SEPTIMUS: No more you can, time must needs run backward, and since it will not, we must stir our way onward mixing as we go, disorder out of disorder into disorder until pink is complete, unchanging and unchangeable, and we are done with it forever. This is known as free will or self-determination. *(He picks up the tortoise and moves it a few inches as though it had strayed, on top of some loose papers, and admonishes it.)* Sit!

THOMASINA: Septimus, do you think God is a Newtonian?

SEPTIMUS: An Etonian? Almost certainly, I'm afraid. We must ask your brother to make it his first inquiry.

THOMASINA: No, Septimus, a Newtonian. Septimus! Am I the first person to have thought of this?

SEPTIMUS: No.

THOMASINA: I have not said yet.

SEPTIMUS: "If everything from the furthest planet to the smallest atom of our brain acts according to Newton's law of motion, what becomes of free will?"

THOMASINA: No.

SEPTIMUS: God's will.

THOMASINA: No.

SEPTIMUS: Sin.

THOMASINA: *(Derisively.)* No!

SEPTIMUS: Very well.

THOMASINA: If you could stop every atom in its position and direction, and if your mind could comprehend all the actions thus suspended, then if you were really, *really* good at algebra you could write the formula for all the future; and although nobody can be so clever to do it, the formula must exist just as if one could.

SEPTIMUS: *(Pause.)* Yes. *(Pause.)* Yes, as far as I know, you are the first person to have thought of this. *(Pause. With an effort.)* In the margin of his copy of *Arithmetica,* Fermat wrote that he had discovered a wonderful proof of his theorem but, the margin being too narrow for his purpose, did not have room to write it down. The note was found after his death, and from that day to this—

THOMASINA: Oh! I see now! The answer is perfectly obvious.

SEPTIMUS: This time you may have overreached yourself.

Buddies

by Mary Gallagher

The Play: Several college "buddies" live life with great cama-
raderie and zest for life. Along the way, however, they
uncover their fears and anxieties and learn much about the
human condition and their love for one another.

Time and Place: A summer night in 1967. A living room of a house.

The Scene: *In this opening scene, Boe brings Theresa (both
late teens) back to his house for some late-night partying, but
once inside, Theresa finds that cleaning is more in order.*

• • •

THERESA: *(As they approach the porch.)* Listen, Boe…it's awfully
late…I think I'll just drop you off and go on home, you
know.

BOE: Hey, we're gonna have a party, right?

THERESA: Well, but I don't want to come barging in all by
myself—

BOE: You're not. You're with me.

THERESA: —and Jerry's probably asleep—

BOE: So we'll wake him up. Hey, Squeaky. How long have we
been buddies and you've never seen our house?

THERESA: Well…just for a minute, then. *(Starts up steps.)* It
really is neat that you guys have a whole big house like
this.

BOE: Yeah. We're great housekeepers, too.
*(Bob holds door for Theresa, flicks on light switch.
Theresa enters, stops dead, surveying the chaos.)*

THERESA: God, Boe.

BOE: I warned you.

THERESA: Yeah, but I thought you were kidding.

BOE: I never joke about sanitation.

THERESA: Don't you guys ever...you know...clean?

BOE: Whadaya mean? We got a broom and everything. Here, this chair is safe. How about a brew?

THERESA: *(Sitting.)* Oh, I don't really want one...

BOE: *(Opening two beers with his churchkey.)* You gotta get over that. You teach me to clean, I'll teach you to drink. But we'll start with the drinking part.

THERESA: Ha!

BOE: *(Hands her opened beers, takes others toward doorway, right.)* I'll stash these babies in the fridge, then I'll wake Jerry up.

THERESA: Oh, no, don't wake him up...

(Boe is gone down the hall. Theresa turns back to room, looks around with some distaste and much curiosity, gingerly begins to pick up litter. Boe reenters.)

BOE: Don't start cleaning, Theresa. You won't get done till Christmas. *(Takes melmac plates from her, throws them into closet.)*

THERESA: Aren't you gonna wash them?

BOE: Nah. I can't get to the sink anyway.

THERESA: You're gonna run out of plates, some time.

BOE: We use 'em again. We need a plate, we get one outa the closet.

THERESA: Oh, right, Boe. So you *never* wash them?

BOE: Right. We got a more efficient system. Except I screwed it up just now. I didn't mark the plates. *(Reaches into closet, gets two plates, gets Magic Marker from bookshelf.)* See, after we eat, whatever we had, we write it on the plates. Like "EGGS," you know, or "BEANS," this looks like beans... *(Writes on plates.)* Then we toss the plates in here. *(Tosses them into closet, closes door.)* Next time we wanna eat eggs and beans, we go to the closet, we take out the plates... *(Takes them out, examines them for writing.)* ..."EGGS AND BEANS!" All right!

THERESA: *(Laughing.)* That's disgusting.

BOE: Yeah. *(Tosses plate in closet, heads for stairs.)*

THERESA: Listen, don't wake Jerry up.

BOE: Huh?

THERESA: I mean, you know, don't bother him. He must be really tired, working all day in the hot sun like that—

BOE: Are you kidding? All he does is watch nymphets all day. If anyone drowns, forget it. An old lady or a fat little kid could struggle and yell for half an hour, old Jerry wouldn't even notice. He's sitting up there in his high chair with his tongue hanging out.

THERESA: But you said he started training. He must have to quit partying and stuff—

BOE: Not Jer. He's just gotta quit drinking beer for a week to get down to his wrestling weight. He'll wait till a week before weigh-in, then he'll start jogging six hours a day all wrapped in Saran Wrap and sweat it off. The guy's a maniac. *(Starts upstairs again.)*

THERESA: Really, *don't*, Boe. This is queer. *(Sits on couch.)*

BOE: *(Comes down, sits next to her.)* Hey. If I didn't wake him up, he'd beat me up tomorrow. He hates to miss a party.

THERESA: Some party. You and me.

BOE: Whadaya mean? You and me, that's the best.

THERESA: But you live here, you're not a party. And me...he sees me all the time, down at the Barrell. So I happen to be in his house, big deal.

BOE: Hey. What have I been telling you? He thinks you're great. He's told me that lots of times.
    (Pause. Theresa shrugs.)

BOE: Hey. Squeaky. Would I lie to you?

THERESA: Yeah, you would, if it would make me feel good.
    (Boe laughs. Suddenly he grabs her, throws her over his shoulder, starts for stairs.)

BOE: Hey, Jer! There's someone here to see ya! I'll show her right up!

THERESA: Boe! You creep, I'll kill you! Put me down! You pea-head, you moron, I'll murder you!
    (Laughing, Boe sets her down.)

Class Action
by Brad Slaight

The Play: A collage of encounters and solos occurring outside the classroom, reveals the difficulties of coming-of-age in the complex environment of high school.

Time and Place: A year in the 1990s. An urban high school.

The Scene: *Two chairs, side by side, represent a parked car where Tina (seventeen) and Robby (seventeen) sit. It is prom night. The mood is romantic, but their expressions are not.*

• • •

TINA: Haven't we been here long enough?

ROBBY: I say we give it another five minutes. *(Pause.)* Look who just pulled up...

TINA: That surprises you? Gale and Lyle come here to make out all the time.

ROBBY: I know...I just thought that tonight maybe they'd get a motel room or somethin'.
(Pause.)

TINA: This dress has some kind of wires in the bra...it's starting to cut into my skin.

ROBBY: Yeah, well this tuxedo sucks. I told the guy the cumberbum was too small.

TINA: Cummerbund...it's called a cummerbund.

ROBBY: Whatever...it's too small.

TINA: Just take it off.

ROBBY: Hey, with what I paid for it, I'm gonna wear it until I take it back.
(Tina nudges him and nods toward another part of the stage.)

TINA: Look, Susie and Tom are doin' it.

ROBBY: How can you tell?

TINA: The fact that their car is rocking back and forth is a pretty good clue.

ROBBY: Think we should get this thing rockin', too?

(She gives him a look.)

ROBBY: I didn't mean for real, I meant pretend...like we've been doin' it all night.

TINA: Nah, people would really get suspicious then. We've never even dated before.

ROBBY: I don't see why we have to pretend at all. Why don't we just tell everyone that we didn't want to go to the prom alone, so we decided to go together?

TINA: Because that makes us look like a couple of losers.

ROBBY: We are a couple of losers.

TINA: Speak for yourself.

(Pause; suddenly Robby pulls her in tight.)

TINA: What are you doing?

ROBBY: Karla and Jonathan are just two cars away...they can see us.

TINA: So?

ROBBY: So, I asked Karla to go to the prom with me and she turned me down. I don't want her to think we're just sittin' up here.

TINA: She turned you down? Who does she think she is?

ROBBY: Yeah, right. Who does she think she is? *(Pause.)* Man, I feel so stupid.

TINA: How do you think I feel?

ROBBY: Hey, you could have at least gone with another girl. Lots of 'em paired off. But if I went with a buddy, I'd be gay. Talk about your double standards.

(She nudges him again.)

TINA: Look, Connie and Tim are making out and this is only their second date.

ROBBY: Yeah, two weeks ago they didn't even know each other. *(Robby looks at Tina for a moment.)*

TINA: By the way, the corsage is very nice. I'll reimburse you for it tomorrow.

ROBBY: No hurry.

TINA: Minus what I paid for your boutonniere.

ROBBY: My what?

TINA: The flower I gave you.

ROBBY: Oh, right. (Pause.) Uh…Maybe we should, you know… you know.

TINA: No I don't know. Maybe we should what?

ROBBY: Well, if anyone is lookin' at us, like we're lookin' at them…I thought maybe we should kiss or something.

TINA: I don't know?

ROBBY: Only a pretend kiss.

TINA: You may be right…it would certainly remove any doubt, in case we are being watched.

ROBBY: Alright, go ahead.

TINA: You're the guy, you're supposed to be the kisser…I'm the kissee.

ROBBY: Right. *(Robby awkwardly puts his arm around her; gives her a quick peck on the lips.)*

TINA: I get more romantic kisses from my little brother. If you're going to do it…do it right.
(Robby hesitates, then really lays one on her. It is a long, compassionate kiss. When they come up for air, they've both been affected by it.)

TINA: *(Overwhelmed.)* That was better.

ROBBY: *(Also affected.)* Yeah.
(Pause.)

TINA: Look, there's Melanie…maybe we should kiss again so…
(Before she can finish her sentence, Robby kisses her again. Even longer than before. Finally they pull away from each other and recover.)

ROBBY: *(Looking at watch.)* Well, I think it would be okay if we left now.

TINA: We've certainly proved our point.

ROBBY: Yes we have. *(Robby reaches to start the car.)*

TINA: You start that car and you're a dead man! *(Tina pulls him in for another kiss.)*

• • •

The Scene: *Joni (sixteen) approaches Jack (seventeen), who sits in a quiet corner of school, writing in a notebook.*

• • •

JONI: I saw you writing in your notebook, you can't fool me.

JACK: Hi, Joni.

JONI: You haven't finished your English assignment, have you?

JACK: Uh...not really.

JONI: I know you so well, Jack Heller.

JACK: Yeah...

JONI: You always wait until the last minute.

JACK: What were we s'pose to do?

JONI: Poetry! Remember, we have to turn in a poem? Mrs. Vernon only told us five or six times.

JACK: Guess my head was somewhere else.

JONI: Want to hear mine?

JACK: Sure.

(Joni takes a paper out and reads from it proudly.)

JONI: "Love...by Joni Mendez:
    I was riding in my car,
    I was riding all alone
    I was riding in my car
    Going through the radar zone.
    The policeman clocked my speed,
    At 80 miles per hour
    He asked me why I sped like that
    Calling me a wild flower.
    So I told him that I hadn't seen
    My guy for over a week
    And I was rushing to see him
    So the two of us could speak.
    The cop he smiled and said okay
    He understood my longing heart.

And let me continue on my way
So my love and me would no longer be apart.

JACK: Wow...that's great.

JONI: I guess I just have a way with words.

JACK: Wish I could write like that.

JONI: You just concentrate on winning the game tonight. I've already taken care of your assignment...I wrote your poem for you, so you can stop worrying.

JACK: Really?

(She holds up paper.)

JONI: It's called "Broken Heart" and it's almost as good as the one I wrote for myself. I better hold it for you until class, you'll probably lose it.

(She kisses him on the check, and then exits. Jack makes sure she is gone; opens his notebook back up and reads from it.)

JACK: "Winterscape. A Poem by Jack Heller"
A vibrant glaze slips upon the busy hillside
Blowing a blue chill like notes from
An angry saxophone
Upon the unsuspecting hollow heart world
Hunkering down the brown leaf child of fall
And causing a pond frog to scream
His protest at the dormant mud.
And with a simple dark shade
Closes the lid
Closes the winterscape
Closes the world
For now.

(Jack tears the poem from his notebook; shoves it in his back pocket. Picks up his notebook and spins his football in the air as he exits.)

Darcy and Clara
by Daisy Foote

The Play: A family struggles to hold onto precious land and survive inner crisis. Both parents and children in the Chancy house face conflict and failure as they deal with a greedy world and crushed hopes and dreams.

Time and Place: The present. New Hampshire farm country.

The Scene: *Darcy Chancy (seventeen) is the fraternal twin of Clara who is in the hospital with kidney failure, a result of her severe diabetes. In this first scene from Act II, Darcy returns home from her first date with Tom Clark (twenty-three), who works with Darcy and Clara's father in the logging business.*

• • •

(End of the evening. Darcy and Tom come through the door to the kitchen.)

TOM: I don't want to bother.

DARCY: It's no bother. *(A beat.)* Dad's not here. He's on the mountain, I think. He'll probably be there all night.

TOM: It's not that I'm afraid of your father. It's just that... well...I don't see the point in crossing him...when we've had such a good evening. At least I think it's been good...have you had a good one?

DARCY: Yes. I have.

(Tom goes to the window.)

TOM: I always wondered what he did up there all night.

DARCY: I don't know. Drinks beer. Looks out over the town... *(A beat.)* It was something he and my grandfather did together. They'd go up after supper with their beer, and a lot of times they'd just stay out all night. *(She goes to the refrigerator.)* Would you like a beer?

TOM: No thanks. *(A beat.)* But I wouldn't mind a cup of coffee...

DARCY: All right... *(She goes to make the coffee.)*

TOM: He asked me to spend the night up there with him once. About six months ago...when we lost another big clearing contract to Rene Lemay. It had been the third one in a row. And your father had about a case of beer, and he was madder than usual.

DARCY: And did you?

TOM: No. No...I'm not real comfortable doing that sort of thing. I just think it ends up making you madder than you already are. *(Tom looks over at the rocking chair.)* How long ago did he die?

DARCY: Five months ago.

TOM: I never did know him very well. By the time I started working in the mill, he was pretty sick. He'd poke his head in every once in a while, but he never had a whole lot to say.

DARCY: Clara says he's still here. She says she sees him in the room watching us.

(Tom has no idea how to react to this statement.)

DARCY: But then that's just Clara. And you know how Clara is... *(A beat.)* Grandpa Joseph used to say that I was just a piece of Clara's extra energy that broke off when she was born. And if it weren't for Clara, I wouldn't even be here.

TOM: That's not true. It seems to me you're very much your own person...

DARCY: But Clara...

TOM: Clara's Clara, and you're Darcy. And I'm glad you're you...and not her...I'm glad...

(They both become very self-conscious.)

DARCY: The coffee is ready.

(She starts to pour their coffee. Tom moves shyly toward her.)

TOM: You enjoy that movie?

DARCY: Yes. *(A beat.)* And the burgers were good too...

TOM: Oh I enjoyed the burgers. They do a good burger...

(They take their coffees and sit at the table. Tom looks around the room.)

TOM: Something looks different...

DARCY: Ma cleaned...

(Some more silence as they continue to drink their coffee.)

DARCY: I suppose you've heard...

TOM: Heard?

DARCY: About selling everything.

TOM: Yes, I've heard... *(A beat.)* But I thought I'd wait for you to bring it up... *(A beat.)* Rene Lemay and his sister are buying it?

DARCY: Yes.

TOM: For them to put up a bunch of houses...

DARCY: To pay for an operation for Clara for a kidney transplant... *(She gets mugs out of the cupboard. She brings them and some sugar to the table. She goes to the refrigerator. She opens it.)* Do you take milk in your coffee?

TOM: If there is some...I wouldn't turn it down...

(She takes it out of the refrigerator.)

DARCY: There's plenty. Ma went shopping today. *(She puts it on the table.)*

TOM: Darcy...

DARCY: Yes...

TOM: Maybe now's not the best time to tell you this, but I think you should know... *(A beat.)* I'm gonna quit working for your father. *(A beat.)* It's getting harder and harder for him and me to make any money. Rene Lemay keeps winning all the contracts. *(A beat.)* If you'd rather not go out with me anymore, I'll understand.

DARCY: No. I want to go out again...if you want to...

TOM: Oh...sure...I want to...if you do...

DARCY: I do...yes...

TOM: You do?

DARCY: Yes. *(She goes over to the coffee pot.)* Coffee's ready...
(She brings it over to the table and pours the coffee.)

TOM: Sometimes...when we're in the mill...or in the woods...

I'll catch your father talking to someone...like he could be talking to himself...only he's not. He's talkin' to someone else, but there's no one there...just him and me. *(A beat.)* I'm worried about him, Darcy. I think he might be losing it...

DARCY: Can we please not talk about this any more?
(Tom looks confused.)

DARCY: It's been such a nice evening. Dinner at the Riverside... and the movies. I liked talking about other things...what were we talking about?

TOM: Graduating...you were telling me about graduating... and how you want to be a nurse...

DARCY: A nurse practioner...

TOM: A nurse practioner?

DARCY: There's a big difference.

TOM: Is there?

DARCY: Oh sure...a nurse practioner requires a lot more train-ing and can make a lot more money...
(He reaches out and takes her hand. She becomes flus-tered and loses her train of thought.)

TOM: How much school do you need for something like that?

DARCY: It's four years of college and then two years of school after that...
(The lights fade.)

Early Dark

by Reynolds Price

The Play: Rosacoke Mustian and members of her family struggle with life in northeastern North Carolina, attempting to seek love and purpose amidst complex internal and external turmoil.

Time and Place: Summer, fall, and winter 1957. Warren County, North Carolina and Mason's Lake, Virginia.

The Scene: *Rosacoke (twenty) seeks commitment from Wesley (twenty-two), the young man she stayed loyal to during his three-year absence while he was in the Navy. Wesley resists a permanent arrangement, although his passion for Rosacoke is unflagging. Wesley sits on his front porch, playing the harmonica. Rosacoke approaches and listens. Wesley stops playing.*

• • •

ROSACOKE: Don't stop.
  (He plays on a little, the song unfinished.)
ROSACOKE: Is that all you know?
WESLEY: No. Oh no. *(Smiles.)* But it's all I'm giving. Got to save my strength.
ROSACOKE: *(Tries for lightness.)* For what?
WESLEY: My life. *(Waits, smiles again.)* My pitiful life.
ROSACOKE: I heard you playing almost to Mary's. *(Points behind.)* I've been to Mary's to see Mildred's baby.
  (Wesley laughs gently. It whines through his harp.)
ROSACOKE: If you managed everything good as you manage a harp, wouldn't none of your friends ever be upset.
WESLEY: Wesley's friends got to take Wesley—lock, stock, and block—or leave him alone.
ROSACOKE: Doesn't make his friends' life easy, does it?
WESLEY: *(Still smiling.)* Who did I beg to be my friend?

ROSACOKE: You've spent your life—or the last seven years—drawing people to you.

WESLEY: They don't have to come. I don't carry a gun.

ROSACOKE: That may well be. *(Looks up to the sky—a night sky now.)* Can I use your phone? It's darker than I counted on.

WESLEY: To get home, you mean? I can carry you.

ROSACOKE: Can you? I wonder.

WESLEY: I've wondered myself.

ROSACOKE: Reached any conclusions?

(Wesley faces her plainly but does not speak.)

ROSACOKE: Then while you're waiting, do me a favor—say "Rosacoke."

WESLEY: Why?

ROSACOKE: A gift to me.

WESLEY: Rosacoke.

ROSACOKE: Thank you. That's my name. Bet you haven't said it since late July.

WESLEY: *(Smiles.)* I don't talk to trees and shrubs like some people if that's what you mean.

ROSACOKE: It's not what I mean. You're Wesley—is that still right?

WESLEY: Unless the law has changed it and not notified me.

ROSACOKE: Just checking. I know such a few facts about you that sometimes I wonder if I even know your name.

WESLEY: Yes ma'am. Rest easy. It's Wesley all right and is Wesley walking you home or not?

ROSACOKE: I'd thank you—yes.

WESLEY: And you'd be welcome. *(Reaches behind on the porch, finds a flashlight, descends toward her.)* Won't cost you a cent.

(Wesley offers his hand, she takes it; they leave. Slowly they walk through changes of light—time and place. In dark spots Wesley does not use the flashlight and makes no sound. Rosa stops at last.)

ROSACOKE: Might as well be on the motorcycle for all we've said.

WESLEY: What you want to say?

ROSACOKE: *(Waits.)* I want to say you are half this trouble, that

you've never talked to me, and now you're gone, and I
don't know— *(Breaks off, shamed, in her old harangue.)* I
want to say I've said it *all*, till my teeth ache with shame.

WESLEY: You haven't—not all. I've answered every question the
best I could, best *I* could. There's one left for you—
(A sudden crashing in the near woods halts them.)

WESLEY: Jesus, Rosa!

ROSACOKE: Wesley!

(As the sound retreats, they wait a stunned moment.)

WESLEY: *(Half-whispers.)* All my life I waited on that—

ROSACOKE: A deer? Me and Mildred saw one years ago.

WESLEY: A grown buck leading two does to water. They were
killed all through here before you were born.

ROSACOKE: What water, Wesley?

WESLEY: Mr. Isaac's spring. I've seen tracks there. I scared them,
talking.

ROSACOKE: Will he try again?

WESLEY: If he doesn't hear us.

ROSACOKE: We could wait.

WESLEY: You want to?

*(Rosa thinks a moment, nods. They sit on a low rise and
silently wait. Then the deer cross toward the spring—del-
icate sounds. Wesley watches closely; Rosa watches him. A
moment to realize they are gone; then Wesley moves to
stand. Rosa touches his arm.)*

ROSACOKE: Since it's not too cold, we could walk behind them—
find the spring.

WESLEY: If you want to. We won't see the deer.

ROSACOKE: If we went gently—
*(Wesley studies her, takes her hand, and rises. Slowly—
together, silent—they move inward. Deeper darkness.
Rosa at last pulls back on his hand.)*

ROSACOKE: Listen.

WESLEY: To what?

ROSACOKE: I thought we might hear them. Mildred and I saw
the deer we saw in a field like this.

WESLEY: Not this field.

ROSACOKE: How do you know?

WESLEY: (His voice begins to alter in speed and pitch till it gradually seems a stranger's.) This is my private field. Mr. Isaac doesn't know he owns this field. Nobody knows this field but me.

ROSACOKE: I never knew it.

WESLEY: You know it now.

ROSACOKE: I know it now.

(They stand, hands joined, but she cannot see him. She begins to feel fear but tries to speak lightly.)

ROSACOKE: It's night all right—dark early now. Wesley, switch on your light. I can't see you. (She moves away.)

WESLEY: (Waits.) You mean to take pictures?

ROSACOKE: No.

WESLEY: Then if you don't need light, this boy doesn't.

(He offers a hand, firm but undemanding. She stands a moment, then goes to accept it. He sets both hands on her shoulders and presses her down. On their knees in near-darkness, they kiss—hands at sides. Then Rosa begins to unbutton his shirt. Wesley waits till she's finished—his chest bare to her; she lays a palm on it. He takes her wrist, pushes her gently to her back. In deeper dark, he opens his belt; slides down his pants and trousers, begins to bare Rosa. Then he lies upon her and slowly moves. Total dark till Wesley can speak.)

WESLEY: Thank you, Lady. (He slowly rolls off, lies on his back beside her and launches a flashlight beam on the sky.) Did you know this light won't ever stop flying? Nothing to block it. Millions of years from tonight—somewhere— people in space will move in my light.

ROSACOKE: Is that something else you learned in the Navy?

WESLEY: Ain't I a good learner?

(He reaches to touch Rosa again. She seizes his wrist and holds him back.)

WESLEY: Why?

ROSACOKE: I got to go home.

WESLEY: What you got at home as good as what's here?
(Wesley takes her hand, pulls it down toward himself. Rosa draws back and stands.)

ROSACOKE: If you won't carry me, I'll gladly walk; but since you know these woods so well, please lend me your light.

WESLEY: *(Sits upright, throws his light on her face, sees the baffling change.)* Are you all right?

ROSACOKE: I'm all right. *(Moves to leave.)*
(Wesley stands and puts his clothes together, then comes up behind her, shines his light at the ground.)

WESLEY: You need to remember—the way you feel is a natural thing after what we've done. You answered me. The sadness'll pass. You'll feel good as you ever did. Gradually better.
(Touches her shoulder; she doesn't turn.)

ROSACOKE: *We* haven't done nothing. I haven't answered nothing. *(Moves on again to the bottom porch step of the Mustian house. The porch light is on. At last she turns.)*

WESLEY: I'm out of my depth. Hell, Rosa, I'm drowning. Stand still and say what you want out of me.

ROSACOKE: I don't want anything you've got to give. I've just been mistaken—

[SISSIE: *(Inside.)* Help me, Milo. Help me please.]
[(Light rises in the upstairs room—now Milo and Sissie's: Sissie in bed, Milo, Emma, Mary Sutton, and Dr. Sledge silently busy round her.)]

ROSACOKE Sissie's started. Please leave. *(Climbs two steps.)*

WESLEY: Are you all right?

ROSACOKE: I answered that once. I was just mistaken. If that's you, Wesley; if that's what you've been, I've been wrong for years.

WESLEY: *(Waits, nods twice.)* It's me and you.
(Rosa shakes her head No, looks to the house, then quickly enters. Wesley stands a moment, then moves away.)

• • •

The Scene: *Wesley has pursued Rosacoke out of her house into the yard. Rosacoke is clearly upset.*

• • •

WESLEY: Please tell me what hurts you.

ROSACOKE: Nothing you can cure.

WESLEY: You don't know that. *I* don't know that till you tell me the trouble.

ROSACOKE: It's *my* trouble and if you don't know by now—

WESLEY: I don't know anything about you, Rosa; and I've known you seven years. Six weeks ago you welcomed me, then turned yourself like a weapon against me—won't answer my letters, won't tell me nothing. You don't have the right. *(With both hands he takes her arms at the elbows, holds her firmly but gently.)* We've got to go practice. Everybody's waiting. Come on with me.
(Rosa shakes her head No.)

WESLEY: Rosa, Willie has gone. You've got to take her part or your mother's show will fail.

ROSACOKE: Marise Gupton can do it.

WESLEY: You haven't seen Marise lately then. She's the size of that house. *(Points behind him, glances back.)*
(Sammy stands in the door. Wesley waves him in.)

WESLEY: It's all right, Sammy.
[(Sammy nods and goes.)]

ROSACOKE: It's not all right.

WESLEY: *(Still behind her, he reaches for her left hand. She lets him hold it.)* Why?

ROSACOKE: *(Frees her hand; turns to face him, calm but tired.)* Marise Gupton is not the only person working on a child.

WESLEY: Who do you mean?

ROSACOKE: I mean Rosacoke.

WESLEY: *(Thinks a long moment.)* And Wesley then.
(Rosa shakes her head No, not fiercely but firmly. With his hand in the air, he asks her to wait.)

WESLEY: Understand this one thing and answer—you don't know nobody but me, do you?

ROSACOKE: I don't know you.

WESLEY: Don't lie to me—you know what's here. *(Waits.)* You don't know anybody else, do you, Rosa?

ROSACOKE: You know I don't.

WESLEY: *(Draws one long breath, slowly exhales it; makes no try to touch her again but extends his offer in a mild half-whisper.)* Come on then. We got to go practice.
(He turns to go and has gone four steps before he knows he is walking alone. He stops and half-turns. Rosa is facing her home but has not moved. Wesley comes back to her; by now his voice is almost happy.)

WESLEY: Rosa, why didn't you tell me sooner?

ROSACOKE: What good would that have done?

WESLEY: Good?—maybe not. But it would've been fair.

ROSACOKE: I can't see I owe you two more words.

WESLEY: Try one. Try *Wesley*. Wesley's my name.

ROSACOKE: *(Smiles.)* I'll try to remember that. *(Takes a homeward step, turns.)* Weapons, Wesley—I have lain down and got up and worked through years with you driven into my chest like a nail.
(Wesley takes that, full face; then slowly comes toward her, begins quietly as if to himself.)

WESLEY: Rosa, you aren't the only human made out of skin. What do you think us others are? What do you think I've been these long years?—asbestos? wood? I'm not, not now if I ever was. I may not have talked as well as you. Or planned as far. I may have disappointed you hundreds of times, but I'm still the person you claimed to love and plan a life on. I've shied from plans. *(Waits.)* I'm not shying now. We'll leave here after the pageant tonight and be in South Carolina by day—we won't need a license;

that's where everybody goes. We can spend a night somewhere, be back by Christmas eve—

ROSACOKE: I'm not everybody. I'm just the cause of this one
baby. It's mine—something really mine from the start; I'll
have it on my own.

WESLEY: And shame your mother and feed it how and tell it
what? Not a hundred percent yours, it's not. Remember
that along with my name.

(Rosa watches him closely but doesn't answer.)

WESLEY: Do something about me. Tell me "Go" or "Stay."
(Silence still.) We can live. I've paid up all my debts; every
penny I make from here on is mine.

ROSACOKE: *(Genuinely thinking aloud.)* Let me get this straight.
You offer to drive me to South Carolina and marry me at
dawn in some poor justice of the peace's living room,
then give me a little one-day vacation and bring me home
for Christmas with my family that will be cut again by this
second blow, then take me on to Norfolk to spend my life
shut in two rented rooms while you sell motorcycles—me
waiting out my baby, sick and alone, eating what we
could afford and pressing your shirts and staring out a
window in my spare time at concrete roads and people
that look like they hate each other—That's what you're
standing here, offering me, after all these years?

WESLEY: Yes. It was all I ever had to offer. I never said I was anything but Wesley. All the rest you made up yourself and
hung on me. Sure, that's one way of seeing my plan; but
if everybody looked at their chances like that, people
would have gone out of style long ago.

ROSACOKE: Maybe they should've.

WESLEY: You don't mean that.

ROSACOKE: I think I do. I haven't been sleeping.

WESLEY: You're talking like the old Wesley now.

ROSACOKE: You said there was just one Wesley all along.

WESLEY: *(Shakes his head slightly.)* There's Wesleys you never
dreamed of, Rosa.

ROSACOKE: *(Opens her mouth to answer, finds only a kernel of what seems knowledge.)* That may be so. But—look—I'm free. I'm standing here seeing you and, Wesley, I'm free.

WESLEY: You're wrong. And I'm sorry. We've got till tonight. Believe I'm serious—whatever it means weeks or years from now—and tell me tonight.

(Rosa starts to answer.)

WESLEY: Please. Tonight.

Full Moon

by Reynolds Price

The Play: Kerney Bascomb attempts to find direction to her life and reconcile her relationship with a young man (Kipple Patrick), complicated by his long-standing involvement with Ora Lee, the daughter of his family's housekeeper. Issues of race and gender inform and deepen Kerney's choices while the adults around her offer advice and reflections from the past.

Time and Place: Late summer, 1938. Eastern North Carolina.

The Scene: *The first scene in the play finds Kerney (nineteen) and Kip (twenty-one) returning from a late Saturday night date. Kip has been drinking heavily. A dramatic full moon illuminates the Bascom front yard. It is midnight.*

KERNEY: *(Hugging her shoulders and shivering.)* This moonlight has got to be *poison.* Everybody knows it'll drive you crazy. *(Waits, bathes her face again in the glow.)* I may already be stark raving nuts. And it's not just the gin—

KIP: Kerney, you were crazy before they *had* moonlight.

KERNEY: Crazy enough to stay in this town—a Christian white lady with nothing to do, locked up indoors. *(Sees the moon again.)* How can people sleep through something fine as this?

KIP: They get as tired as I am now. And you're no lady.

KERNEY: *(Stepping toward him.)* I begin to believe you. And oh sweet Kip, you're too old for me. I'm awake; every cell of my body is singing. And thus I bid you a grateful good night. *(Gives an elaborate bow, nearly falls, then continues toward him.)*

KIP: *Stay.* Stay *there.*

KERNEY: If you don't want me, there's others that do—lady or tramp.

KIP: Lady, I want you but I want you *there,* this instant. *(Studies her.)* Kerney Bascomb, you—look—so—fine.
(Kerney is puzzled for a moment, then moves through a light succession of poses, a silent fluid dance. Then she stops and stands, facing Kip.)

KIP: I—*need*—it.

KERNEY: *It?* Be ashamed. Anyhow, you're familiar with my *it.*

KIP: Forgive me, lady. I want you forever.

KERNEY: I'm no fine lady trapped in your dream. Since school, I've spent a whole two years as a trainee lady—indoor sports like reading novels and having headaches, going out just to weddings and dances.

KIP: *(Waits, then stands.)* You look too good. I may need to join you.

KERNEY: You—are—not—hearing—me. You told me to *stay.* Didn't we promise not to touch anymore, not till we know?

KIP: I know. I need you.

KERNEY: We both said we wanted to think awhile.

KIP: Maybe my advanced age speeded me up. And this fine moonlight and you resigning your ladyhood.

KERNEY: A former lady's not always a tramp.

KIP: You know what I mean.

KERNEY: I honest to God don't know if I do. You're an older man. Hell, I'm just nineteen.
(Kip moves toward Kerney. Through the rest of the meeting, they move round the yard—standing or sitting on the white rock—till they end on the porch steps. Before he speaks again, Kip extends a slow hand toward her. Kerney gives no sign of shying, but his reach barely misses contact, and he chooses not to step closer.)

KIP: I've looked far ahead as my eyes reach. And Kerney, I want us to leave here soon and marry each other.

KERNEY: We could always leave and marry other people.

KIP: *(With sudden calm force.)* Don't talk that trash.

KERNEY: *(Calm too.)* I'll say any goddamned thing I feel.

KIP: Your father'll hear us.

KERNEY: My pa could teach us worlds about swearing.

KIP: All your pa wants to teach Kip is *running* lessons—how to run as far as Bangor, Maine and never see you.

KERNEY: And your pa's not that stuck on me.

KIP: That's a lie. He told me, not two days ago, "Kip, she's an elegant piece of construction with a mind like a steel trap. Don't let her vanish."

KERNEY: *(Laughs and nods.)* Your pa would call a two-headed cross-eyed brunette gorgeous if she kept you home.

KIP: We wouldn't live with him.

KERNEY: But in sight and earshot.

KIP: McDuff is no village. We'd move across town—

KERNEY: Across the tracks maybe? *(Half-sings.)* Out near Sugartown, where the sweet darkies dwell—

KIP: *(Ignoring her hint and fervent to hide the problem she has raised.)* Kerney, my father's been good to me. Now he faces me leaving. I don't see you abandoning yours.
(Kerney thinks through that. It is the first time she has faced the full prospect of leaving home. Her face slowly mirrors the mind's desolation. At no other moment will she seem more alone. When she speaks, she's resolved.)

KERNEY: I—*will*—leave—though, when the time really comes.
(At the end she is smiling. Kip sees it, shivers slightly.)

KIP: Got any hint who you're leaving with?

KERNEY: I've entertained more than one bid and you know it. Yours still in force?

KIP: *(Waits incredulous.)* God on high, woman! Kipple Patrick loves you. He's said it all ways, in more than one language, since you were a child.

KERNEY: Ego amo te. Je t'aime. Yo te amo. And what about African? Mumby-Jumby-Boo! I'll need to learn it in African, won't I?—to keep your attention.

KIP: You're not drunk. Why the hell turn vicious?
(Kerney takes fire from his word vicious. She waits blankly for a moment, then contorts her face and gives a sudden,

muted but impressive cat's warning growl and a single clawing gesture in the air.)

KERNEY: *(Suddenly calm.)* Something mean got in me, some truth-telling demon.

KIP: Get it out fast.

(Kerney prowls in the effort to clear her mind. She has a fierce need to exorcise what she has heard in town gossip but has not discussed with Kip.)

KERNEY: I need to hear you say it again. Make your bid again please.

KIP: You're not at auction. It's a heartfelt proposal.

KERNEY: Say it.

KIP: *(Waits.)* Let's clear out of here. We'll catch a train to South Carolina, get married down there where you don't need a blood test and spare our fathers the cost and worry. What we save, we can put toward buying a house.

KERNEY: Sounds easy as buying a red toothbrush.

KIP: It's not that new an invention, girl—holy matrimony. A man and a woman choose each other and say so in public. Ninety people in any odd hundred have done it.

KERNEY: A hundred people in any odd hundred are going to die. I don't think I plan to be that normal.

KIP: *You* won't be normal—don't lose sleep on it.

KERNEY: Now tell me why I should do what you say?

KIP: Say *we* for once. Why should we elope?

KERNEY: I'm all *for* elopement. Big weddings are nothing but a sinful waste. No, tell me why to get married at all. And why is it holy?

(Through the following Kerney reveals a genuine innocence—she does not know and wants to. Kip shows the delighted patience of a good teacher.)

KIP: I guess most girls learn this from their mothers, so you got left out. But I just thought—Lord, with all we've done, from rafters to floor—you were some great expert on love and life.

KERNEY: I did what you and Jeffer Burns taught me. It didn't seem holy.

KIP: Don't mention Jeffer Burns. *(Waits.)* You enjoyed yourself, true?

KERNEY: I liked being present and helping you out. It seemed like something you needed, right then, to go on living. Like you were out to get my blood.

KIP: I never meant harm.

KERNEY: Never—you didn't. It *seemed* like, seemed that urgent.

KIP: And it's not for you? I'm a young man, girl. Men are built that way. But hurt you? God, I want you to last—here in my life.

KERNEY: Why not another girl—same hills and valleys—that can cook, clean house, do long division? I can't walk straight, much less keep house.

KIP: You, Kerney. You or life alone.

KERNEY: I'm looking at life alone myself. *(Waits, laughs.)* If I die tonight you'd marry by fall.

KIP: Me and my wife'll sweep the dead leaves off you.

KERNEY: *(Laughs.)* See?

KIP: —If you're *dead.* But if you're drawing breath on Earth— with Jeffer Burns or Gary-damned-Cooper—I'll be the most miserable soul upright.

KERNEY: Is it holy though? Why won't you tell me?

KIP: *(Waits, then smiles.)* I can't say I'd ask God to watch every minute. But I think he blesses love, lasting love.

KERNEY: Church love, altar love. Church marriage makes you say "Forsaking all others." You ready for that?

KIP: I've copied the Methodist marriage vows. Once we're joined by the justice of peace, we'll read each other the vows in private.

KERNEY: You didn't! *(Laughs.)* If I know you, there'll be precious little reading. But "Forsaking all others"—talk about that.

KIP: Who's been filling your head with filth? I'll come to you clean.

KERNEY: *(With increasing force.)* I've heard that concubines flourish hereabouts. I'll need an oath that I'm all you've got before I let my body start babies. *(Tries to lighten her tone.)* Now if we perform this private wedding in our honeymoon nest, will you sing "Oh, Promise Me" and other crowd favorites? *(Then quickly.)* Kipple, Kipple—I don't mean to mock. God knows, you can't marry me in church. Orange blossoms and satin just will not hang on skin as wicked as this skin has been.

(Kip thinks, then gently takes Kerney's wrist, kisses it, trails his lips delicately up the skin.)

KIP: Sweet, sweet, sweet.

(Kerney bears him a moment, then pulls away—no harshness or fear. She walks to the dark edge of the pool of moonlight. Kip moves to follow. She stops him with a gesture, then studies him.)

KERNEY: Kip Patrick, I may need you.

KIP: Is that the same as "Kip, I may love you"?

KERNEY: It could well be—any minute, any day.

KIP: You're welcome to phone me collect, from any phone on the planet Earth, if and when you can truly say yes.

KERNEY: I can save you some cash— *(Faces him fully.)*

(Kip is oddly cautious. He waits a moment, then steps to within an arm's length of her. She pulls him down to sit beside her.)

KERNEY: I want to try what you think is right. *(Reaches for his hand.)*

KIP: Kerney, I'm overwhelmed but—hell!—we're in plain view of your father's window.

(Kerney takes Kip's wrist and repeats his kisses. Kip accepts with less than total joy—quick glances at the house. Ending her kisses at his elbow, Kerney smiles in his face and slowly stands.)

KERNEY: We both need sleep.

KIP: Hold on, sweet child—you got me tuned up tight as a harp string. If I break now and lash around, I'll leave thousands homeless.

KERNEY: That's what I said—we both need rest.

KIP: *(Waits.)* Can I take you to church in the morning?

KERNEY: Won't the church cave in? *(She backs away almost into darkness, then blows a slow kiss.)*

KIP: Did you mean all this?

KERNEY: Every word, all night—in spite of this moon.

KIP: Then let's leave now. In less than a day, we can be man and—

KERNEY: *(Smiles.)* Slow down, boy. I can't have you locked in jail—hauling a minor across state lines.

KIP: Nineteen is grown.

(Kerney by now is almost dark.)

KERNEY: No sir, not yet—twenty-two long months. Go take a cold swim for two more years. You need exercise.

KIP: *(Whispers.)* You need not to never drink gin again.

KERNEY: This is on *your* soul. *(Then a Mae West imitation.)* I'm a child, big boy. *(A distinct pause, then trailing off in her own voice.)* A jealous child that demands every drop of your heart's blood and will not share it with any live thing—

(The dim sight and sound of Kerney withdrawing, climbing the porch steps, opening the door. Kip clenches his hands in confusion and leaves.)

• • •

The Scene: *Kip returns to the Bascom yard, after a disturbing and difficult meeting with Ora. The gin he has continued to drink hasn't dulled his pain or offered any answers to his problem.*

• • •

(Kip enters, smoothing his hair and clothes (no tie, open shirt). He goes to the center and cups his hands to call for Kerney, then changes his mind. He lays his seersucker

jacket on the ground and goes toward the window. Quietly he begins to sing "Jeannie with the Light Brown Hair." He lifts his hands in almost mock-prayer—the gin is still in him. Then he pushes the window wider open. After a long wait Kerney appears, full-length in the window. She wears a long nightgown but seems wide awake. It takes her awhile to notice Kip.)

KERNEY: Go *on*—

KIP: Where?

KERNEY: *Fly,* to the stars—I know you can.

KIP: Girl, are you still drunk?

KERNEY: I never was but I know who is.

KIP: Come save me then.

KERNEY: I'm no missionary. Save your own soul.

KIP: My body's the problem.

KERNEY: I thought you'd have that cooled down by now.

KIP: No ma'm, still steaming. I've been out seeing to the orders you gave me.

KERNEY: Pa and Walter Parker are asleep. You ought to be.

KIP: *(Holds up his arms for her to join him.)* One short look— at just your face—and then I'll fly.
(Kerney thinks, then slowly climbs through her window, crouches on the ledge and—almost dizzy—sits there.)

KERNEY: You'll kill me yet.
(Kip stays in place.)

KIP: That's not my intention.

KERNEY: What is?
(Kip studies her slowly, hoping to calm the sadness from Ora.)

KIP: Watching you, all dazed and helpless.

KERNEY: Get one thing into your dazed head—Kerney's as helpless as a Mexican rattlesnake. *(She springs from the window ledge to the ground and approaches Kip.)* What did you tell her?
(When Kip looks puzzled.)

KERNEY: You said you obeyed some orders of mine.

KIP: The way's clear now.

KERNEY: What did you tell her?

KIP: I'm not here begging for your secrets, notice.

KERNEY: *(Waits.)* Your concubine was never a secret.

KIP: That's a scandalous lie.

KERNEY: I've known it forever. So have Pa and Walter Parker. And all my friends. So's every colored person between here and Raleigh.

KIP: We won't get anywhere, telling lies. I came here to tell you I did what you asked. Think it over in your spare time, hear?

KERNEY: *(Studies him slowly, nods.)* Now go on to bed.
(She moves toward her window. For a moment Kip balks, stunned by her apparent refusal in the face of his news. But then as she reaches to climb back in, he takes her arm. She pulls free and stays by the window. Again Kip is won by her presence and tries to raise the tone.)

KIP: Those Mexican rattlers you spoke about? They look right fine, undressed for bed.

KERNEY: You don't want to corner one.

KIP: You never hurt a gnat. *(Studies her again.)* You need me, girl.

KERNEY: You'd make a nice hat rack to stand in the hall.

KIP: You'd make a fine statue for the Temple of Venus.

KERNEY: *(Takes a step toward him.)* I'll make you a practical proposition, son. Get somebody sober to drive you to Raleigh. Find you an artist and I'll pose for him, long as it takes to make you a perfect life-sized *me*—real hair, china teeth: your own Kerney Bascomb. Then tease her, squeeze her, do anything you need to that I don't have to watch. *(Turns to her window.)*
(Kip's head has begun to clear. His voice is firm.)

KIP: This is so damned childish. I beg your pardon.

KERNEY: I can sleep tomorrow. I'm not as accustomed to gin as you and I'm—

KIP: We're both heading south.

KERNEY: With the wild geese or what?

KIP: With the man you'll spend your grown life beside.

(Kerney moves closer to see his eyes. Then she steps well back.)

KERNEY: I'm no orphan dog. I don't follow strangers.

KIP: You've known me most of the days of your life. I'm your heart's own choice.

KERNEY: (Laughs one note.) Brace yourself, boy. (Waits.) My heart hasn't chose.

(Kip approaches and reaches for her hand. Kerney draws back.)

KERNEY: I'm thinking. But I have not chosen. I've got real duties—I'm all Pa's got.

KIP: He's got his life—his law practice, this house for a home. He's got Walter Parker.

KERNEY: If I leave now he'll howl like the wind through a burnt-out barn.

KIP: Brace yourself now: That's—the—way—life—is. You want to leave here. You said you were trapped.

KERNEY: It's the trap I know—no mean dark corners.

KIP: If it's my dark corner you're worried about, I told you that's gone.

(This late, and near her father's window, Kerney will not deal with the subject of Ora. She shakes her head No.)

KIP: (A new calm tack.) I know for a fact that your father wants you to have a grown life. (Waits.) I asked him.

KERNEY: Don't start a clean day with a lie, Kip Patrick.

KIP: (Raising his hand to swear.) Two whole days ago, in his office. I'd gone in to ask him about a land problem, my family's land. And when we were finished, your father sat back and asked a few questions about my life—any hopes I had. I didn't feel like he was fishing hard, but finally the trust in his face made me tell him. I said "Mr. Bascomb, I'm in love with Kerney."

KERNEY: No wonder he was so blue tonight.

KIP: Blue? No, lord, he was pink with joy. He said "She mentions your name more than seldom." Then we sang your praises in all major keys.

KERNEY: How sad for you both.

KIP: No! By the end we were whooping like monkeys. *(When he sees a sign of anger in Kerney.)* Whooping in *love,* child—pure brotherly love. He told me about you before I knew you—how you set fire to your granddaddy's hair, how you lamed the gray horse, how you took the good rolling pin and squashed your goldfish.

KERNEY: To see how they worked. But you never got serious with him again?

KIP: Sorry. I told him he couldn't change my heart, no matter what terrors he dredged from the past.

(Kerney moves quickly to the edge of dark—her back to Kip, facing the audience. This is hard to hear.)

KIP: Then he finally gave me a reason to hope.

(Kerney crouches to the ground and covers her ears.)

KIP: He said "I'll give her to the man she chooses, no sooner than that." I said "Will you bless him?" He walked all the long way back to his desk. Then he faced me and nodded "It'll be God's will."

KERNEY: *(Faces Kip, stands.)* That proves you're lying. Pa's an old agnostic.

KIP: *(Smiles.)* Ah! I too smelled a lawyer's trick. I said "Sir. you're no church-going man." He said "True, Kipple, but that's owing to the scenery: those ladies' hats, those fat preachers stuffed down in swallow-tailed coats."

KERNEY: *(Nods.)* His voice.

(Disheartened, she moves a little farther from Kip.)

KIP: Marry me.

KERNEY: Why?

KIP: *(With smiling impatience.)* I've done the last big deed you demanded. You're changing ground fast as a Mexican rattler.

KERNEY: *(Waits.)* I need to know what drives a person as smart as you to give up freedom and all his sins and crave wild me.

KIP: *(Waits.)* You know about the beauty part, but there's so much more. *(Tries to see her in the dark.)* —How scary you are, what a daring soul. Everybody else we know is groggy. I've been a stunt pilot all my life and so have you. I need a brave wife.

KERNEY: I'm weak as water.

KIP: You're a damned *power* plant. You glow in the dark. You'd gnaw your arm off, neat at the shoulder, if you got caught. You've got a mind in all that hair, that glorious hair—

KERNEY: Just stay out of the beauty department.

KIP: I can see children all in your eyes, all lovely as you—

KERNEY: No healthy young man ever wants children. Tell that to some sucker-homebody, not wise old Kerney.

KIP: *(Waits, then with new firmness.)* All right, goddammit—I feel like I'm strong and need to bear weight. You're what I want to lift and carry. I want to bear you forward through life, whatever years are left.

(As Kip's explanation grew, it gradually fascinated Kerney with its passion; and eventually it touched her. She moves back nearer, into the moonlight.)

KERNEY: All this moonlight and all that honor—Kip, I think you mean it. And a lot of the time, I want to step toward you. But there's still big trouble, deep back in my head. *(Waits.)* I'm such a part of my father's life, so maybe I've had all the marriage I need. More likely though, I don't have the talent. I just can't say, tonight or next week, where I'm likely to be six minutes from now, much less sixty years.

KIP: Do you love me?

KERNEY: Now you sound like Jeffer.

(Kip turns and begins to leave.)

KERNEY: I may well need you someday soon.

(When he stops to listen.)

KERNEY: But maybe right now, here tonight, it's your age that's the problem. Your glands and all—

KIP: *(Calm but strong.)* My glands cranked up more than eight years ago. By now I've learned how to screen glands out of my hopes and dreams.

KERNEY: *(Nods, in innocence.)* I'll try to answer you soon as I can. Right now my tired runaway mind wants to stand in a field, with shade and a pear tree and no—other—thing.

KIP: You scare me.

KERNEY: I told you I would. I scare myself so bad I can't breathe.

KIP: *(Believing her, relenting a little.)* I've told you my feelings. I won't try again. Remember my question—will you stay by me, through whatever comes, till you or I end? Like it or not, we were both born with faces people fly up against like moths to a light—

KERNEY: Or me to the moon.

(Through the following Kip slowly walks over and stands close to Kerney.)

KIP: So nobody's going to leave us alone. If we don't choose each other soon, we'll be worn down with people coming at us. That's not pride; it's a flat damned fact. *(He takes Kerney's hands.)*

(Suddenly she raises the joined hands and kisses each, entirely sincere. Kip is moved but after a moment he withdraws both hands and steps back.)

KERNEY: Soon, soon. You've got my word.

(Kip turns and walks away slowly, As he sinks into darkness, Kerney can't help teasing.)

KERNEY: Take several more words—all my favorites. Take— *(Waits, then with hushed but exaggerated relish.)* Alabaster. Chamomile. Resurrection. Take *cellar door.*

KIP: *(At a distance.)* Get serious; that's two.

(Kerney reaches for her window ledge.)

KERNEY: Take *forsaking all others.*

KIP: Take *hush your mouth.*

(At the sound of Kip's car, Kerney waves once. Then she makes the small leap and enters her window.)

Hidden Parts

by Lynne Alvarez

The Play: A gifted young pianist comes home to the Midwest to celebrate his success with his mother, father, and young cousin. The reunion is charged with the secrets and lies that abound. Abuse and betrayal poison the lives of this family. As the truth unravels, surprise lurks within the farmhouse, where the father is consigned to never leave, and in the field of eight-foot-tall corn, where the young cousin goes for time alone.

Time and Place: All action takes place during five days in the present in and around a cornfield on a farm in the Midwest

The Scene: *It is the first evening. Daria (fifteen) is at work in a small clearing deep in the cornfield creating exotic umbrellas by stripping the frames and attaching new special fabric. Through the dense corn stocks bursts Daria's cousin, Justin (twenty-one).*

• • •

(We hear "Blue Moon" from a great distance. We are in the clearing in the cornfield where Daria works. Several open umbrellas, a cot, a moon overhead. A lantern. Daria is stripping a frame. Rustling in the field. Daria stops. She slowly rises to get an umbrella, which she holds as a weapon.)

DARIA: Okay now...all right, boy...come here...here, boy... here, boy...
(Justin bursts through the corn. His coat covers his face. He looks like a giant crow.)

JUSTIN: Jesus, how do you expect anyone to find you. It's a maze in there. *(He laughs.)*

DARIA: What the hell are you laughin' at?

JUSTIN: Maize corn, maze labyrinth. A play on words. *(Pause.)* I made a joke.

DARIA: I thought you were a goddamn dog. *(She puts her umbrella away.)* I got to work.

JUSTIN: Umbrellas!

DARIA: These umbrellas sell like goddamn hotcakes. I'm making a lot of money. Charlie takes them to fairs and bazaars for me, that sort of thing.

JUSTIN: Charlie?

DARIA: Jericho.

JUSTIN: Ahhh yes, those sweaty, hardworking Jericho boys.

DARIA: I made forty-six bucks last week plus I got a big order from a lady in Brighton who wants three wedding shawls. I already got the idea for them. All fish and seaflowers 'cause her daughter's a Pisces.

JUSTIN: I see everything's under control, eh?

DARIA: Sure.

JUSTIN: Nice place you got here.

DARIA: I love nature.

JUSTIN: Spartan, but peaceful. Beats the madhouse back there.

DARIA: The house?

JUSTIN: Yes. The mad-angry, mad-crazy house.

DARIA: Stop it!

JUSTIN: Come here little one.

DARIA: I hear you're going to England. They say it rains a lot there. *(She presents him with a closed umbrella.)* I made you a present. What do you think?

JUSTIN: Give me a minute. *(He opens it.)* It's amazing. I can't believe a squirt like you made this.

DARIA: I didn't make the frame. Charlie found it. You know Charlie.

JUSTIN: Um-hmm.

DARIA: I thought of every mean creature I possibly could. Hawks and eagles and sharks. But look at this. *(She turns it for him.)* Ain't this a bitch? The dragon! If you turn it, the wings sparkle. Crushed the mother-of-pearl myself.

That's seashells, you know. And look at his fangs and the fire rolling out. I think he's goddamn beautiful. Fierce, breathin fire. So fierce…and he's beautiful…like you. You like it?

JUSTIN: Are you kidding? Of course I like it. I love it.

DARIA: Cross your heart?

JUSTIN: Cross my heart. Hope to die.

DARIA: I think artists can carry it off, right?

JUSTIN: Right. Tell me how you're doing? Really.

DARIA: Every time you open it, you'll be someplace beautiful and you'll think of me.

JUSTIN: Then I don't need to open it now, do I?

DARIA: Justin, you're a jerk.

JUSTIN: Like Pop?

DARIA: No.

JUSTIN: Do you think all men are like Pop?

DARIA: Do you think all girls are like me?

JUSTIN: I take it that was a stupid question.

DARIA: Yeah.

JUSTIN: Tell me how to talk to you then. I don't know how anymore.

DARIA: If you were here for more than fifteen seconds you would.

JUSTIN: I'll make it up to you.

DARIA: It's beautiful out here. I seen spring and summer. It's fall. Winter's comin'. Do you think I can get out of here, Justin? I don't have much time. Winter's comin' early this year. I can tell. See over there. The trees are full of sparrows. Hundreds of 'em. They're going south already. The geese are leavin'. The leaves are gone, the grass is white. It's gonna be cold and I don't want to go back to that house again…that madhouse. Justin, I think this is a desperate situation.

JUSTIN: Not so desperate. I can help.

DARIA: No one can help.

JUSTIN: I'll subsidize you. I'll buy all your umbrellas—past, present, and future.

DARIA: It's like I can't move. My goddamn heart weighs a million pounds.

JUSTIN: A heavy heart, eh? Weighted down by your long dark past.

DARIA: Why are you laughing? It is dark. And I need something dark to get rid of it. *(She shivers.)* I scared myself. *(She lights her lantern.)* Look at that fire. Pretty little dancing thing.

JUSTIN: So you are a gypsy after all. Fire, mystery, romance. What would a gypsy be without a long dark past. That shouldn't stop you. We all have our troubles, sweetheart, I left when I was your age.

DARIA: You weren't raped!

JUSTIN: Don't ever say that again! We've all had our troubles!

DARIA: Yeah, well you had scholarships, and teachers and places to go.

JUSTIN: Sure, I had music. I could pull it out like a pocket mirror and blind folks with the flash...but of course, I also had a heavy heart.

DARIA: It was different for you.

JUSTIN: All right. No parallels there. Let's find another example then. Closer to home. Your mother. Nothing stopped her. She left. Seventeen, husband dead, living with strangers, a babe in arms and then...then what? She left. Whatever happened to her, whatever made her leave suddenly without a word, without a warning, whatever dark and painful thing happened to her didn't weigh her down. It freed her. She left. She left a trail for you to follow.

DARIA: She didn't leave a trail. She left me! She's dead as far as I'm concerned.

JUSTIN: I don't want to get you upset. I just don't want to come back in a year and find you angry and bald and swearing like a sailor.

DARIA: You're never goddamn serious.

JUSTIN: Aren't I? Listen to my concert tomorrow night and you'll hear serious, I assure you. Boulez at nine. The university station.

DARIA: FM right? All goddamn culture's on FM.

JUSTIN: And wait up. I want to see you. I'll quiz you on the program notes.

DARIA: What?

JUSTIN: *(Opens the umbrella.)* Great umbrella. Just great. Wait here tomorrow. And no bullshit. *(He exits whistling.)*

DARIA: *(Calls after him happily.)* You got bullshit on your shoes, farmboy!
(Lights fade.)

• • •

The Scene: *The fifth day. Late afternoon. Daria is waiting for Justin. She holds one large black umbrella over her head or perhaps it floats there. The clearing is clean. Daria is dressed neatly, a Sunday quality to her appearance.*

• • •

(Late afternoon. Justin appears.)

JUSTIN: All right. We're even. You paid me back. I stood you up and now you've stood me up.

DARIA: I thought you'd left.

JUSTIN: I should have.

DARIA: You didn't come by last night. I waited up for you. You were pissed, right?

JUSTIN: Not really. However, it did take quite a while to change the car rental, the plane tickets, the hotel reservations, a couple of taping sessions, and a rehearsal.

DARIA: I'm sorry.

JUSTIN: Good.

DARIA: You were plenty mad at me, weren't you?

JUSTIN: Yes, I was. Actually, I was more hurt than mad. But I'm over it. Cool, calm. *(Holds out his hands.)* See? *(Roughly.)* Let's go.

DARIA: There's more to say.

JUSTIN: In the car.

DARIA: I am leaving. I can't tell you how glad I am. Everything's over. Look at those old witchy trees across there. I didn't even see the sparrows leave. Did you? The geese even took off. You can still hear them calling to each other. We all should leave, don't you think?

JUSTIN: Is there a bag or something?

DARIA: Not really. I sold all my umbrellas. Look—I made a hundred and fifty-eight dollars yesterday. I wanted to leave with money, you know?

JUSTIN: You're scared, aren't you, little gypsy? You don't have to be scared. I'll take care of you. You are pretty. I don't think I've ever seen you so pretty.

DARIA: That's a real compliment when you say it. You have lots of experience. Charlie says it too, but he's never had a girlfriend so I don't think he knows what he's talking about.

JUSTIN: Why are we talking about Charlie? I don't really feel like talking about Charlie. I arrange to come halfway across the continent—I insist on these stupid broadcasts to corn pickers and dairy farmers—just to see you and you're off with Charlie. You can't even see your way to meeting me on time! Well, I apologize. I really do. I thought I was just a wee bit more important to you. Well, I'm sorry. My mistake.

DARIA: Justin, that's not it.

JUSTIN: And there I was, packed and nervous like some idiot teenager, waiting for you—and you're off selling these *(Grabs her umbrella.)* ridiculous umbrellas—

DARIA: Hey careful!

JUSTIN: —with some local hick! Jesus!

DARIA: I thought you weren't mad.

JUSTIN: I'm not.

DARIA: Oh yeah?

JUSTIN: I'm not. I'm furious!

DARIA: Did you really come here just for me?

JUSTIN: Yes.

DARIA: That's the sweetest thing anyone's ever done.

JUSTIN: "I am no pilot, yet wert thou as far as that vast shore wash'd with the furthest sea, I would venture for such merchandise…"

DARIA: That's the Bible, right?

JUSTIN: It's Shakespeare. Romeo to Juliet.

DARIA: I'm leaving, but I'm not going with you, Justin. Charlie's offered to drive me to Missouri to see if I can locate my mother. I want to see what she's like. I want to see if she has gypsy hair and gypsy eyes. You were right again, see? She left a trail and I want to follow. I want to see her, Justin. And it isn't as crazy as it seems. We're going to hit all the flea markets along the way and the county fairs. This is the season. My mom might be at one of the fairs reading cards. She'd be easy to spot. There can't be too many gypsies in Missouri.

JUSTIN: A lovely girl like you. Of course you'd have someone. How stupid of me! You should have told me sooner. You let me go on and on like a fool!

DARIA: Not you, Justin. You could never be a fool. You're wonderful. So cool and handsome. Trailing secrets. I know you think you've come all this way for nothing, but you don't know how much you've done for me. You don't know. I couldn't do any of this without you. You brought the world to me. I was as stuck here as some dumb old crow in a cornfield. I couldn't step through the open door of a public bus, never mind ride in a truck alone with a boy. But you came here so cocky and sure of yourself, I thought, nothing's stopping him, right? Well, nothing's stopping me neither. It was my thoughts all along, just like you said. And you know what, I bet that's just how my mother felt too. Free. Walking down the road to who knows where.

JUSTIN: For God's sakes, Daria, you're not going to leave me for an eighteen-year-old boy!

DARIA: You're not taking this right.

JUSTIN: You know what the trouble is? You don't know what the fuck you're doing. You never have. You don't have a clue about other people's intent or your effect on them, and that's going to get you into a mess all over again. Now, let's look at this rationally, okay? Okay?

DARIA: Okay. But you're mad.

JUSTIN: No. I'm not. Now look, this Jericho boy, who the hell is he?

DARIA: Charlie.

JUSTIN: This Charlie kid, he's taking you around the country for free because he's such a kind, generous person. Is that right?

DARIA: It isn't free. I'll pay him for gas and stuff.

JUSTIN: But what does he really get?

DARIA: I guess about full value for gas and oil.

JUSTIN: Don't play the hick with me, little one.

DARIA: He gets my friendship. That's what he gets. He's helping me out.

JUSTIN: People don't do things for nothing. You're helping him out too, aren't you?

DARIA: Don't say it like that. You make it sound dirty and nasty. Like I'm selling myself or something.

JUSTIN: Do you love him?

DARIA: It's nothing like that!

JUSTIN: It's something! There's something. What is it? What's the matter?

DARIA: Your questions make me feel like a criminal.

JUSTIN: You're hiding something. Don't hide things from me.

DARIA: You get mad now. You never used to get mad.

JUSTIN: You're right. I won't get mad.

(Daria looks at him skeptically.)

JUSTIN: I won't. Cross my heart.

DARIA: I asked Charlie to lie down on top of me to see if I could get near a man. But I couldn't do it. As soon as I felt him pinning me down, I wanted to scream and tear his eyes out. You should have seen him jump back.

JUSTIN: Daria, you just can't do those things.

DARIA: I'll never be a proper woman.

JUSTIN: You are a proper woman. You're perfect.

DARIA: I'm going with him anyways. He thinks we'll try again, I can tell. Maybe I should. But inside me, I don't know. But you would know, Justin. Tell me, am I doomed? Will I ever be like any woman with any man?

JUSTIN: Yes, yes. Of course you will.

DARIA: Maybe I'll always feel pinned down. Maybe I'll always feel that terror in my chest. Maybe every man who lies on top of me will be the man who raped me cold in that field.

JUSTIN: Charlie's virtually a stranger. You can't jump into bed with a stranger.

DARIA: Yeah, you should talk. You've had lots of girls, right? I bet you don't even remember half of their names?

JUSTIN: Girls and girls and girls.

DARIA: And they didn't make you want to scream, did they?

JUSTIN: Are you so sure? Are you so very sure, little one? What about my first love? Surely you remember. She was such a lovely girl. I was as close to her as I've been to any human being in my life. But she was young, wasn't she? That was a problem. She didn't know what she was doing. She sure was pretty. She had long silky hair, beautiful hair that fell smooth as water along her face. But she tortured me. Never gave it a second thought. She'd look at me with those black eyes and tell me about the boys she wanted to kiss. We'd go for walks—she'd take my hand and look up at me and ask if she'd ever "really, truly" fall in love. Can you imagine? With me standing there half dead on my feet for her? It killed me. I hated her. I tore up everything she ever gave me—cards, photos, little presents. She gave me a baby field mouse once, and I drowned it!

DARIA: Why I...gave you a baby field mouse...

JUSTIN: But every conscious moment of my life, I've been bound to her. And it's very ironic, Daria. I must tell you how ironic it is. It didn't destroy me. I've become a big success! I use it. Endlessly. In my music. That fury slices through me so I bleed in public until they applaud. It all comes from her, isn't that funny? And I've become quite well known. And it doesn't matter! Because no matter how many thousands and thousands of people sit at my feet, no matter how many lights burn over me on stage, it's always dark and cold and I'm alone.

DARIA: That girl you're talking about is me, isn't it?

JUSTIN: Yes.

DARIA: I don't want that girl to be me.

JUSTIN: It just happened. I couldn't help it. But I swear. I promise you. I can make things better. I swear. It won't be like Charlie or whatever his name is. You'll make love again. Under the sky with the stars spinning. I swear to God.

DARIA: I don't want it this way.

JUSTIN: Yes you do.

DARIA: No I don't, Justin.

JUSTIN: Everything about you tells me you do. The way you move, the way you take my hand and laugh, the way you swear—even your goddamn swearing. Christ! I miss your hair though, your long beautiful hair like a rippling stream along a smooth white shore. *(He touches her neck.)*

DARIA: Don't do that. Hell, Justin. It was you. It was. Why did it have to be you?

JUSTIN: Wait. Listen to me, Daria. Please!

(Daria turns and runs through the field to the farm.)

High Tide
by Brad Slaight

The Play: Two young men attempt to sort out their feelings after the death of their best friend. Into their private conversation come two young women who provide the moment for a startling revelation.

Time and Place: Late Fall, 1990s. A Southern California beach.

The Scene: *Connie (seventeen) has stepped on glass and cut her foot. Her friend, Lisa, and Brian's (eighteen) friend, Keith, have gone for help. Left alone, Brian tells Connie of the tragic death of his friend, Kirk.*

• • •

BRIAN: He bought a new surfboard last week. Used the money he was saving for college. He didn't need a new board... already had three of the best and a big company was talking to him about sponsorship. But he just got up one day and decided to buy another one. *(Pause.)* It was the last one he ever rode.

CONNIE: That's sad.

BRIAN: The day before he died, I stopped at his house after school. He missed two days in a row and I was going to give him the old "no diploma, no surf tour" speech. He just laughed it off. *(Pause.)* We came down here and I watched as he broke in his new board. Rolling, shooting, pitching back and forth. The guy was incredible. Perfect balance. He had so much talent. *(Pause.)* We sat for an hour and talked about his upcoming tournament. Girls. School. The usual stuff. *(Breaking a bit.)* And I said to myself...I've never seen Kirk so happy. But he wasn't. There was something inside of him that was tearing him up. And I just don't understand why he couldn't have talked to me about it. Instead of letting it push him over the edge.

CONNIE: Over the edge?

BRIAN: Kirk's drowning was no accident. He committed suicide. *(There is a moment of silence. Connie is a bit awkward with this new information. Brian pulls a letter from his jacket.)*

BRIAN: The day after he died, I found this letter in our locker at school. *(Angry.)* Didn't leave it with his Mom, or his girlfriend...no, he chose me to be the one to find it.

CONNIE: You sure you want to tell me this? I mean, it was pretty obvious that Keith wants people to think it was an accident.

BRIAN: That's because Keith thinks it was.

CONNIE: You haven't told him yet?

BRIAN: I haven't told anyone. Except you.

(Connie looks at him for a moment.)

CONNIE: Why?

BRIAN: I don't know.

CONNIE: Not even his parents?

BRIAN: Especially not them.

(Connie is not sure what she should say. Decides to say nothing.)

BRIAN: When I read his letter, my first impulse was to run to his parents. But I just kinda walked around for a few hours. And then when I went to the funeral home that night and saw them all there...crying and talking about how great of a kid he was... *(Brian breaks a bit. He takes a few steps away.)* Goddamn him for doing this to me. For doing this to everyone.

(Pause.)

CONNIE: I don't know what to say.

BRIAN: And neither did I. So I just didn't say anything. *(Pause.)* What would you have done?

CONNIE: I don't know. I can see how hard it would be. I mean, it's not the kind of thing people would want to hear. But sooner or later they would have to be told.

BRIAN: Today at the funeral, I wanted to stand up in the middle of the service and just scream it out...you know, take care of it all at once. And then I looked around at the faces. And I heard the crying again. When a young person dies the crying is always louder...more painful.

CONNIE: Well I can understand how that wouldn't have been the place...

BRIAN: I even thought about not telling anyone...ever. He's dead. This can only hurt the ones who are already in pain. If I never said anything...at least they wouldn't have to go through what I'm going through. Maybe it's best just to keep it to myself.

CONNIE: But you're telling me.

BRIAN: It just came out. Maybe Keith's Mother was right... maybe it is easier to talk to strangers. *(Brian looks at Connie for a moment.)* God, I'm sorry. This really isn't fair to dump on you.

CONNIE: It's alright. I understand.

BRIAN: But you didn't know Kirk. And you don't know me. It's just that...well I had to tell somebody. *(Pause.)* I thought I could tell Keith...I thought if we came down here, away from all of those people, I'd show him the letter and talk with him about it...but every time I tried, the words seemed to choke up in my throat.

CONNIE: He could help you get through this.

BRIAN: Keith looked up to Kirk. We all did. Something like this...what if he decides to do the same thing? What if it pushes him over the edge, too? *(Brian turns away and faces the ocean.)* They're going to blame me for what happened to Kirk.

CONNIE: Why would anyone blame you?

BRIAN: Because I didn't see it coming. I knew him better than anyone else. I should have known.

CONNIE: But you didn't.

BRIAN: Why couldn't he have given me a clue? Some kind of sign. Even his letter...doesn't really say why. *(Reads from letter.)* "Brian, By the time you get this letter I will be dead. I'm sorry for putting you through this. I can't go on. Kirk." *(Pause.)* Can't go on? What the hell is that supposed to mean? Why couldn't he have gone on? Why?

CONNIE: There's nothing you could have done.

BRIAN: I keep going over and over the last time I saw him. Trying to remember everything we talked about...something he said that might have been a clue. But there was nothing. *(Pause.)* He kept everything inside...and he took it all with him.

CONNIE: And if you do the same thing...you've learned nothing from his mistake. *(Quickly.)* I'm sorry...I shouldn't have said that.

BRIAN: Don't be sorry.

CONNIE: But I have no right to criticize you. I mean, I have no idea what you're going through right now.

Jack, or the Submission

by Eugene Ionesco, translated by Donald M. Allen

The Play: In this absurdist play, Jack, a petulant young man, frustrates his family when he refuses to marry the girl of their dreams.

Time and Place: A somber, gray, messy room with pictures that don't represent anything and furniture that is dilapidated; the time is neither wrong nor right.

The Scene: *Dressed in a wedding gown, Roberta II, a big, majestic girl—though shy and timid—with three noses (and nine fingers) has been attempting to interest and then seduce a bemused Jack.*

● ● ●

ROBERTA II: Listen, I have some horses, some stallions, some brood mares, I have only those, would you like them?

JACK: Yes, tell me about your horses.

ROBERTA II: In my place, I have a neighbor who's a miller. He had a mare who dropped two sweet little foals. Very sweet, very cute. The bitch also dropped two little puppies, in the stable. The miller is old, his eyesight isn't very good. The miller took the foals to drown them in the pond, in place of the little puppies...

JACK: Ah! Ah!

ROBERTA II: When he realized his error, it was too late. He wasn't able to save them.

JACK: *(A little amused, he smiles.)* Yes? Hm.

(As Roberta tells her story, Jack's smile becomes a full laugh, but he's still calm. During the following scene both Roberta and Jack develop—very slowly at first—a declamatory style; the rhythm intensifies progressively, then slows down toward the end.)

ROBERTA II: No, he wasn't able to save them. But it wasn't really the foals either that he drowned. In fact, when he returned to the stable, the miller saw that the foals were there with their mamma; the little puppies were there too with their mamma, who was barking. But his own child, his baby who had just been born, was no longer beside his mother, the milleress. It was really the baby that he'd thrown into the water. He ran quickly to the pond. The child held out his arms and cried: "Papa, Papa"…It was heartrending. Only his tiny arm could be seen which said: "Papa, Papa! Mamma, Mamma." And then he sank, and that was all. And that was all. He didn't see him again. The miller went mad. Killed his wife. Destroyed everything. Set fire to it. Hung himself.

JACK: *(Very satisfied with this story.)* What a tragic error. A sublime error!

ROBERTA II: But the foals frolic in the meadow. The little puppies have grown big.

JACK: I love your horses. They're intoxicating. Tell me another about a dog, or a horse.

ROBERTA II: The one who was engulfed in the marsh, buried alive, so that you could hear him leaping, howling, and rolling in his grave before he died?

JACK: That one or another.

ROBERTA II: Would you like the one about a horse of the desert, of a city in the Sahara?

JACK: *(Interested, as though in spite of himself, and louder and louder.)* The metropolis of the desert!…

ROBERTA II: All of bricks, all the houses there are made of bricks, the streets are burning…the fire runs through underneath…the dry air, the very red dust.

JACK: And the fiery dust.

ROBERTA II: The natives there have been dead for a long time, their cadavers are desiccating in the houses.

JACK: Behind the closed shutters. Behind the red iron grills.

ROBERTA II: Not a man in the empty streets. Not a beast. Not a bird. Not a blade of grass, not even a withered one. Not a rat, not a fly...

JACK: Metropolis of my future!

ROBERTA II: Suddenly, in the distance, a horse whinnies...han! han! Approaches, han! han! han! han!

JACK: *(Suddenly happy.)* Oh yes, that's it, han! han! han!

ROBERTA II: Galloping at full speed, galloping at full speed...

JACK: Haan! haan! haan!

ROBERTA II: There he is on the great empty square, there he is...He whinnies, runs around, galloping, runs around, galloping...runs around, galloping, runs around, galloping.

JACK: Han! han! haan! at full speed, galloping, at full speed, galloping...Oh yes, han! han! han! galloping, galloping, galloping as hard as he can.

ROBERTA II: His hooves: click clack click clack, galloping, striking sparks. Click...clack...clack...clack...vrr...

JACK: *(Laughing.)* Oh yes, yes, bravo, I know, I know what's going to happen. But quickly...quickly...go on...hurrah...

ROBERTA II: He trembles, he's afraid...the stallion...

JACK: Yes, hurrah...He whinnies, he cries with fear, han!... Han!...He cries out his fear, han! han! let's hurry...let's hurry...

(A blazing horse's mane crosses from one end of the stage to the other.)

ROBERTA II: Oh! he won't escape...never fear...He turns around and around, gallops in a circle...

JACK: Bravo, that's it! I see...I see...a spark in his mane...He shakes his head...Ah! ah! ah! it burns him! it hurts him!

ROBERTA II: He's afraid! he gallops. In a circle. He rears!...

JACK: His mane is blazing! His beautiful mane...He cries, he whinnies. Han! han! The flame flashes up...His mane is blazing. His mane is burning. Han! han! burn! burn! han! han!

ROBERTA II: The more he gallops, the more the flame spreads.

He is mad, he's terrified, he's in pain, he's sick, he's afraid, he's in pain...it flames up, it spreads all over his body!...

JACK: Han! han! he leaps. Oh, what flaming leaps, flaming flaming! He cries, he rears up. Stop, stop, Roberta. It's too fast...not so fast...

ROBERTA II: *(Aside.)* Oh...he called me by my given name...He's going to love me!

JACK: He's burning too fast...It's going to end! Make the fire last...

ROBERTA II: It's the fire that goes so fast—the flames are coming out of his ears and his nostrils, and thick smoke...

JACK: He screams with fear, he screams with pain. He leaps so high. He has wings of flame!

ROBERTA II: How beautiful he is, he's turning all pink, like an enormous lampshade. He wants to fly. He stops, he doesn't know what to do...His horseshoes smoke and redden. Haan! Through his transparent hide, we see the fire burning inside him. Han! he flames! He's a living torch...He's only a handful of cinders...He's no more, but we hear still in the distance the echo of his cries reverberating, and weakening...like the whinnyings of another horse in the empty streets.

JACK: My throat is parched, this has made me thirsty...Water, water. Ah! how he flamed, the stallion...how beautiful it was...what a flame...ah! *(Exhausted.)* I'm thirsty...

ROBERTA II: Come on...don't be afraid...I'm moist...My necklace is made of mud, my breasts are dissolving, my pelvis is wet, I've got water in my crevasses, I'm sinking down. My true name is Liza. In my belly, there are pools, swamps... I've got a house of clay. I'm always cool...There's moss... big flies, cockroaches, sowbugs, toads. Under the wet covers they make love...they're swollen with happiness! I wrap my arms around you like snakes; with my soft thighs... you plunge down and you dissolve...in my locks which drizzle, drizzle, rain, rain. My mouth trickles down, my legs trickle, my naked shoulders trickle, my hair trickles, everything trickles down, runs, everything trickles, the sky trickles down, the stars run, trickle down; trickle…

JACK: *(In ecstasy.)* Cha-a-arming!

ROBERTA II: Make yourself comfortable. Why don't you take off this thing that you're wearing? What is it? Or who is it?

JACK: *(Still in ecstasy.)* Cha-a-arming!

ROBERTA II: What is this, on your head?

JACK: Guess! It's a kind of cat. I put it on at dawn.

ROBERTA II: Is it a castle?

JACK: I keep it on my head all day. At table, in the parlor, I never take it off. I don't tip it to people.

ROBERTA II: Is it a camel? A capricorn?

JACK: It'll strike with its paws, but it can till the soil.

ROBERTA II: Is it a catapult?

JACK: It weeps sometimes.

ROBERTA II: Is it a catarrh?

JACK: It can live under water.

ROBERTA II: Is it a catfish?

JACK: It can also float on the waves.

ROBERTA II: Is it a catamaran?

JACK: You're warm.

ROBERTA II: Is it a caterpillar?

JACK: Sometimes it likes to hide in the mountain. It's not pretty.

ROBERTA II: Is it a catamount?

JACK: It makes me laugh.

ROBERTA II: Is it a cataclysm, or a catalog?

JACK: It screams, it splits my ears.

ROBERTA II: Is it a caterwaul?

JACK: It loves ornaments.

ROBERTA II: Is it a catacomb?

JACK: No!

ROBERTA II: The cat's got my tongue.

JACK: It's a cap.

ROBERTA II: Oh, take it off. Take it off, Jack. My Jack. With me, you'll be in your element. I have some, I have as many as you want, quantities!

JACK: ...Of caps?

ROBERTA II: No...of cats...skinless ones!

JACK: Oh, my cat... *(He takes off his cap, he has green hair.)*

ROBERTA II: Oh, my cat...

JACK: My cat, my catawampous.

ROBERTA II: In the cellar of my castle, everything is cat...

JACK: Everything is cat.

ROBERTA II: All we need to designate things is one single word: cat. Cats are called cat, food: cat, insects: cat, chairs: cat, you: cat, me: cat, the roof: cat, the number one: cat, number two: cat, three: cat, twenty: cat, thirty: cat, all the adverbs: cat, all the prepositions: cat. It's easier to talk that way...

JACK: In order to say: I'm terribly sleepy, let's go to sleep, let's go to sleep...

ROBERTA II: Cat, cat, cat, cat.

JACK: In order to say: Bring me some cold noodles, some warm lemonade, and no coffee...

ROBERTA II: Cat, cat, cat, cat, cat, cat, cat, cat.

JACK: And Jack, and Roberta?

ROBERTA II: Cat, cat. *(She takes out her hand with nine fingers that she has kept hidden under her gown.)*

JACK: Oh yes! It's easy to talk now...In fact it's scarcely worth the bother...

(He sees her hand with nine fingers.)

JACK: Oh! You've got nine fingers on your left hand? You're rich, I'll marry you...

(They put their arms around each other very awkwardly. Jack kisses the noses of Roberta II, one after the other, while Father Jack, Mother Jack, Jacqueline, the Grandparents, Father Robert, and Mother Robert enter without saying a word, one after the other, waddling along, in a sort of ridiculous dance, embarrassing, in a vague circle, around Jack and Roberta II who remain at

stage center, awkwardly enlaced. Father Robert silently and slowly strikes his hands together. Mother Robert, her arms clasped behind her neck, makes pirouettes, smiling stupidly. Mother Jack, with an expressionless face, shakes her shoulders in a grotesque fashion. Father Jack pulls up his pants and walks on his heels. Jacqueline nods her head, then they continue to dance, squatting down, while Jack and Roberta II squat down too, and remain motionless. The Grandparents turn around, idiotically, looking at each other, and smiling; then they squat down in their turn. All this must produce in the audience a feeling of embarrassment, awkwardness, and shame. The darkness increases. On stage, the actors utter vague miaows while turning around, bizarre moans, croakings. The darkness increases. We can still see the Jacks and Robertas crawling on the stage. We hear their animal noises, then we don't see them any more. We hear only their moans, their sighs, then all fades away, all is extinguished. Again, a gray light comes on. All the characters have disappeared, except Roberta, who is lying down, or rather squatting down, buried beneath her gown. We see only her pale face, with its three noses quivering, and her nine fingers moving like snakes.)

The Kentucky Cycle
by Robert Schenkkan

The Play: A series a nine short plays, this Pulitzer Prize–winning cycle of plays spans two centuries and seven generations of Kentuckians. The plays focus on the lives of the turbulent Rowen family as they evolve through the years, and probes the myths of American expansion and growth that have produced what we are today.

Time and Place: Eastern Kentucky. 1775–1975.

The Scene: *In the opening of the third play in Part One,* The Homecoming *(set in 1792 on a ridge overlooking a vast expanse of mountains), Rebecca Talbert (sixteen) sneaks up on Patrick Rowen (sixteen), who—hunting rifle in hand—is quietly contemplating life and the wilderness before him.*

• • •

REBECCA: If I was an Injun, you'd be dead six ways from Sunday by now.

PATRICK: *(Unperturbed.)* Ain't been no Injuns round here for five years.

REBECCA: Well, if there was, I'da had your scalp for sure.

PATRICK: *(Laughs.)* I heard you comin' days ago.

REBECCA: Oh, yeah? How'd you know it was me?

PATRICK: 'Cause as much noise as you were making, it had to be you or some pack of razorback hogs. I'm sittin' downwind of you and decided early on it couldn't be them hogs.

REBECCA: Well. That's a nice thing to say.

PATRICK: Coulda been a lot worse. I coulda said I was still guessing till I saw you!

(She swings at him. He ducks and laughs.)

PATRICK: I take it back!

REBECCA: You better. *(Beat.)* Pretty up here. Maybe we oughta have us a house up here when we get married. Whatya think?

PATRICK: Don't stand there.

(She ignores him. He pulls her down beside him.)

PATRICK: I said, don't stand.

REBECCA: Why not?

PATRICK: 'Cause we're on a ridge, facin' the sun, and you stand there you stick out like a sore thumb. Might just as well fire off a cannon for folks.

REBECCA: What's to worry? "Ain't been no Injuns round here for five years." Not countin' you or your ma.

PATRICK: There's worse things than Injuns.

REBECCA: I been missin' you somethin' fierce. You miss me?

PATRICK: Yeah. I reckon.

REBECCA: "You reckon?" Well, whyn't you gimme some sugar and we'll find out for sure. Come on.

(He kisses her.)

REBECCA: Well, what you think?

PATRICK: Yeah. I missed you.

(Beat.)

REBECCA: I knew you'd be up here. Know how I knew? When you weren't in the fields I asked Star...

PATRICK: *(Concerned.)* I told you, you shouldn't oughta bother my ma like that...

REBECCA: All right by me! Didn't so much as give me back a how-do-you-do. Just grunted and pointed off toward the woods. She don't like me much.

PATRICK: She likes you fine.

REBECCA: Shoot! She'd just as soon put that gimpy leg of hers up against my backside as look at me.

PATRICK: Don't make fun of her!

REBECCA: I wasn't...makin' fun of her.

PATRICK: Just don't talk about my ma like that.

REBECCA: Well, how come she don't like me? I ain't never done nothin', ain't never looked crossways at her, but whenever

she come visitin', you'd think I was a chair or somethin'
for all the notice she give me.
(Beat.)
PATRICK: *(Surprised.)* My ma's been visitin' over to your place?
REBECCA: Sure. Coupla times.
PATRICK: She don't visit nobody. Ain't never been acrost to the
other side of the Shilling as far as I ever knew.
REBECCA: Well, it warn't no social call you understand. My
daddy, he had a cut on him that went bad and everythin'
and I thought maybe he was gonna lose that arm or die,
maybe. Well, it ain't no secret round here that your ma
got healin' hands. I guess Jeremiah gone and fetched her,
'cause she just shows up—bled my daddy and cooked him
up a poultice o' herbs and his arm healed up just fine, nice
as you please. *(Beat.)* Since then, she been back, oh, I
don't know, a buncha times—to look in on him, I guess.
Sure wasn't to say howdy to this girl.
PATRICK: She ain't never said nothin' 'bout that to me.
REBECCA: So?
PATRICK: So nothin'. It s just…nothin'.
(Beat.)
REBECCA: Anyways. So, you know how I found you? I knew you
was out here somewheres, but I didn't know exactly
where. And like I said, your ma wasn't goin' to be any
help. So, I did that thing you talked about. I tried to think
like you—like you was some kind of animal or something?
I thought, "Now, where would I go if I was you?" And
then, I just had the strangest feelin', like a goose stepped
on my grave or somethin', and—
PATRICK: Don't have nothin' to do with thinkin'.
REBECCA: What don't?
PATRICK: When I hunt, I don't "pretend" I'm a deer or nothin'.
I just *am*. I'm out here in the woods and things just get
real…still…or somethin'…
REBECCA: You talk like that, you sound like your ma when she
conjures over them herbs of hers.

PATRICK: It ain't magic or nothin'. It's just... *(Then shyly.)* When I reach that place, when I just am, there, with the forest, then it's like I can call the deer or somethin'. I call 'em and they come. Like I was still waters and green pastures, 'stead of hunger and lead.

(Rebecca strokes his face.)

REBECCA: Nobody hunts as good as you, that's a fact, not in these hills.

PATRICK: My pa can hunt.

REBECCA: Shoot! He can't hold no candle to you.

PATRICK: Yeah?

REBECCA: Oh yeah.

(He kisses her. She pulls him down on top of her.)

REBECCA: I want lots of kids, don't you?

(He moans assent.)

REBECCA: Bunches and bunches.

(He kisses her throat.)

REBECCA: What'd your pa say when you talked to him?

(He freezes.)

REBECCA: You talked to him, right?

(He rolls off her onto his back.)

REBECCA: You didn't, did you! You promised you would and you didn't! I swear, sometimes I think you're just scared of him!

PATRICK: I ain't scared!

REBECCA: Well, fine, then. Talk to him about it!

PATRICK: It ain't all that easy.

REBECCA: What's so hard about it? You just tell him—"Pa, me and Rebecca Talbert's wantin' to get married."

PATRICK: You don't know him. You can't just say nothin' like that to him.

REBECCA: Well, don't say nothin' then! Let's just run off! Get outta here! We don't need 'em.

PATRICK: I AIN'T LEAVIN' THIS LAND! It's *mine!* I don't want any-wheres else!

(Beat.)

REBECCA: Then talk to him.

PATRICK: I will.

REBECCA: When?

PATRICK: Soon.

REBECCA: When?

PATRICK: As soon as he gets back from Louisville!

REBECCA: When'll that be?

PATRICK: Any day now. He's late. We spected him back last week. *(Beat.)*

REBECCA: You think mebbe he got kilt or somethin'?

PATRICK: Not unless a mountain fell on him.

REBECCA: What's that supposed to mean?

PATRICK: It's just...he ain't dead, that's all. I'd know it if he was.

REBECCA: Well, how come your pa's so late gettin' back, you suppose?

PATRICK: I don't know. Cain't never figure him. Maybe...Ever year, on each of these trips to Louisville, he makes a big show outta buyin' somethin' for Ma. Maybe that's what's takin' so long.

REBECCA: Well, that's nice.

PATRICK: No it ain't. There's always some meanness in his givin'. First time, it was a hand mirror.

REBECCA: So?

PATRICK: Well, Ma ain't never seen a glass before, and it scared her half to death. She thought it was bad magic or some- thin'. He said not to worry—any old devil she saw in there, he'd been lookin' at for years and it ain't never kilt him yet! Well, she threw that mirror at him, busted it into a thousand pieces. This is a *two-dollar* mirror, mind you!

REBECCA: No!

PATRICK: Next trip, he brung her that big tin tub that sits up in the yard there so's she could soak her leg whenever it stiffens up on her.

REBECCA: What's so mean about that?

(He hesitates, then looks away.)

PATRICK: Nothin'. *(Beat.)* He got somethin' special in mind, this time—been thinkin' hard on it all winter. I watch him. He's figurin' somethin' out.

REBECCA: How come you talk about him like that?

PATRICK: Like what?

REBECCA: Callin' him "him" and "he" instead of "my pa" or "my daddy." You never call him nothin' like that. It's like you ain't really kin or something.

(Beat.)

PATRICK: I had me a sister, once. 'Bout tore my ma inside out, havin' her. Tore her up fierce. I never saw so much blood.

REBECCA: And the baby?

(Beat.)

PATRICK: He took her away, somewheres.

REBECCA: Your pa?

PATRICK: He said he was doin' her a mercy. Said she was sick and wouldn't goin' to last. But she looked fine to me. Star had beaded this piece of buckskin for her so fine, it looked like she pinned all the stars in the sky to it. He wrapped the baby up innit and took her away and we never saw her agin. Only time in my life I ever seen Ma beg him. Usually she just quiet as the grave no matter what he do or say, but she cried and begged him for that baby. Didn't seem to make him no never mind. (Beat.) He ain't never even told Ma where she's buried. I usta look for her grave all the time, but I ain't never found nothing. (Beat.) Waste of time.

REBECCA: Gimme goosebumps just thinkin' about it. You reckon mebbe she ain't at rest, bein' buried like that?

PATRICK: You mean, is she a haint, or somethin'?

(She nods.)

PATRICK: Nah. I seen a whole lotta death, and I ain't never seen nothin' dead get up and walk agin. I don't worry none about the dead. (Beat.) What're you supposed to be doin' over this way, anyhow?

REBECCA: (Indicating the basket.) Huckleberries. My daddy's

real partial to 'em. Well, leave a few! I gotta look like I been doin' somethin' when I get back or he'll tan my hide.

PATRICK: *(Eating the berries.)* Good.

REBECCA: 'Course, gettin' round *my* daddy's not all that hard. But Jeremiah? Now, he's a nosy one. Always wantin' to know where I'm goin', when I'll be back.

PATRICK: He's just lookin' out for you.

REBECCA: That's what he says! But he's just lookin' out for himself. Have a fit if he thought I was gettin' away with somethin' that he wasn't.

PATRICK: I'm sure he ain't that bad. Probably real nice to have a brother.

REBECCA: Well, you can have Jeremiah if your heart's so set on it!

PATRICK: Hold on! *(Beat.)* See that?

REBECCA: What?

PATRICK: In the gap there.

REBECCA: I don't see nothin'.

PATRICK: There's a glint there. Like metal. There it is agin! Somebody's comin' through there. In a hurry.

REBECCA: Is it your pa?

PATRICK: More 'n likely. I'm gonna go finish up, then git back to home. *(He rises, starts to exit.)*

REBECCA: You gonna talk to him about us?

PATRICK: I said so, didn't I?

REBECCA: When?!

(He stops and thinks.)

PATRICK: I'll do it tonight. He's always feelin' good when he gets back from one of these trips. Gets good and likkered up, anyway. You bring your pa over after dark 'n they can make a deal.

REBECCA: What's your pa gonna want, you think?

PATRICK: *(Smiling.)* What's your pa got? *(He kisses her.)* I love you.

(She bends down to get her basket, and as she does so he disappears into the woods.)

REBECCA: It's gonna be fine, I know it. I just gotta feelin'. I...

(She looks up, but he is gone. Then, to the trees and the darkness around her.) I love you.
(Fade out.)

• • •

The Scene: *In the first play of Part Two, Tall Tales (set in 1885 on the Rowen homestead), Patrick and Rebecca's great-granddaughter Mary-Anne Rowen (early teens), kneels by a brook when she is startled by an older man (early twenties).*

• • •

JT: Friend. I'm a friend.

MARY ANNE: Shouldn't sneak up on a body like that!

JT: No, you're quite right, young lady, I shouldn't have. And under any other circumstances, my rudeness would merit your harshest disapprobation.

MARY ANNE: Huh?

JT: You'd a right to be pissed off. But the fact of the matter is, if you hadn't been in mortal danger just now, I probably would've walked right on by, 'stead of savin' your life.

MARY ANNE: My life?

JT: Well, your immortal soul at least.

MARY ANNE: How you figure that?

JT: Why, starin' into that stream like that. I've heard it said from them that knows, that the devil himself hides his bleak heart in the muddy bottom of slow-movin' pools, just like this.

MARY ANNE: *(A little uncertain.)* You're just foolin'.

JT: Would that I were, ma'am. But 'tis a widely known fact that the Father of Lies often assumes the shape of an *Ictalurus punctatus* and—

MARY ANNE: A what?

JT: Channel catfish.

MARY ANNE: You use more twenty-five-cent words when a nickel word would do than any man I ever met.
(JT grimaces, mimes being shot by an arrow, pulls it out, and hands it to Mary Anne.)
JT: I think this is yours.
(Both laugh.)
JT: Where was I? Oh yeah...And thus disguised, he lies in wait for an innocent virgin to come along.
MARY ANNE: Devil hafta wait a might long time for one of those in these parts.
JT: Well, he's a mighty patient fella, the devil is.
(They both laugh.)
MARY ANNE: There *is* an old catfish in this crick.
JT: Oh yeah?
(He sits close beside her and they both look into the stream.)
MARY ANNE: I ain't never seen him, but my daddy has. Almost caught him once. So's Tommy, but I think he was lyin'.
JT: That your brother?
MARY ANNE: Naw, he's my boyfriend.
(JT moves away slightly.)
MARY ANNE: Leastways, he thinks he is.
(JT moves back.)
JT: Mighty pretty here.
MARY ANNE: Yeah.
(Both are quiet for a moment.)
MARY ANNE: I jist love them old trees. Specially that oak there. That's my favorite.
JT: That's a beaut all right.
MARY ANNE: Folks round here call that the Treaty Oak, 'cause my great-great-granddaddy, Michael Rowen, that's where he bought this land from the Injuns.
JT: That a fact?
MARY ANNE: That's what my daddy says. I don't think there's a tree in these hills comes close to touchin' it for size. Leastways, I ain't never seen one. When I was a kid, I used

to think that tree was all that kept the sky off my head. And if that tree ever fell down, the whole thing, moon and stars and all, would just come crashin' down. I think sometimes how that tree was here way before I was born and how it'll be here way after I'm gone and that always makes me feel safe. I think this is just about my favoritest spot in the whole world. Not that I seen a lot of the world, but my daddy took me to Louisville once when I was six. You ever been there?

JT: Well, it just so happens I was in Louisville three weeks ago.

MARY ANNE: Yeah? I bet you been a whole heap of places, way you talk 'n' all.

JT: Oh, I been here and there.

MARY ANNE: Where?

JT: Well, places like…Atlanta.

MARY ANNE: You been to Atlanta, *Georgia!?*

JT: Hell, that ain't nothin'. I been to *New York City!*

MARY ANNE: *(Almost inarticulate with wonder and envy.)* Nooooo.

JT: Yes ma'am, I have. And lived to tell the tale.

MARY ANNE: What's it like?

JT: Well, I tell you, it's…it's pert near indescribable. It's hundreds of buildings, each and every one taller'n that ole granddad oak of yours. "Skyscrapers." That's what they call 'em. Sky*scrapers.* Clawin' up at the very fabric of heaven, threatening to push old Jesus Christ himself off his golden throne! And not more 'n two months ago, I's standin' in the top a one of them golden towers and John D. Rockefeller himself shook me by this hand.

MARY ANNE: No.

JT: Yes ma'am, he did. And me, just a poor boy outta Breathitt County. Said to me, he said, "JT, you've got a future here," and then he clapped me on the back! Imagine that—the richest man in the country—the "Standard Oil King" himself—standin' no further from me than you are now.

(Beat.)

MARY ANNE: *(Shyly.)* Is that your name?

JT: *(Still lost in reverie.)* Huh?

MARY ANNE: JT. I was wonderin' what your name was.

JT: Oh Lord, isn't that just like me? Here I get to jawin' so much I clean forgot to introduce myself. JT Wells at your service. The "JT" stands for Just Terrific. And who do I have the honor of speaking to?

MARY ANNE: *(Mumbling, embarrassed.)* Mary Anne Rowen.

JT: Say what?

MARY ANNE: Mary Anne Rowen. *(Quickly.)* Most folks just call me Mare, though.

JT: "Mare"? Well, I don't know. Don't seem right somehow. I mean, isn't that what you call a horse or something? "Mare"? That's not a proper name for a pretty thing like you. Let me see here. Mary Anne. You know what your name is in Spanish?

MARY ANNE: No.

JT: *(Savoring it.)* Mariana.

MARY ANNE: *(Delighted.)* Yeah?

JT: Now, that sounds about right, don't it? Got all the right colors in it and everything. Mariana.

MARY ANNE: Mariana. *(She giggles.)*

(Beat.)

JT: Mariana.

The Less Than Human Club

by Timothy Mason

The Play: A troubled young man recreates a turbulent year in his life (1968) with the hopes of finding answers to paths that have led to today. The journey back replays the complexities of relationships, the crisis of sexual identity, the bonds of truthful friendship, and the search for purpose.

Time and Place: Fall of 1967; winter and spring of 1968. Minneapolis, Minnesota.

The Scene: *Dan (seventeen) has a crush on Amanda (seventeen), who heretofore has shown no interest. Tonight, however is Homecoming. Rather than go to the dance (she wasn't asked), she has invited Dan over. A candle burns, and in the background sitar music plays.*

• • •

DAN: So there was this lake we always used to go to, my sisters and my and my parents, when we were camping up north.

AMANDA: Uh-huh.

DAN: And it was called Tame Fish Lake.

AMANDA: Yeah.

DAN: And it was called Tame Fish Lake because all the fish in it were tame.

AMANDA: Danny.

DAN: I prefer "Dan," actually.

AMANDA: Is this a joke? 'Cause I don't like jokes.

DAN: No, I swear, its true!

AMANDA: Right.

DAN: Honest! See, these three old brothers bought this lake, years and years ago.

AMANDA: You don't *buy* a lake, people don't buy lakes.

DAN: These guys did. Come on.

AMANDA: You wanna eat the roach?

DAN: No, you have it.

AMANDA: You can have it.

DAN: No, you have it.

AMANDA: I don't need it.

DAN: You have it.

AMANDA: Really?

DAN: Really.

AMANDA: Honest?

DAN: Really.

(Amanda eats the tiny stub of the marijuana cigarette.)

DAN: So these guys bought this lake when they were young, they were from Oklahoma or somewhere, and they all lived together and they never got married and they lived all alone on this lake and they tamed all the fish in it and then it got to be called Tame Fish Lake and every summer when we were camping north of Brainerd we'd drive over one afternoon to see the fish in Tame Fish Lake.

AMANDA: You are so stoned.

DAN: No, really! It's true. We'd drive up this gravel path about I don't know fourteen miles long and finally you'd come to this tarpaper shack where these three old brothers from Oklahoma or somewhere lived and there was this big bell mounted in this big stone thing down by the shore, it was made of big stones put together with cement or something and if you knocked on the door of the tarpaper hut one or two or three of the old brothers would finally come out and they'd say I guess you're here to see the fish.

AMANDA: You are killing me.

DAN: Good. You believe me, don't you?

AMANDA: Sure, why not.

DAN: Thanks for inviting me over.

AMANDA: So?

DAN: So I guess I'm your Homecoming date.

AMANDA: So one or two or three of the big brothers would come out and say...

DAN: Old brothers. They were old, they weren't big.

AMANDA: God, I am dying.

DAN: Really? 'Cause if you don't like this story, I know lots of others.

AMANDA: So it is just a story, right?

DAN: My stories are true, Amanda. Okay?

AMANDA: Okay, okay. So?

DAN: What?

AMANDA: Tell your damned true story!

DAN: Do you want me to go?

AMANDA: No! I want you to tell your story!

DAN: Do you like me at all?

AMANDA: God, Danny.

DAN: Dan.

AMANDA: Dan. Yes. Okay? Tell the story!

DAN: Which one?

(She moans or falls into helpless laughter, however it strikes her.)

DAN: Oh! Tame Fish Lake! Great! I love that story!

AMANDA: So do I, babe.

DAN: I love you.

AMANDA: Shut up and tell your story.

DAN: I mean it.

AMANDA: So do I.

DAN: You like Davis, don't you. He's an intellectual. Like you.

AMANDA: I am not an...God, why does it all have to come down to crap like that?

DAN: Because it does.

AMANDA: Dan? Don't.

DAN: Okay. Okay. These old guys would look at us like we were from Mars or something, even though they saw us every summer, us and about a thousand other tourists. Then one of them, whichever one it was, he'd sort of shrug, and he'd walk down to the shore where this big bell thing was, made of stone and cement, and he'd reach under and yank on the rope and the bell would ring this deep sound, like "Bong, Bong, Bong," and at first you didn't see anything and my sisters would be saying "Where are the tame fish, where are the tame fish?" and then you'd see a little ripple and then a whole lot of ripples and then dozens and hundreds and thousands of fish would come swimming up to shore and whichever old guy it was, he'd toss out bread crumbs by the handful and the fish would jump and splash and the water would just go crazy and the tame fish would eat every crumb.

(Pause.)

AMANDA: Wow.

DAN: It's on the map and everything. Tame Fish Lake.

(Lights change.)

• • •

The Scene: *We are at the Snow Daze Dance. Kirsten (seventeen), a shy but intelligent girl, sits on a staircase in the school. We hear music from the gymnasium P.A. system. Davis (seventeen), our central character, intense, grappling with his sexuality, approaches with hot cider in Dixie Cups. They are both dressed up for the dance.*

• • •

KIRSTEN: Oh, thanks!

DAVIS: Look out, they're hot.

KIRSTEN: Steaming. It's my Dad's recipe multiplied by a couple hundred. Heavy on the cinnamon.

DAVIS: It smells great.

KIRSTEN: Thank you. I made the fruit salad, too. You're a wonderful dancer.

DAVIS: Thanks, I'm not that...

KIRSTEN: I mean, you never go to dances, where did you learn to dance like that?

DAVIS: I don't know.

KIRSTEN: You're just amazing.

DAVIS: You tired or anything?

(Beat.)

KIRSTEN: My dad helps me with so much, he's such a great guy, I mean, he's a little quiet, he's a mailman.

DAVIS: Uh-huh.

KIRSTEN: They tend to be quiet, letter carriers, they think a lot, I don't think people generally realize that.

(Beat.)

DAVIS: And walk, they walk a lot.

KIRSTEN: Oh, yes. Walk and think, think and walk.

DAVIS: Really. Is there, you know, wax or something floating in your cider?

KIRSTEN: Oh, no, I just knew it! I knew Dixie cups were a mistake!

DAVIS: I mean, its not a lot or anything.

KIRSTEN: Miss Borders said she didn't think it would be a problem and I said, "Oh yes it will, you just wait."

DAVIS: It's only a little wax.

KIRSTEN: That woman just doesn't listen. Sorry, I shouldn't criticize.

DAVIS: Why not?

KIRSTEN: Well. It's like Thumper's dad was always saying to him, "If you can't say somethin' nice, don't say nothin' at all."

DAVIS: Thumper's dad?

KIRSTEN: In *Bambi.* The movie?

DAVIS: Oh, yeah.

KIRSTEN: It was my favorite movie when I was a kid. Remember it?

DAVIS: Yeah, I think so.

KIRSTEN: If you want to go, Davis, I'll understand.

DAVIS: What?

KIRSTEN: I know you're thinking this was a mistake.

DAVIS: No! Honest. No.

KIRSTEN: You're a kind person, you always have been. But I'll understand.

DAVIS: Hey, I don't know what you're talking about, really. I'm having a great time.

KIRSTEN: You're really so sweet. But you sure as hell don't have a crush on me.

(Beat.)

DAVIS: I don't think I ever heard you use a four-letter word before.

KIRSTEN: I'm never going to win a Nobel Prize or anything, but I'm not a damn fool.

DAVIS: Wow.

KIRSTEN: Girls. I don't know, they're different. They get crushes.

DAVIS: Boys do too.

(Beat.)

KIRSTEN: And I'm not kidding, I think the two of you would be so perfect.

DAVIS: Who?

KIRSTEN: You and Amanda.

DAVIS: Oh, God!

KIRSTEN: Let's go.

DAVIS: No! Kirsten. Please. Let's go back in there and dance some more. Or we could stay here if you like. Talk to me.

(Pause.)

KIRSTEN: My dad was so nervous tonight, you'd think he was the one going on a…To the dance. And a little proud, too, I think, you know? But mostly just nervous. He felt better when he met you, I could tell. Did he give you the old third degree while I was upstairs?

DAVIS: No. He didn't say much really.

KIRSTEN: Oh.

DAVIS: I mean, we talked. He gave me a Coke. Mostly he read the paper.

KIRSTEN: I think my dad's a lot more like Thumper's dad than Bambi's dad. Of course Bambi's dad was a great big stag and the King of the Forest and my dad's a lot more like an old rabbit. Bambi's mom died around the same time mine did, I mean, that's about when I saw that movie, right round the time my mom died, and we both missed our moms terribly. I think of all the things I should have said to her but didn't I guess that's why you mourn. Then you go on. Like Bambi did. This is the first time I ever went out with a boy. I think my dad was afraid I was going to get all twitter-pated tonight and that's why he was so nervous.

DAVIS: Twitter-pated?

KIRSTEN: You'll have to see the movie. At Luther League at church they pair you off for parties or hayrides but that's different. A boy tried to kiss me once on a hayride but I didn't like him so I didn't let him. There was one boy at church I sort of liked but he moved.

(Beat.)

DAVIS: Should I kiss you?

KIRSTEN: I don't know.

(Davis kisses Kirsten.)

KIRSTEN: It's not Amanda? I won't ask. When I talk to myself I sound interesting but when I say things out loud I don't.

DAVIS: I'm interested.

KIRSTEN: And that's a real problem because what you say out loud is important, it's like a bridge, and if you don't have it you're all alone. So whatever you've got to say, Davis, whoever you've got to say it to, you better say it. I would like to go to the girls' room now. *(She starts off and turns back.)* Let me take these, they're undrinkable.

(Kirsten takes Davis's Dixie cup and her own and leaves. Maybe Davis puts his head in his arms.)

Life Under Water

by Richard Greenberg

The Play: A biting yet amusing look at upper-middle-class values through the lives of two attractive college girlfriends, Amy-Beth and Amy-Joy, and Kip, the handsome preppie divorcé they encounter one summer. Set against this triangle is the young man's mother and her conceited married lover.

Time and Place: The present. Summer. Various locations on Long Island's Southern Fork.

The Scene: *Amy-Beth (early twenties) in a chaise lounge, reading. Kip (early twenties) enters, twirling a beach ball on his finger. They are in the process of approaching the unapproachable.*

• • •

BETH: I thought you were supposed to be working. I haven't seen it.

KIP: I've been bathing the kids, feeding them, washing the dishes, windexing the glass...which in this house is a chore, believe me. What kind of people build a glass house on the edge of a hill in front of an ocean?

BETH: Facetious people.

KIP: Why are you playing with that string?

BETH: Why not?

KIP: Whenever I see you, you've got something...string, marbles, a daiquiri glass. Your hands are never unoccupied, why is that?

BETH: Do you have money for train fare yet? It can't be more than ten dollars to the city from here.

KIP: I've decided to stick around for a while. Until I've got enough to get started. It's not the best idea to arrive in Manhattan empty-handed. Lots of people on the street waiting for you if you do that. Terrible types on the streets of Manhattan. Muggers. Rapists. Mimes.

(Amy-Beth laughs.)

KIP: Ah-hah!

BETH: That was a spasm.

KIP: No, it wasn't.

BETH: I promise you it was.

KIP: I don't believe you.

BETH: I don't care.

(Pause.)

KIP: Amy-Joy tells me you went to Radcliffe for a while. I got kicked out of a lot of schools, too.

BETH: I did not get kicked out. I left.

KIP: Really? Why?

BETH: Reasons. Amy-Joy never understood why I went in the first place. She said, "Once you get in, why bother?"

KIP: *(Laughs.)* I like her.

BETH: Of course. Everybody does.

KIP: I like you, too.

BETH: That's a less common reaction.

KIP: Why don't you ever talk to me?

BETH: Kip, listen. You're here because Amy-Joy wants you here. You're her boy, not mine.

KIP: I like you better. I like her a lot, but I like you better. *(Pause.)* What did I say? Did I offend you? I didn't mean to offend you.

BETH: I want you to leave soon.

KIP: Look—I'm sincere. Utterly. I think we have a lot in common. I have trouble with people too. I look as if I don't, but I do. *(A beat.)* Do you know before I came here I used to gaze up at this house? I used to wonder about it. There's a green light that burns all night at the end of your dock...

BETH: That's the goddamn *Great Gatsby.* I can read! Oh, you sensitive boys with your quotations—I don't trust you as far as I can throw you.

KIP: You should. I only tell nice lies. The past five days here I've been looking for a method to approach you. I think unapproachable people like us have a responsibility to seek each other out. The only thing I've come up with is to tell you exactly how I feel. But it's hard to express something like this. You must know how hard it is.

BETH: Meaning?

KIP: I'd like to get you between the sheets.

BETH: I'd like to get you between the eyes.

(Blackout.)

Merton of the Movies

by George S. Kaufman and Marc Connelly

The Play: In this 1922 satire of the movie industry, Merton Gill, a film-struck, small-town clerk, loses his job and heads for Hollywood, where he is quickly befriended by a bathing beauty in a slapstick film series. Before long Merton becomes disillusioned, but he perseveres and eventually lands a good part in a slapstick himself. He becomes a star and marries the bathing beauty.

Time and Place: Waiting Room outside the Holden (motion picture) lot in Los Angeles, 1922.

The Scene: *Merton (early twenties) has arrived at the studio in hopes of landing a part in "serious" motion pictures. He is quickly befriended by a girl (early twenties) eager to educate him about the business.*

• • •

GIRL: *(Crosses right to Merton.)* Hello, Kid!

MERTON: *(Compelled to reply, but keeping his dignity.)* Good morning.

GIRL: How about a little dialogue? Name your own weapons.

MERTON: I—haven't anything to say.

GIRL: Sure you have—you're just modest. Come on over here and talk it over.

(Merton goes unwillingly. He and the girl come downstage.)

GIRL: That's the stuff—be sociable. Now tell me, what have you got against poor Jeff Baird?

MERTON: *(Compelled to defend himself.)* I don't like his comedies. They degrade a—an art.

GIRL: Well, now we're getting some place. *(She turns to him suddenly and whispers.)* What art?

MERTON: *(With dignity.)* The art of the motion picture.

GIRL: *(Changing her key.)* You haven't been around here long.
   (Merton is silent.)

GIRL: Huh?

MERTON: I—I don't care to discuss my—private affairs. *(Crosses right, turns back.)*

GIRL: All right, kid. Only take an old trouper's word for it—it's a tough game. Work is few and far between, and when it does come, it's generally pretty cheesy. You take even an old-timer like Pa. Last month he got a job in a moonshining play.

MERTON: You mean where the revenue officer falls in love with the moonshiner's daughter?

GIRL: That's it. Well, anyhow, Pa gets this job and they won't stand for the crepe hair, so he has to go and raise a garden. *Gives a month to raising it*—all his spare time—and what happens?

MERTON: I'm sure I don't know.

GIRL: *After four days' work* they go and have him killed off. Pa goes around for a week and tries to rent the garden, but by that time nobody was doing anything but Chinese pictures. That's what you're up against in *this* game, kid.

MERTON: But I couldn't raise a beard anyhow.

GIRL: *(A pause.)* You win.
   (Merton starts to turn away. Crosses left. She follows.)

GIRL: Say!

MERTON: Well?

GIRL: You understand I'm not inquisitive or anything, but— don't you think I've been doing a lot of talking?

MERTON: Oh, I don't know.

GIRL: How long you been around here?

MERTON: About—three weeks.

GIRL: Funny I didn't see you before.

MERTON: I wasn't—I didn't know about this place.

GIRL: Where were you?

MERTON: Out there.

GIRL: On the street? For three weeks?

MERTON: *(Melting a little.)* Oh, I didn't mind it.

GIRL: You're hell on being an actor, ain't you?

MERTON: I expected I'd have to struggle.

GIRL: Well, don't say I didn't warn you.

MERTON: Thanks. *(He is about to turn away left.)*

GIRL: Hold on—don't go. *(She sits.)* That's right. Come on over here and sit down.

(He does so. He halts.)

GIRL: Where'd you come from—before you come here?

MERTON: I—came from a little town. *(Sits left of her.)*

GIRL: Still afraid of me, ain't you?

MERTON: Oh, no, I'm not.

GIRL: Well, don't you be. I'm just a poor mug the same as you, only I've been at it a little longer, that's all. I like you.

MERTON: *(Very fussed.)* Well, it isn't—I don't want you to think I don't appreciate—

GIRL: That's all right. You're a nice kid, only you're awful green. Don't think I talk to all of them like this, but somehow there's something about you that made me do it; if you want somebody to pilot you around, maybe introduce you at the other studios—

MERTON: Oh, no—thanks. I—I'm going to work just at this studio, if you don't mind.

GIRL: What's the big notion?

MERTON: Well, you see—what I want— *(Laughs—crosses to center. He is quite fussed.)* I mean, this is the company where Beulah Baxter is, and I figured—

GIRL: *(Rises—regarding him closely.)* Say, kid, look at me.

(He does so.)

GIRL: You haven't gone and fallen in love with a picture, have you?

MERTON: *(Gulping.)* I—I didn't say that.

GIRL: I know you didn't, but I'm awful quick.

MERTON: It is merely that I am a great admirer of Miss Baxter's art, and regard her as the wonder woman of the silver screen.

GIRL: Honest?

(Ready 'Phone.)

MERTON: You—of course you were only joking about starring with her, weren't you? Because she doesn't ever have anybody. She doesn't even have anybody ever double for her, the way some of them do when it's dangerous.

GIRL: Oh!

MERTON: So I thought if I could only get with her company, I mean no matter how small a part it was, why, I thought I'd rather do that than go to one of the other studios and maybe with somebody who—whose ideals weren't as fine as hers.

GIRL: I see.

MERTON: You—you don't know of anybody whose ideals are as fine as hers—do you?

GIRL: No. She's got the finest set of ideals on the lot.

(The phone rings. Casting Director answers—her voice is unheard in the beginning.)

GIRL: She's certainly the—What was it you called her?

MERTON: The wonder woman of the silver screen.

Miss Lonelyhearts

by Nathaniel West (Adapted by Howard Teichman)

The Play: A dark story of young reporter who is assigned to write a "lovelorn" column. The young man—"Miss Lonelyhearts" —has only contempt for his readers and revels in his clever replies, however, as time goes on, the real pain in the lives of those who follow him takes its toll.

Time and Place: A small one-room apartment in a big city, evening, 1957.

The Scene: *In this opening scene, the soon-to-be Miss Lonelyhearts (early twenties) arrives at the apartment of his girl, Betty (early twenties), for an evening of relaxation.*

• • •

GIRL: Who is it?

BOY'S VOICE: *(Offstage.)* Joseph Pulitzer.

GIRL: Who?

BOY'S VOICE: William Randolph Hearst! *(More knocking at door.)*

GIRL: Stop pounding. The lady downstairs will complain again.

BOY'S VOICE: This is Adolph Ochs. Colonel Robert E. McCormick and I *must* come in.

GIRL: What do you want?

BOY'S VOICE: A byline and an unlimited expense account. I also want you.

GIRL: *(Frantically taking curlers out of hair.)* Well, you can't come in! I haven't got a stitch on my back. *(She pulls off her sweater.)* Stop it! Do you want to break the door?

BOY'S VOICE: Definitely.

GIRL: *(Removing her skirt.)* Why didn't you call? I'd have been ready.

BOY'S VOICE: What's taking you so long?

GIRL: *(Removing her oxfords.)* I'm dressing! *(She hurries into mules and a white house coat. The pounding begins anew at the door.)* You be quiet or they'll cancel my lease. *(Lipstick.)* Really. The way you carry on. What'd you come here for tonight anyhow? Yelling and kicking the door and...I don't remember inviting you.

(Rushes a comb through her hair, dabs cologne onto both sides of her neck, and then flies to answer the door as the bell rings. There stands the Boy wearing a topcoat and hat. He is carrying a bottle of liquor in a brown paper bag and is grinning.)

BOY: Hello.

GIRL: Hullo yourself. Come on in.

(He does so.)

GIRL: I think the only reason you come around here is because there's a liquor store downstairs.

BOY: You smell good tonight. Look good, too.

GIRL: *(Kissing him lightly.)* Thank you.

(As he takes bottle out of paper bag and hands it to her.)

GIRL: This is going to be a celebration, is it?

BOY: Uh huh.

GIRL: In honor of what? The coming of Spring? Income tax time? Me?

BOY: In honor of maybe I'm going to get a new job tomorrow.

GIRL: You don't mean it!

BOY: *(Kissing her long and hard.)* Did I mean that?

GIRL: *(Fanning herself with a handkerchief.)* Whew...Give me your coat. Now—tell me about your job.

BOY: It isn't mine yet. But with any luck, by this time tomorrow you'll be calling me Miss Lonelyhearts.

GIRL: *(She grimaces.)* Miss who?

BOY: Advice To The Lovelorn is what the *Chronicle* is going to chronicle from now on. A Friend In Need Is A Friend Indeed—beginning Monday in the second section.

GIRL: That kind of trash?

BOY: You never thought a paper like the *Chronicle* would stoop to it, did you ? Neither did I. Answer is circulation.

GIRL: *(Handing him a drink.)* We drink to circulation.

BOY: *(Raising his glass.)* And William W. Shrike.

GIRL: Who?

BOY: William W. Shrike.

GIRL: *(Touching his glass with hers.)* Glad to meet him.

BOY: You will be. He's going to give me the job. I hope.

BETTY: You'll get it. You get everything you go after.

BOY: *(Taking her into his arms.)* I can think of a few things I haven't been able to get yet.

BETTY: Don't let that word "yet" trick you into believing it means "eventually."
(They kiss.)

BETTY: Now unwind a bit and tell me about the job.

BOY: Well, Ned Gates told me...By the way, Gates said to give you his regards.

BETTY: That's nice. Thanks.

BOY: Anyhow—Gates told me Shrike said he didn't want any birdbrained psychologist handling the Lonelyhearts column. He wants a writer. He said that to Gates today. And Mary, *Mrs.* Shrike, told me last night, he thinks I've got the makings of a writer.

BETTY: She works there, too?

BOY: Nah. She just hangs around. Mostly at Delehanty's.

BETTY: I've wondered where you've been. And with whom.

BOY: I'll ignore that. Strictly business. She's the one who introduced me to Shrike. Quite an operator, yes, sir.

BETTY: Shrike or *Mrs.* Shrike?
(He kisses her.)

BETTY: Are you finished work for this evening?

BOY: Nope. Gotta cover Night Court.

BETTY: That's a shame.
(He kisses her.)

BOY: It's a lousy assignment.

BETTY: For both of us.

(He kisses her.)

BETTY: You'd better go to Night Court.

BOY: Too early. *(Takes her in his arms again.)*

BETTY: Get your feet off my coffee table, you. You'll scratch it.

BOY: *(Softly.)* Are you practical about everything?

BETTY: Almost.

BOY: What *aren't* you practical about?

BETTY: A reporter on the *Chronicle.*

BOY: What do you feel about *him?*

BETTY: That I should be *more* practical.

> *(He kisses her. Her arm goes around him. She fishes a book out of his pocket.)*

BOY: Just a little paperback number. Compliments of the house.

BETTY: When are you going to stop swiping these books? Don't you have *any* sort of a conscience?

BOY: What's a conscience? Did you ever see one? Touch one? Taste one? You never even *heard* one. You've just heard people talking about hearing a conscience. Besides, I don't think of it as swiping. I just help tidy up the book review department. Do you know how many novels they get a week? And volumes of poetry? And biographies? If some of us don't clean out that place every so often the book section people wouldn't be able to get inside to work. They really ought to pay us for helping out.

BETTY: *(Laughs.)* You're dreadful.

BOY: You're fooling yourself.

BETTY: I know.

BOY: Because if I'm dreadful, so're you. If I steal those books, you read 'em. So what's the difference? Morally, I mean.

BETTY: I don't know.

BOY: Sure you do. There's no difference. We're *all* corrupt. Some of us hide it better than others, that's all. Did you finish that last one I got for you?

BETTY: Not yet. It's too long to read in two days. *(She holds up a thick volume.)*

BOY: Oh. That one. He always overwrote. Let's see. *(Remembering.)* "Love a man even in his sin, for that is the semblance of Divine Love and is the highest love on earth. Love all God's creation, the whole and every grain of sand in it. Love the animals, love the plants, love everything. If you love everything, you will perceive the divine mystery in things. Once you perceive it, you will begin to comprehend better every day. And you will come at last to love the whole world with an all-embracing love." Have you come to that chapter yet?

BETTY: No; but it's beautiful.

BOY: It's junk.

BETTY: Now *you're* the one who's kidding himself.

BOY: The hell I am!

BETTY: Then why did you memorize it! And don't shout!

BOY: How should I know why I memorized it? I do a lot of things I don't understand!

BETTY: Like taking a job that's beneath you?

BOY: *Nothing's* beneath me!

BETTY: After all the talking you've done in this room about what you wanted to be, what you wanted to make of your life? A Miss Lonelyhearts column?

BOY: It can put me on the road toward being a big man.

BETTY: A big man? What're you trying to prove? That you're better than your father?

BOY: *(Rises abruptly.)* Why don't you stop reading books! Go back to double crostics!

BETTY: Oh. You actually *do* have a father problem. I didn't know.

BOY: To hell with that! I don't have any problems. Except that my glass is dry.

BETTY: I'm sorry; I'll put something into it. *(Rises, makes drink returns.)* Listen, you—ever since we met, you and I have had an understanding of each other that's—well, a bit less ordinary than drinks and dates, and boy-girl. You haven't thought of me as just a stupid blonde, and I've always told myself that there was more to you than a flip tongue and a press pass. There are a lot of extras in you, and I like 'em. I'm not always sure what the extras are, but I know they're there. Somehow, we've hit it off on almost all levels, so let's not stoop to bickering. I'm responsible for this and I apologize. So if you *want* that kind of a job, I suppose you ought to take it.

BOY: I do want it. It's phoney and ridiculous and it's less like newspaper work than anything except the want ads. But I want it bad because it's a chance to crack into Features and out of the City Room.

BETTY: I thought you liked reporting.

BOY: There are reporters and reporters. The kind of reporter I am isn't a reporter. I'm a leg man. Now before you say anything, let me give you the advantages of being a leg man. For instance: If you're a leg man, you have the opportunity of leaving your soft, warm girl and her soft, warm lips and her soft, warm sofa, and dragging your tail down to Night Court to look at the bums. You also have the chance—and a good one, too—of getting up at 6:30 to look at *more* bums in the morning lineup at Centre Street. I've got to get out of there, Betty! That column can do it for me. It can be the beginning of everything for us! Betty—if Shrike gives me the job tomorrow, you and I'll get married. What do you say?

BETTY: *(Softly.)* How many drinks have we had?

BOY: Don't be a clown.

BETTY: I'm sorry. It came a little too fast for me, that's all.

BOY: Weren't you expecting, sooner or later, I'd say it: Let's get married?

BETTY: Yes.

BOY: Too soon?

BETTY: I don't think so.

BOY: Not interested?

BETTY: Now *you're* the clown. I'll marry you tonight if you want me.

BOY: *(Taking ring off his finger.)* I wish I had an heirloom to give you, but my family never had enough money for my mother to pass on an engagement ring. *(Slips ring onto her finger.)*

BETTY: I could swim in it. I never realized you had such big fingers.

BOY: You can have it cut down.

BETTY: *(Taking ring off, placing it on table.)* It's a beautiful ring. I wouldn't want to spoil it.

BOY: Don't you want to keep it?

BETTY: I'll wear it around my neck, on a ribbon, for a while.

BOY: Why? Why not on your hand?

BETTY: Oh…

BOY: What does "oh" mean?

BETTY: A ring, to me at least, no matter what kind of ring it is, stands for an engagement. I want you to make sure that's what you want.

BOY: You also want to make sure it's what you want, too! *(Angrily sweeps ring off table. She catches his hand.)*

BETTY: A long life and a lot of kids—yours—are what *I* want. *(She opens his fist slowly, takes ring, drops it into the bosom of her housecoat. Then puts her arms about him and kisses him. Still kissing they sink down into couch.)*

BOY: Maybe I'll skip Night Court.

BETTY: I'd like that. Will it be okay with your boss?

BOY: I'll think of something.

BETTY: *(Out of his arms.)* I hate to do this, but…Up! *(She stands and offers him her hands. He rises.)*

BETTY: You're going to stay in the City Room until Mr. Shrike comes through with the other job. No, no more of that. Into your coat and down to Court.

BOY: I guess you're right. *(Into coat.)* You're also as practical as a bottle opener.

BETTY: *(Opening the door for him.)* I'm more than practical. I'm a little high and a lot in love.

BOY: *(Taking her into his arms.)* What do you want me to do about it?

BETTY: You know the song that says button up your overcoat?...Well, do it. You belong to me, now! *(She eases him out and returns to room, hugging herself with happiness.)*

One Flea Spare

by Naomi Wallace

The Play: A wealthy couple, quarantined in their home during London's historic plague, harbor a girl and a sailor. As death rages beyond their door the four lives entwine and disintegrate within.

Time and Place: 1665. A comfortable house in Axe yard, off King Street, Westminster, in London.

The Scene: *Snelgrave (elderly man of the house) has been tied to a chair by the sailor (Bunce), who sleeps in a corner of the room. Morse (twelve) sits and plays with two small cloth and stick dolls. She wears an ill-fitting, once elegant dress belonging to Mrs. Snelgrave.*

● ● ●

MORSE: And the two lovers were happy and the sky a blue grape and the birds sang. *(To Snelgrave.)* Can you make the tweet of the birds?

SNELGRAVE: If you untie me.

MORSE: *(Uses the doll to speak.)* I can't, Mr. Snelgrave. If I let you go you will break me in half with your cane. *(Beat.)* If you don't want to play, then shut up. *(Beat.)* And the two lovers were happy and the sky a fat apple and the birds sang. And the world—
(Snelgrave begins to make bird sounds. Morse listens a moment. She approves.)

MORSE: And the birds sang sweetly and the world was good and— *(She looks at Snelgrave's bare feet.)* —even the rich had shoes. But one day the world changed. *(Morse strikes a tinderbox.)* And it never changed back. *(She holds one of the dolls near the flame.)*

SNELGRAVE: Don't do that. *(Beat.)* Please.

MORSE: The young man said. But the fire-angel would have her heart.

(She lights the stick doll on fire and sets it on the floor to burn. They watch it burn out.)

MORSE: Even her voice was burned, but still he heard her say "Hold me" and the young man came to her and—

SNELGRAVE: No. He didn't come to her. He was a coward, your man.

(Darcy almost enters the room, but then stops and watches them. They are intent on the story and do not see her.)

MORSE: He knelt down beside her—

SNELGRAVE: He walked away.

MORSE: —and put his hand into the ashes that were her body.

SNELGRAVE: He turned his back.

MORSE: The young man sifted the ashes until he found what was left of her heart.

SNELGRAVE: Small and black and empty it was—

MORSE: But it was her heart.

SNELGRAVE: And the young man put the burnt organ—

MORSE: No bigger than a walnut shell—

SNELGRAVE: Into a glass of his own blood.

(While Morse speaks the following, Snelgrave again whistles softly as before.)

MORSE: And there the heart drank and drank until it was plump once more. And though the prince could never hold her in his arms again, she being now only the size of his palm, he could caress her with his fingers and when it was winter the heart lay against his cold breast and kept him warm.

(Darcy exits. They do not notice.)

SNELGRAVE: I'm an ordinary man. I never meant to be cruel.

MORSE: Neither did Sir Braithwaite. And yet when my mother, a maid in his house for fourteen years, came to him one morning with the black tokens on her neck, he locked her in the root cellar. He was afraid they'd close up his house if they found out someone had taken sick. Neither food nor water he gave her. I lay outside the cellar door. With the door between us, we slept with our mouths to the crack so that we could feel each other's breath.

SNELGRAVE: We didn't lock up our maids. We called for a surgeon.

MORSE: She said "Hold me" because she was cold but the door was between us and I could not hold her.

SNELGRAVE: Enough of this. Get me some water, child.

MORSE: Did you bring them water when they were dying?

SNELGRAVE: Yes.

MORSE: You lie. You sent your boy to do it. You never looked on them once they were sick.

SNELGRAVE: I couldn't help them. It was God's wish.

MORSE: You locked them in the cellar.

SNELGRAVE: That's not true.

MORSE: And they died in the dirt and filth of their own bodies. And their last cries blew under the door and found your fat mouth and hid inside it and waited for the proper moment to fill your throat.

SNELGRAVE: You are an evil, evil girl. If your mother were alive—

MORSE: My mother lives in your mouth and one day she will choke you.

SNELGRAVE: Who's your father, girl?

MORSE: I was born from a piece of broken star that pierced my mother's heart.

SNELGRAVE: More likely Sir Braithwaite. Masters make free with their maids. I'll be honest. I've done so myself. Perhaps this gentleman you despise and ridicule was your own father. Heh? How about that little girl? Ever thought of that?

(Morse stands staring at him some moments. Then she slowly, slowly lifts the long dress and flashes him. This action is not seductive. For Morse it is as though she were pissing on him. After a moment, he turns his head away. She picks up the doll that played the prince. The remains of the burnt doll on the floor she scatters with a kick.)

Only You
by Timothy Mason

The Play: Big-city life and complex labors of love find this group of young people trying to sort out each others' problems—with little success. Eveyone's expectations are beyond any realistic reach, and the attempts are deliciously funny.

Time and Place: The present. A large metropolitan city.

The Scene: *Heather (twenties) and Eddie (twenties) meet at a local coffee shop.*

• • •

HEATHER: The coffee here is terrific.
EDDIE: I know.
HEATHER: You come here?
EDDIE: For years.
HEATHER: I'm here constantly. *(Beat.)* We must come at different times.
EDDIE: That must be it.
  (Beat.)
HEATHER: So what are you going to have?
EDDIE: The tea, I think.
HEATHER: The coffee here is...
EDDIE: Terrific. I know.
HEATHER: But you prefer the tea.
EDDIE: At this particular moment.
HEATHER: Waitress? Two teas, please.
EDDIE: *(To the Waitress.)* Milk and sugar.
HEATHER: *(To the Waitress.)* Milk and sugar.
  (Beat.)
EDDIE: So.
HEATHER: So.
EDDIE: I usually sit there by the window.

HEATHER: I used to have a terrible weight problem.

EDDIE: Oh, really.

HEATHER: I usually get that off my chest when I'm getting to know someone.

EDDIE: Good, good.

HEATHER: I really weighed a lot.

EDDIE: Congratulations. On your loss.

HEATHER: I weighed a ton.

EDDIE: That's a lot.

HEATHER: I'd eat whenever I felt things in my life weren't going right.

EDDIE: I think a lot of people probably...

HEATHER: And for the most part nothing went right.

EDDIE: I'm sorry.

HEATHER: I didn't want the people in the shops knowing how much I ate, so I'd go from one deli to the other, buying one thing here, another there, and then I'd take it all home and eat it.

EDDIE: Sometimes I sit over against that wall.

HEATHER: I could go through a chocolate marble cake in the time it takes you to open the box.

EDDIE: Golly.

HEATHER: And start right in on another.

EDDIE: That's a lot of cake.

HEATHER: I finally went to my doctor to see if I had that condition where you eat a lot...

EDDIE: Oh, yeah—what's that called?

HEATHER: But I didn't, I just ate a lot.

EDDIE: Ah-huh. *(Beat.)* And what do you do now when you feel these yearnings?

HEATHER: Brazilian folk dancing.

EDDIE: In the summer, of course, I sit outside.

HEATHER: I met this wonderful teacher who has really become probably the most influential person in my life, a Brazilian who I ran into in a deli and although I didn't realize it then, I realize now that I was really looking for a father, and since he was looking for a daughter, we hit it off.

EDDIE: He's a folk dancer.

HEATHER: A cellist.

EDDIE: A cellist?

HEATHER: Studied with Casals.

EDDIE: Pablo.

HEATHER: Before him I was with this really extraordinary orthopedic appliance salesman but I can't talk about it because it still hurts a little.

EDDIE: Pablo Casals.

HEATHER: Physically, he's this gorgeous man who has had terrible taste in choosing life-partners.

EDDIE: This is the salesman? No—the folk dancer.

HEATHER: The cellist. He's on his fifth wife right now, but I'm his make-believe daughter and he's my make-believe daddy, and he calls me his "little girl" and I call him my "papi."

EDDIE: Do you think we should get our check?

HEATHER: You're leaving?

EDDIE: No. No. Eventually.

HEATHER: Suit yourself.

EDDIE: No, no, no. We haven't even had our tea, have we?

HEATHER: Waitress! I'll take the bundt cake.

(Blackout.)

Private Contentment

by Reynolds Price

The Play: On leave from the military to attend his mother's funeral, Logan (twenty) learns that his father has for seventeen years maintained a completely separate life with another woman. During a time of shared grief between father and son, Logan meets the other woman and the girl, Gail (fourteen), who is his newly discovered stepsister.

Time and Place: 1945, eastern North Carolina.

The Scene: *Gail and Logan in a garden behind Gail's house planting strawberries. They work intently. This is the first time Gail and Logan have an opportunity to talk alone.*

• • •

GAIL: *(Not looking up.)* Don't let Remus bite you.
LOGAN: Who?
GAIL: The snake that lives here. Black as old Uncle Remus.
LOGAN: Too early for snakes. Anyhow, a black snake's the least of my worries.
    (They work another long silent moment. Then Logan looks to Gail. His strong response to her open beauty is hindered by thoughts of his likely future.)
GAIL: What would be the most of your worries?
LOGAN: *(Thinks.)* —Ending the war.
GAIL: You'll have a lot of help. You're not the only soldier.
    (Logan pauses, then laughs.)
GAIL: *(Looking up.)* Are you?
LOGAN: No, there's several million more. They kill us one at a time, just the same.
GAIL: *(Pauses, looking round toward the distant woods.)* Seems pretty safe to me.
LOGAN: I'll be leaving here. *(In all that follows, his vulnerability*

to Gail's magnetism is shown in small helpless gestures of attraction—any move that will bring his hands nearer to her.)

GAIL: That wouldn't worry *me.*

LOGAN: You been here all your life?

GAIL: More than fourteen years. We moved here right after my father died—I was six months old. My mother had to work, and she only knew music, so she got a job here. They're crazy for music. *(Waits.)* I wish it could have been in a lot bigger place.

LOGAN: *(Looks round.)* Seems big enough here—plenty air, plenty trees.

GAIL: *(Smiles.)* Trees mostly don't talk.

LOGAN: What you want to talk about?

GAIL: Just *talk,* to hear myself. Mother's always too tired. Everybody else is children.

LOGAN: Dive in. I'm grown and I'm not a bit tired.

GAIL: How old are you?

LOGAN: Twenty.

GAIL: *(Kneels in the row of plants and faces Logan.)* Does it ever get better?

LOGAN: *(Kneeling also.)* What?

GAIL: I don't know—life.

LOGAN: What's wrong with life?

GAIL: *(Thinks.)* Oh, it's *taking* too long.

LOGAN: *(Laughs.)* What you want it to do?

GAIL: Make me grown up—soon.

LOGAN: *(Studies her a moment.)* You're what?—fifteen? You're moving right along.

GAIL: *(Unselfconsciously runs a hand across her breasts, half-whispering.)* Claudia Spencer, one grade ahead of me, is pretty sure she's pregnant.

LOGAN: *That's* life—speeding up. Where'd she find a father? All boys are in the army.

GAIL: That's what *you* think. We've got plenty boys. I wish they'd draft them sooner.

LOGAN: Don't wish that on anybody, Gail.

GAIL: It's doing *you* good.

LOGAN: *(Laughs.)* How's that?

GAIL: You've grown on up. You look a lot better.

LOGAN: Thank you, I guess. But where've you seen me?

GAIL: *(Points quickly to the house.)* Your father—pictures of you—he's shown us your pictures long as I remember.

LOGAN: Have you known him that long?

GAIL: *(Nods.)* Longer.

LOGAN: *(Mildly curious.)* He's worked with your mother.

GAIL: *(Nods, returns to planting.)* We heard about your mother.

LOGAN: How well did you know her?

GAIL: We never saw her.

(Logan's initial sense, in the schoolroom, of something strange begins to deepen now. But Gail, still planting, forestalls him innocently.)

GAIL: You haven't even planted enough to earn your supper.

LOGAN: *(Returning to work.)* Are we eating here?

GAIL: *(Nods.)* Are you married?

LOGAN: I thought you knew about me.

GAIL: Not much—just your face.

LOGAN: No ma'am. I'm single. I'll wait to get free. Then I have to finish college.

GAIL: Are you lonesome?

LOGAN: *(Laughs and stops again, facing Gail.)* Not now—not this minute.

(Gail looks up, smiles quickly but points him to work again. Soon she turns her back and moves away to another row. When she's worked there a moment, she speaks without looking.)

GAIL: If second cousins marry each other, what happens?

LOGAN: *(Laughs.)* Beg your pardon?

GAIL: You know—do they have two-headed babies?

LOGAN: I haven't tried it yet. But there's no big shortage of strangers to love.

Scenes for One Female and One Male • 113

GAIL: In the army?

LOGAN: —Army *towns.* And in the whole world.

GAIL: *(Thinks.)* That's why I want to get out of this place.

LOGAN: You in love with your cousin?

(Gail turns back to study him carefully, her face entirely neutral.)

GAIL: I could probably love you.

LOGAN: *(Touched, almost shaken.)* Not now. I may not last.

GAIL: We're just second cousins—maybe even third.

LOGAN: *(Puzzled but still in the grip of her offer.)* We're no kin at all, to the best of my knowledge.

(Gail shakes her head No. Logan slowly stands. Gail stays in place, a plant in her hand. He begins to move toward her. When he's four steps away, Gail looks back quickly to the distant house—no one in sight. Then she rises to meet him. Logan's hands stay down; but he pauses a moment, looking past her (though not to the house). Then he leans to kiss the crown of her head. Gail accepts that, unmoving. Logan takes a step backward. Gail studies him, then closes the gap and cranes up to meet his lips—long but cool. His hands have stayed down. Gail steps back and bends to collect her trowel. Logan does the same. They rise together.)

GAIL: What happens if cousins *kiss?*

LOGAN: Big babies in loud colors—red, green, orange—that come out talking and can sing on-key.

GAIL: *(Thinks, then sings softly.)* "Over hill, over dale,
We have hit the dusty trail,
And those caissons go rolling along.
In and out, hear them shout,
'Counter-march and right about,'
And those caissons go rolling along."

(She has hit upon the song of the Field Artillery, and Logan shows some initial resistance; but as she nears the end of the verse and moves toward the house, he falls in beside her and joins the chorus.)

LOGAN AND GAIL: "Then it's hi! hi! hee! in the field artillery,
Sound off your numbers loud and strong—One! Two!
Wher'er you go, you will always know
That those caissons are rolling along.
Keep them rolling!
And those caissons go rolling along."

• • •

The Scene: *Evening. A dark woods beside a creek. Gail's private place. Logan and Gail enter, Logan with a flashlight, which he soon places on a rock pointing the light at a spot on the ground. He then kneels and unearths a doll buried in shallow soil. He brushes off the doll and hands it to Gail.*

• • •

LOGAN: Remember now?

GAIL: Maybe so. There's a lot I forget.

LOGAN: Dad said you and he left it here when it broke. *(He quickly smoothes the dirt, then stands.)*

GAIL: He was always bringing me dolls—dolls, dolls. They were meant to make me like him.

LOGAN: Did they work?

GAIL: *(Studies the doll's face.)* No. *(Touches the ruined eye.)* I liked him anyway. We didn't get a whole lot of people through here—still don't, I told you. I like everybody I possibly can.

(Logan smiles and steps back to sit on the center stone.)

GAIL: Let's don't stay here please.

LOGAN: Got homework to do?

GAIL: *(Nods.)* Latin—but that's not why.

LOGAN: *(Smiles.)* Scared of Nazi bombers?

GAIL: *(Laughs.)* I *used* to be. When the war first started, I thought every plane passing over at night had me in the bombsight. Now I doubt even *Germans* would want this place.

LOGAN: Seems nice to me.

GAIL: It's better right down by the creek.

LOGAN: I could build a fire here—

GAIL: *(Suddenly firm.)* I said I couldn't stay here.

LOGAN: *(Shrugs, gestures.)* Lead the way, Lady.

GAIL: Don't make fun. This is where I was miserable.

LOGAN: What happened here?

> *(Gail pauses then turns and walks from the ring. In three steps she's vanished. Logan turns on the flashlight. The doll lies skewed at his feet, dropped by Gail. He stands, leaving it, and follows Gail. She is kneeling on the creek bank, her right hand in the water. Logan moves up beside her and stands four feet away.)*

LOGAN: Is it cold?

GAIL: No, warm for some reason. You can sit down here.

LOGAN: Thank you. I'm tired. *(Puts a hand in the water, pulls it back quickly.)* Gail, it's cold as glaciers!

GAIL: I knew you wouldn't like it.

LOGAN: *(Laughs.)* I just told a simple truth. *(Blows on his hand to warm it.)*

GAIL: I used to love it here.

LOGAN: You said you were miserable.

GAIL: That's *why* I loved it. I came here and talked to what couldn't talk back—rocks, leaves, lizards, frogs.

LOGAN: What would you say?

GAIL: I'd ask for things—a life like everybody else: some sisters maybe.

LOGAN: Wouldn't God be the one to ask? Do lizards answer prayer?

GAIL: In stories, sure. No, we don't go to church; so God's not something I think much about.

LOGAN: Everybody else is—praying for peace. Stuff like that.

GAIL: God made lizards. They can carry the message.

LOGAN: They never do seem to have got you the *sisters*.

GAIL: Too late now.

LOGAN: Why?

GAIL: *(Searches his face.)* Boy, where have you been?

LOGAN: All over—here to Idaho.

GAIL: I got you instead.

LOGAN: *(Lost.)* Ma'am?

GAIL: You—not a sister.

LOGAN: *(Smiles.)* Thank you, ma'am.

GAIL: Stuck-up—

LOGAN: O.K. then, I'm sorry.

GAIL: *(Searches him again and leans a little closer.)* I'm not— any more. *(She slowly leans farther.)*
(Logan waits in place. She brushes her lips against his, then retreats.)

LOGAN: *(Touching his mouth.)* You know I'm not your cousin?

GAIL: I know what they *told* me. *(Points toward the house.)*

LOGAN: Do you think they've told us the whole truth now?

GAIL: I don't much care, do you?
(Logan thinks, then reaches a hand toward her face. His thumb strokes her brow, smoothing the hairs again and again. Gail accepts it calmly.)

LOGAN: I guess I do—I plan to be a lawyer.

GAIL: People won't blame *you.*

LOGAN: *(Smiles.)* I didn't mean that. I'll just need to know plain facts someday. I may have to manage all this if Dad dies.

GAIL: He won't. And forget about *facts*—I've been told more versions of them and who they are than the Bible tells of Moses and the Jews.

LOGAN: By Lena?

GAIL: *(Nods.)* —They've known each other from the time they were *children*—they never saw each other till after I was born—you used to live with us when I was a *baby*—we're cousins; we're not—we're sister and br—
(Logan stops her with a hand to her lips. They stay a moment silent. Then they sit back a little from one another. Logan lies back on the ground.)

LOGAN: *(To the dark trees above.)* Let's let the facts wait.

GAIL: For what?

LOGAN: To see if I get back.

GAIL: From where?

LOGAN: Wherever I go tomorrow—home to my mother's old house, then Idaho, then the whole blue Pacific, then God knows where.

GAIL: What if you don't?

LOGAN: Lena said I would.

GAIL: Lena says a lot—she's a *schoolteacher,* Logan. They can talk lawyers down.

(Logan takes that in silence, staring up. Gail moves over, knees almost against his side. He reaches blindly for her wrist, lays her hand on the center of his chest. They stay thus, silent. Then.)

LOGAN: You've talked *me* down anyhow. You a teacher too?

GAIL: No, I'm a doctor. *(Feels for his heart, then counts the beats.)* One—two—three—four. *You're* still alive.

LOGAN: And strong?

GAIL: —As a bear.

LOGAN: But with much better manners.

GAIL: I thought people didn't have to have manners now—the war and all.

LOGAN: Well, *war*time manners. I try to have those.

(Gail nods but stays in place, her hand now flat on his heart. Logan reaches slowly for the crown of her head and bends that gently toward him. Gail stops the move eight inches from his lips and searches his eyes.)

GAIL: You sure about this?

LOGAN: No.

GAIL: What if you come back?

LOGAN: Then I'll have to *get* sure. I'll be another man.

(Gail waits a long moment. Then his hand brings her lightly to rest on his lips—a long still kiss.)

The Reincarnation of Jaime Brown
by Lynne Alvarez

The Play: The separate quests of a young New York street poet seeking fame and fortune, and a wealthy entrepreneur who will stop at nothing to find his son who committed suicide nineteen years before, collide with astrological proportions, helped by a mystical and androgynous couple.

Time and Place: The present in New York City and the Hamptons.

The Scene: *Jaime (nineteen) has met David (twenties), a musician, while selling her poems in New York's crowded Port Authority. When David's girlfriend dumps him he catches Jaime's eye. After an impromptu date in Central Park, Jaime invites David to her apartment in a funky part of the City.*

• • •

JAIME: This neighborhood is the pits. They always ask if it's affordable. No one asks if it's livable.
(The apartment or rather room is assembled. Jaime points to different corners.)
JAIME: No bathroom. But McDonald's is two doors down and they're open all night.
DAVID: Starving artist, eh?
JAIME: Yeah. I find it therapeutic to refer to different corners of the same room as the living room, dining room, kitchen...
DAVID: Bedroom.
JAIME: Yeah. It's the bedroom. So?
DAVID: Nothing. *(Pointing to a poster.)* Who's that?
JAIME: Rimbaud. The French poet.
DAVID: Didn't Sly Stallone do him? *(Imitates Rambo with a machine gun.)*
JAIME: You're thinking of Rambo you jerk—

DAVID: I know honey. I know.

JAIME: Well I like him. He did his best work by twenty-one, quit to run guns and leave graffiti on the pyramids. Great poets die young you know. I'm going to die when I'm twenty-seven, maybe twenty-eight tops.

DAVID: Really?

JAIME: And this is...

DAVID: Let me guess.

JAIME: Shut up.

DAVID: My psychic energy, my spiritual guide tell meee...Bob Dylan. Greatest rock poet ever born...

JAIME: And a great outlaw. I love outlaws.

DAVID: *(Checking out her windows.)* You must. These windows are an open invitation to any outlaw who happens by. Put some bars on the windows—eh. Then you can chose which outlaws come into this pad.

JAIME: How sweet. You want to protect me.

DAVID: Do you bring just anyone up here?

JAIME: Do you go up to just anyone's pad—dude?

DAVID: You seem pretty sure I'm not going to jump you or anything.

JAIME: You seem cool. I'm a good judge of character.

DAVID: So was Jesus and Judas nailed him.

JAIME: Right.

DAVID: That was a joke.

JAIME: I know. It was good. Smart.

DAVID: Hey. What's up?

JAIME: Nothing. I'm great.

DAVID: We were having a great time and now you're like...

JAIME: Like what?

DAVID: Down, beat. I don't know. Shall I leave?

JAIME: No.

DAVID: Fine.

(They stand awkwardly.)

JAIME: I'm nervous.

DAVID: What's the matter?

JAIME: I like you.

DAVID: *(Moving closer.)* Great!

JAIME: I mean really. And now that I got you up here. I don't know what to do.

DAVID: What do you usually do?

JAIME: Usually? Are you nuts? With all the disease-ridden, murderers, punks, pimps and perverts out there—do you think I'd be stupid enough to bring anyone to my room? Let alone have them know where I live?

DAVID: So I'm the first?

(He moves away from her. Jaime nods.)

JAIME: Don't sweat it. I've been deflowered. Cowboys.

DAVID: Cowboys?

JAIME: *(Hooks her fingers in her jeans.)* Walllll ma'am, been real nice, but I gotta be movin' on. Cowboys! How about you?

DAVID: Me?

JAIME: Are you in love now?

DAVID: Let's just say I'm a cowboy, ma'am. Better steer clear of me.

JAIME: Really?

DAVID: The only thing I know how to do is play music.

JAIME: So play.

DAVID: Right. *(Takes out his keyboard.)* Just happen to have my little keyboard.

JAIME: What kind of stuff do you play?

DAVID: Sorta post-punk, semi-funk, hillbilly-hardcore with a bluesy edge.

JAIME: Oh.

DAVID: *(Setting up.)* I have a new song.

JAIME: Groovy.

DAVID: Groovy? What's this sixties shit?

JAIME: I'm a purist. I'm trying to preserve classic language. Play.

DAVID: It doesn't have a title yet. *(He plays.)* So...what do you think?

JAIME: I think you're the real thing.

DAVID: Thanks.

JAIME: It's in your blood, isn't it?

DAVID: Yeah I guess. My dad was a jazz drummer. You know the kind in bars, plays, smokes pot with his friends—what people in jazz do. Didn't really know him too well.

JAIME: My mom was into country. She was an Elvis freak. We're pretty different.

DAVID: Very. *(He goes to kiss her.)*

JAIME: Do you believe in love at first sight?

DAVID: You're going to spoil this, aren't you?

JAIME: I thought that was romantic.

DAVID: Romantic? Love? Love's a responsibility. Now sex— that's romantic.

JAIME: I don't just go around saying that, you know.

DAVID: Why did you just say it now?

JAIME: Cause that's what I was feeling. Cause I thought you'd dig it. I've never been in love before.

DAVID: And you're not afraid to tell me this?

JAIME: Well shit, yeah!

DAVID: Jaime, you're too open. You got to protect yourself. Look, I don't have a lot of experience with heart-on-the-sleeve kind of people. Maybe I should leave.

JAIME: Maybe you shouldn't take it so hard. Maybe I was just trying to nail you against the wall to see what you'd do— rip your skin off a little before I decide whether to put salt or ice cream on you. Do you want to leave?

DAVID: No.

JAIME: I could read you some of my stuff?

DAVID: No love poems.

JAIME: Right. This one's great. I based it on a man I overheard downstairs… *(Reads.)*
"I just like to see 'em fall, slow
like in the movies,
drops of blood spread,
sailing through the air
as if they don't belong nowhere

and land, spla—a—at, like rain
on the river..."

DAVID: Uh...no. I don't think so.

JAIME: That's just how he said it.

DAVID: I believe you.

JAIME: You said no love poems.

DAVID: You need a sense of humor.

JAIME: I thought that was kind of funny. "Spla—a—a—at, like rain on a river."

DAVID: But you're talking about blood, sweetheart, What's this?

JAIME: Don't read it now.

DAVID: I don't like women who tell me what to do. *(He opens it and reads.)* "When you are old." When did you write this?

JAIME: In the park. Look...

DAVID: When you are old
And mysterious to me,
a dim figure on a
fragile horizon,
Think back
Across the years,
That on one summer night
we broke out of ugliness
and fled
Two conspirators
with bottles full of
Wine and joyous music
on the radio
and remember,
if
you
can
That it was right and
fine and sometimes
More, and we left

Pain.
That interminable fire,
only scorching
Our heels."
(Silence.)
JAIME: It's not funny.
DAVID: No. *(He kisses her.)*

• • •

The Scene: *Sammy (ageless) and Hughie (ageless) have been hired by Wilson to find his son, who he believes has been reincarnated. They believe Jaime is Wilson's son, come back to life as a girl. In this scene, Sammy and Hughie have a private moment to reflect on the state of their own relationship.*

• • •

SAMMY: I'm glad we don't fight.
   (Hughie says nothing.)
SAMMY: We talk things over. For instance, there is the matter of failing Mr. Meredith.
HUGHIE: Have we failed?
SAMMY: We've failed. The girl is not the right person…
HUGHIE: Ahhhhhhh.
SAMMY: You're no help. We've failed. Where are your suggestions?
HUGHIE: Where are your suggestions?
SAMMY: We've found the person. We always find the person. But we haven't identified him!
HUGHIE: Or her?
SAMMY: We have the big picture. Orphans, Pisces, midtown Manhattan, August. Eighth house of legacies in a water sign.
HUGHIE: Wasn't it the fifth house of hidden karma in a fire sign?

SAMMY: No! Well, maybe...But that's not it. There is something we've overlooked.

HUGHIE: Do you really think we've failed?

SAMMY: We've failed. It's the beginning of the end.

HUGHIE: Of what?

SAMMY: Of us, you nincompoop. We don't work well together, we've run out of rope, out of ideas, out of steam.

HUGHIE: Are you kidding me?

SAMMY: I need someone decisive, energetic. Someone who can come up with answers, make statements, take the bull by the horns.

HUGHIE: Do you mean that?

SAMMY: Tell me something!

HUGHIE: What?

SAMMY: Something. Anything!

[BORIS: *(Worriedly.)* Tina! Tina!]

HUGHIE: What do you want from me?

SAMMY: Decisions. Action.

HUGHIE: Don't you know by now what I'm like? Do you know what you're asking?

SAMMY: Yes.

HUGHIE: Sure?

SAMMY: Yes. I'm asking for...

HUGHIE: What?

SAMMY: My needs are different. We're facing a crisis. I need someone who confronts reality. I need someone different.

HUGHIE: Haven't we always worked well together?

SAMMY: Until now.

HUGHIE: Why throw out a perfectly good partnership?

SAMMY: Is that all you can say?

HUGHIE: Do you want me to leave?

SAMMY: Do you want to leave? Answer. Yes or no. Do you want to leave?

HUGHIE: *(Crestfallen.)* Why are you doing this? Can't you see you're making me miserable? Aren't you miserable too? Don't you have any feelings? What's wrong with you?

SAMMY: That's it? All right. I can't stand it. Leave. Go. Get.

HUGHIE: Do you really mean it?

SAMMY: Fight for what you want, you fool! Can't you say anything?

HUGHIE: *(Leaving sadly.)* What's there to say?

(Hughie exits. Sammy slumps in his seat.)

Sally's Gone, She Left Her Name

by Russell Davis

The Play: The story of seventeen-year-old Sally Decker and her parents, Henry and Cynthia, and Christopher, her brother. Mom and Dad are not what they used to be, nor is the family, life is changing—nothing seems connected anymore.

Time and Place: Summer. The present. A large kitchen in a suburban home. Late morning.

The Scene: *In scene three of Act I, Sally (seventeen) and her brother, Christopher (fourteen), play at the adversarial relationship so common among siblings of opposite genders.*

• • •

SALLY: When we were riding in the car, all of us saw that other car. I saw it. You saw it. We saw it coming a long time. I even saw you put your arms in front, brace yourself, and I did too. So did Dad. Only Mom. Only Mom just watched it coming, she just stared, and then took off through the windshield. *(Pause.)* There has to be a reason why Mom took off through the windshield. *(Pause.)* You're quiet, Christopher.

CHRISTOPHER: Huh?

SALLY: I've never seen you so quiet.

CHRISTOPHER: I can be quiet.

SALLY: Sure.

CHRISTOPHER: I don't have to be on the spot all the time. Active.

SALLY: I know.

CHRISTOPHER: I can be private too. You should appreciate when I'm private.

SALLY: I do. *(Pause.)* So what are you private about?

CHRISTOPHER: Nothing particular.

SALLY: Thinking about Dad?

CHRISTOPHER: Nope.

SALLY: Mom?

CHRISTOPHER: No.

SALLY: What are you thinking about?

CHRISTOPHER: None of your business.

SALLY: Okay. *(Pause.)* Pretty quiet.

CHRISTOPHER: Uh huh.

SALLY: Like there's a storm. Are you about to have a storm?

CHRISTOPHER: No.

SALLY: That's good.

CHRISTOPHER: Probably you're the one's going to have a storm.

SALLY: Yeah?

CHRISTOPHER: You're the one upset about Dad. About Bruce, college. You're the one getting picked on.

SALLY: I'm not getting picked on.

CHRISTOPHER: Act like it, Sally. If I were Dad, I'd kick your ass.

SALLY: What?

CHRISTOPHER: I heard your attitude this morning.
    (Pause.)

SALLY: I was just upset, Christopher. About last night, that's all. I got to steer clear of everybody for a few days. Stay out of the way. Til I can get used to it.

CHRISTOPHER: Used to what?

SALLY: You're already used to it, aren't you?

CHRISTOPHER: Me?

SALLY: Seems like you're used to it.

CHRISTOPHER: Nah.
    (Pause.)

SALLY: Christopher, are you naive?

CHRISTOPHER: Huh?

SALLY: Are you naive?

CHRISTOPHER: Naive? I'm not naive.

SALLY: No? You touched a girl's breast?

CHRISTOPHER: Yeah, sure. I touched.

SALLY: You did?

CHRISTOPHER: Sally, you aggravating me?

SALLY: No, I'm not, Chris. Really.

CHRISTOPHER: Okay.

SALLY: What did it feel like?

CHRISTOPHER: Like a lump.

SALLY: It felt like a lump?

CHRISTOPHER: Yeah, and it was baggy. It moved.

SALLY: You didn't like it?

CHRISTOPHER: I thought it was okay.

SALLY: Okay?

CHRISTOPHER: I mean, yeah, I liked it. I just wasn't so sure about getting my lips wet with this particular girl. But I was practicing on her anyway.

SALLY: You were practicing?

CHRISTOPHER: Yeah, you got to practice. You never practiced?

SALLY: What for?

CHRISTOPHER: Well, you got to know what to do in case a girl comes along that I like.

SALLY: And what are you going to do with a girl if you like her?

CHRISTOPHER: All the things I've been practicing.

SALLY: Uh huh.

CHRISTOPHER: Except this time I'll like it. I mean, I hope I like it. Otherwise, then, I don't know what everybody's making such a big deal about.

SALLY: You're going to like it, Christopher.

CHRISTOPHER: Yeah, I figured I would.

SALLY: It's going to make you nervous.

CHRISTOPHER: Me? Nervous?

SALLY: Yeah, a lot of guys are. They're being brave, playing baseball and football, but a lot of it's cause they're nervous.

CHRISTOPHER: No, I don't think so.

SALLY: Could be.

CHRISTOPHER: Why'd I have to be nervous because of a girl?

SALLY: Don't you act up a little bit in front of girls?

CHRISTOPHER: Nah, I just say hello, or don't, depending on the girl, which one.

Scenes for One Female and One Male • 129

SALLY: Then how come you have to practice?

CHRISTOPHER: Huh?

SALLY: How come guys have to practice?

CHRISTOPHER: Girls don't practice?

SALLY: Not like guys.

CHRISTOPHER: I guess because guys have to teach girls.

SALLY: That's not why.

CHRISTOPHER: Who's going to teach them, huh? Their mothers?

SALLY: There's not a lot to teach.

CHRISTOPHER: Okay, why?

SALLY: It's because they're nervous.

CHRISTOPHER: They're not nervous. I haven't seen one guy nervous, at least any of my friends.

SALLY: Then how come they practice so much?

CHRISTOPHER: I told you.

SALLY: No, they're practicing to be calm about it. Casual. They're practicing so they don't care too much. But if you practice enough times with just a bunch of people, then you're going to practice all the care out of you.

CHRISTOPHER: What's the matter, Sally, Bruce doesn't care about you?

(The phone rings. Pause. Sally picks it up.)

SALLY: *(Into phone.)* Hello?...Oh, yeah. Doctor Heisel. Mom's out...Yeah, shopping. Shopping with Dad. That's right... Okay...I'll tell her...I will. Okay. *(Sally hangs up.)* Mom's not at her appointment.

CHRISTOPHER: Her headache appointment?

SALLY: Right. Her headache appointment.

CHRISTOPHER: Oh.

SALLY: Mom's in trouble, Chris.

CHRISTOPHER: Uh huh.

SALLY: She's in trouble cause, for example, Mom's got these beautiful long nails. Which are painted nice with colors that go together all the time with her eyes, and what she's wearing, or the weather. They look so pretty lying on the table, or holding a fork. And when Mom used to scratch my back, or sometimes even touch my arm, I would get goosebumps. Or walking down the street, and if Mom held my hand, it made me feel everybody'd know that she's my mother. Cause Mom's much prettier than anyone else in this house. Much prettier, cause Dad's kind of ugly and we got more Dad than Mom. But did you ever take a look at Mom, Christopher? At all her clothes, did you?

CHRISTOPHER: Yeah, I did.

SALLY: Okay, what about her shoes, her high heels? Did you ever notice them, and all the cream, and makeup, her hair, everything makes her prettier, but, also, it makes her like somebody else has to step in and do stuff for her. Did you notice that? Okay, for example, how's she going to run away from something chasing her if she's wearing high heels, Christopher?

CHRISTOPHER: Who's going to chase Mom?

SALLY: Anything could chase Mom. It could be a dog. Or a robber.

CHRISTOPHER: Yeah, okay.

SALLY: Well, she can't run fast, can she?

CHRISTOPHER: No?

SALLY: Not wearing high heels. So she has to have somebody pick her up instead and run for her.

CHRISTOPHER: Who's going to run for Mom?

SALLY: Somebody not wearing high heels.

CHRISTOPHER: All she's got to do is kick off her heels.

SALLY: Then she's going to ruin her stockings, and she's going to hurt her feet, cause they're stupid things to run in, and how's she going to kick a robber? Or run in one of those dresses? How's she going to do anything with her nails if she's going to break them? How's she even going to sweat if it makes her makeup fall off? I think a robber could do anything he wanted with Mom. And I bet you Mom's been getting more and more tired inside her head, cause all she's been doing is making herself pretty and nothing else.

(Pause. Christopher crosses to the kitchen table. He looks at the empty chair next to him.)

SALLY: I think women make themselves pretty so's to make up for all the practicing guys've been doing. I think we're supposed to do anything we can to make a man nervous again, even if it means he's got to save us from a robber. *(Pause.)*

CHRISTOPHER: *(To the empty chair.)* Mom's prettier?

SALLY: Chris?

CHRISTOPHER: *(To the empty chair.)* Yeah? She is?
(Blackout.)

Sorry

by Timothy Mason

The Play: The complexities of urban existence is tested in a surprisingly comic picture of an extremely dangerous encounter— a shooting in a residence.

Time and Place: The present. An August night, New York City, an apartment in the East Village.

The Scene: *Thinking he was a burglar, Pat (twenties) has shot Wayne (twenties)—through the closed door of her apartment. Realizing the mistake she has made, Pat tries to give aid to a confused, angry, terrified Wayne, who considers fleeing the scene or returning the violence.*

• • •

PAT: Honest to God, I am really sorry. *(Beat.)* Can I get you anything? *(Beat.)* Shouldn't I be calling someone? I mean, really. *(Beat.)* Tea? Toast? Have you eaten? *(Beat.)* You look like someone.

WAYNE: You aren't real, you can't be.

PAT: How's that chair? You could stretch out on the sofa, I wouldn't mind, I'll put down newspapers. *(Beat.)* This is just like me, you know that? This is exactly like me. God. What an idiot. I'm a waitress. Actress really, but. *(Beat.)* I could make some tea, it'd be no problem whatsoever. *(Beat.)* Earl Grey? Chamomile?

WAYNE: You just don't exist!

PAT: Mint?

WAYNE: Jesus.

PAT: Look, I was alone, I was scared. *(Beat.)* How do you feel now? Are you feeling any better? You look a little better.

WAYNE: I feel like shit.

PAT: I know the feeling. Some days it's all I can do to get out of bed and through that door.

WAYNE: Put the gun down.

PAT: Oh, my God, I didn't realize! Of course. Oh. I feel like such a fool. You sure you don't want me to call an ambulance?

WAYNE: Yes! No! Do not. Call. Anyone.

PAT: So what's your name?

WAYNE: You're unreal.

PAT: I'm Pat. Aspirin! *(She starts for the bathroom door.)*

WAYNE: Put down the goddamned gun!

PAT: Just make yourself comfortable. *(Pat exits, still carrying the pistol.)*

WAYNE: Oh, boy. *(He explores his leg, tenderly.)* Ohhh, boy. *(He tries to stand.)* Agggh! *(He falls back into the chair.)*

PAT: *(Calling from offstage.)* Two aspirin, coming right up!

WAYNE: Shit. Oh shit.

(Pat enters with a glass of water and a couple of aspirin.)

PAT: I have the worst time swallowing these things, you wouldn't believe. Here you go.

(Wayne turns his head away.)

PAT: Go on, there's nothing to worry about, they're buffered.

WAYNE: Where's the gun?

PAT: Ah. I don't know, around here somewhere. Here's looking at you.

(He takes the aspirin and the glass.)

WAYNE: Aspirin, wow. *(He swallows the aspirin.)*

PAT: I grind them into powder and stir them into a glass of Tab. Tastes awful, but. *(She takes the glass from him.)* How are you feeling now?

WAYNE: I just took them, for Chrissake!

PAT: Hey, there, Mister, I *said* I was sorry.

WAYNE: You shot me!

PAT: So what am I supposed to do, kill myself?

WAYNE: It's an idea.

PAT: You don't mean that and you know it.

WAYNE: I've got to get out of here.

PAT: So how long have you been with the Little Brothers of Charity? *(Beat.)* They really call you that?

WAYNE: You're weird. You are so weird.

PAT: Talk about weird, you won't even go to the hospital.

WAYNE: It's a flesh wound.

PAT: Most wounds are. What's your name?

WAYNE: I just want to go home.

PAT: You can't even walk, for heaven's sake. What's your name? *(Beat.)*

WAYNE: Wayne.

PAT: You have got to be kidding.

WAYNE: Okay, that's it, I'm going. *(He tries to stand and falls back into the chair with a moan.)*

PAT: Take it easy.

WAYNE: What's wrong with Wayne?

PAT: Nothing, nothing. Nothing.

WAYNE: You know, you don't really *grow* on a person.

PAT: Okay, I'm sorry, I shouldn't have said anything.

WAYNE: Damn right!

PAT: Sorry!

WAYNE: Yeah, right.
    (Pause.)

PAT: It's just always struck me as a very wimpy sort of name.

WAYNE: Oh, you're making me feel great, you know that? You got a real knack for making a guy feel at home. You should put it down in a book. How to Meet Men.

PAT: What was I supposed to do? It's dark, I hear this noise outside my door…

WAYNE: First date: Get yourself a .45.

PAT: Oh, come on—it's just a little .22.

WAYNE: God, get me out of here.

PAT: Anytime you want. Wayne.

WAYNE: Believe me, lady, if I *could.*
    (Beat.)

PAT: How's that leg doing?

WAYNE: How do you think?

PAT: Let's see.

WAYNE: You keep away from me.

PAT: Attitude is going to get us nowhere. Now let's have a look at that leg. *(She begins to gently unwrap the towel from his thigh.)*

WAYNE: Ow!

PAT: What do you Little Brothers do, exactly?
(Wayne whimpers softly.)

PAT: You bring food to people, something like that? Meals On Wheels sort of thing? Oh, God, your leg is a mess.

WAYNE: Tell me about it.

PAT: I am so terribly sorry.

WAYNE: If you apologize one more time I swear I'll kill you.

PAT: I think the bleeding's stopped anyway, but it's hard to tell. Those pants are going to have to come off.
(Beat.)

WAYNE: Not. On. Your. Life.

PAT: Look at you, dressed in black from head to toe, what was I supposed to think.

WAYNE: You didn't even see me, you shot right through the door!

PAT: I was holding it, it went off.

WAYNE: People like you should not have guns. People like you should not have anything! Forks!

PAT: Okay, *you* try living in this city.

WAYNE: I am, I am.

PAT: It's terrifying out there.

WAYNE: If you ask me, it's kind of scary right here.

PAT: The sound of a footstep behind you. A cough in the dark.

WAYNE: Bam! Another chest-cold victim bites the dust.

PAT: Look. Wayne. I am a woman alone.

WAYNE: It's no wonder.
(Beat.)

PAT: This apartment has been broken into twice in the past six months. In the past two years I've had my purse snatched on the F train, the double R, the Lexington Avenue line, and the crosstown bus. And for the past month there's been some, jerk on the roof across the courtyard, *staring*. With *binoculars*. At *me*. So if I'm just the littlest bit jumpy, pardon me!

WAYNE: Okay, okay. I'm sorry. You've had some bad breaks.

PAT: What I've had is a crime wave.

WAYNE: So you got yourself a gun.

PAT: My mother sent it. All the way from Seattle. That's where I'm from.

WAYNE: In the mail? That's illegal.

PAT: What other people do to me is illegal, what my mother does is blameless. What were you doing out in the hall, anyway?

WAYNE: I was trying to read the number on the door, lady— that's all.

PAT: The light out there's burned out.

WAYNE: I noticed.

PAT: So who were you looking for?

WAYNE: Not you.

PAT: Mr. Fischer? He used to get charity people. Someone came from the Synagogue twice a week, but he's dead now.

WAYNE: You plugged him, right?

PAT: You know, you're beginning to annoy me? I liked Mr. Fischer.

WAYNE: God. I feel weak.

PAT: Well, of course you do, you've lost a lot of blood.

WAYNE: How do you know it's stopped bleeding?

PAT: It's not dripping like it was before.

WAYNE: If I die here, lady, so help me...

PAT: The name is Pat and nobody's going to die, for goodness sake. And if you're so worried about it, why won't you go to the hospital?

WAYNE: Well, for one thing, what do you think would happen to you if I did? You got a permit for that thing?

PAT: It was Mother's.

WAYNE: Tell it to the judge, Annie Oakley.

PAT: So you're saying you're doing me a favor?

WAYNE: Damn right I am.

PAT: An act of charity.

WAYNE: Yes, as a matter of fact.

PAT: Well I can't tell you how grateful I am. *(Beat.)* You look pale.

WAYNE: I *feel* pale. How do you know he's looking at you?

PAT: Who?

WAYNE: The guy on the roof.

PAT: Every now and then he waves.

WAYNE: Maybe he's lonely.

PAT: Maybe *I'm* lonely, I don't take it to the rooftops.

WAYNE: Maybe he's just trying to get to know you.

PAT: Maybe it should occur to him to send flowers.

WAYNE: You sure the bleeding's stopped?

PAT: There's only one way to tell.

WAYNE: Oh, Lord.

PAT: Come on, come on. *(She starts to take off his tennis shoes.)* Do you really think I could be, like, arrested? For this?

WAYNE: If there is a God, yes.

PAT: I was protecting myself!

WAYNE: From what?

PAT: And you'd press charges against me?

WAYNE: This is why I'm here instead of there, because I wouldn't— get it?

PAT: Charity.

WAYNE: Why not?

PAT: I like your sneakers.

WAYNE: Thanks.

PAT: Can you stand?

WAYNE: I think so.

(He does so, slowly. She begins to take off his trousers.)

WAYNE: This is making me very uncomfortable.

PAT: So pretend I'm a nurse. Where'd you get them?

WAYNE: What?

PAT: Those hightops.

WAYNE: I don't know. That shop on First Avenue and St. Marks, right across from Spillacci's.

(Beat.)

PAT: You live around here, don't you. *(Beat.)* Don't you.

WAYNE: Ow!

PAT: Don't try to change the subject.

WAYNE: It hurts!

PAT: Of course it hurts, you've been shot. So where do you live? *(She eases the trousers out from under him.)* I knew I'd seen you before. You live right here in the neighborhood, don't you.

WAYNE: So what?

PAT: So nothing. Your pants are finished, there's no getting out these stains.

WAYNE: Right.

PAT: Besides, there's a hole in them.

WAYNE: Right.

(She looks at his bloody thigh.)

PAT: Can't see a thing. You wait right there, I'll go get the alcohol.

(She exits into the bathroom. Wayne sits and examines his thigh. Pat reenters with a bottle of rubbing alcohol and a cotton swab.)

WAYNE: You know, I really don't think it's so bad?

PAT: Really?

WAYNE: Yeah, I think maybe you just grazed me.

PAT: Oh, good!

WAYNE: Anyway, it hardly hurts at all anymore.

PAT: Great. Let me see. *(She daubs the thigh tenderly with the alcohol soaked cotton.)*

WAYNE: Aaaaaagggghhh!

PAT: You've got to expect a little sting.

WAYNE: *Oh! Oh! Oh!*

PAT: Big baby.

WAYNE: Oh! Oh, God! Do you have any salt? Maybe you could rub some salt in it!

PAT: We're killing germs here, mister.

WAYNE: You're killing *me* here, lady!

PAT: Look at that. It's nothing. It's nothing. It's a scratch!

WAYNE: It's my body!

PAT: You have ruined two towels and a carpet for a scratch!

WAYNE: *Sorry!*

PAT: Where did all that blood come from?

WAYNE: Me!

PAT: What are you, some kind of bleeder?

WAYNE: Okay, I'm going. Now.

PAT: What do you plan to wear?

WAYNE: Oh, Lord.

PAT: You'd look great out there in your Fruit of the Looms.

WAYNE: They're not Fruit of the Looms.

PAT: What are they then?

WAYNE: Will you stop looking at my underwear!

PAT: I am not looking at your underwear!

WAYNE: You were too!

PAT: So big deal! You think this was all a plot in order to get a peek at your skivvies?

WAYNE: Just…let me have something to wear out of here and we can forget about the whole thing.

PAT: Would you like a jumper or a plain cotton skirt?

WAYNE: You're not even funny.

PAT: You're not even civil.

WAYNE: Jeans, slacks…

PAT: I'll take care of you, don't worry.

Tango Palace

by Marie Irene Fornes

The Play: In this dark, ominous ritual, Isidore, an ageless androgynous clown, taunts and plays with Leopold, an earnest, handsome young man, as a matador does with a bull before the kill.

Time and Place: The present. A room. The door is bolted with an oversized padlock. There is a big filing cabinet, an armchair, wall mirror, a water jug, a radio, three porcelain teapots, a large vase, a blackboard. A recess in the back wall serves as a shrine. Within the recess, hanging from nails, are a guitar, a whip, a toy parrot, a Persian helmet, two swords, a cape, a compass, a muleta, a pair of bulls horn, six banderillas, two masks in the form of beetles' faces.

The Scene: *Isidore has been dancing about the room, tossing playing cards at Leopold, who has been begging him to stop.*

• • •

ISIDORE: And a one and a two. One, two, three, dip and turn... You still have to be punished. Don't think I forgot.
(Isidore takes Leopold by the hand and walks him to a corner. Leopold leans against the wall.)
ISIDORE: Straighten yourself up. Are you hearing things again? I'm jealous. I want to hear too. *(Putting his ear against Leopold's ear.)* Where is it? I can't hear a thing. *(Talking into Leopold's ear.)* Yoo hoo. Where are you? Say something. Talk to me. It won't talk to me. *(To Leopold.)* Tell me what it says. I'm angry. *(Isidore sits on the shrine, crosses his legs and his arms, and turns his head away from Leopold.)* I'm angry. Don't talk to me. I said don't talk to me. Don't you see I'm in the typical position of anger?...Do you want to say something to me?

LEOPOLD: No.

ISIDORE: Well. I want you to tell me what that awful voice was telling you.

LEOPOLD: It said, "Isidore deceives you." It said, "Don't listen to Isidore."

ISIDORE: Oh. Horrible. Horrible. Treason in my own house.

LEOPOLD: Let me tell you...

ISIDORE: Oh. Don't say any more, treason. Oh.

LEOPOLD: Let me tell you what I think, Isidore.

ISIDORE: No.

LEOPOLD: Please.

ISIDORE: You've said enough.

LEOPOLD: I haven't said...

ISIDORE: Treason!

LEOPOLD: Isidore!

ISIDORE: *(In a whisper.)* Don't talk so loud.

LEOPOLD: *(In a whisper.)* I haven't said...

ISIDORE: I heard you already. Treason!

LEOPOLD: I want to leave.

ISIDORE: Bye, bye, butterfly.

LEOPOLD: I want to get out.

ISIDORE: See you later, alligator.

LEOPOLD: Give me the key.

ISIDORE: Pretty parrot.

LEOPOLD: I want the key.

ISIDORE: He wants the key.

[PARROT: He wants the key.]

ISIDORE: There is no key.

[PARROT: No key.]

LEOPOLD: You're lying.

ISIDORE: I always tell the truth. I worship truth and truth worships me. Don't be so stubborn. There is no key.

LEOPOLD: There must be a key.

ISIDORE: I see what possesses you. It's faith!

LEOPOLD: So what?

ISIDORE: Faith is a disgusting thing. It's treacherous and destructive.

Mountains are moved from place to place. You can't find
them. I won't have any of that.

LEOPOLD: Well, I do have faith.

ISIDORE: Infidel. I'm too upset. I can't take any more of this.
(Covers his face.) It's the devil. I can't look at you. Tell me
you'll give it up. Tell me you have no faith.

LEOPOLD: But I do.

ISIDORE: Well, I'm a mountain. *Move me.*

LEOPOLD: I know there is a way out because there have been
moments I have been away from here.

ISIDORE: That's not true. You get ten demerits for telling lies.

LEOPOLD: It is true. There are moments when you have just vanished...

ISIDORE: Vanished? I have never vanished.

LEOPOLD: I don't mean vanished...exactly...I mean there are
moments when I've felt this is not all there is.

ISIDORE: What else is there?

LEOPOLD: Close your eyes...Imagine...that all is calm.

ISIDORE: I don't like playing childish games. I'm supposed to sit
there imagining a field of orange blossoms and then
you're going to pour a bucket of water on my head. Let
me tell you, young man, that I played that game when I
was five. Let me tell you that it was I who invented that
game. And let me tell you that I didn't invent it to sit
there like a fool and get the water on *my* head. I invented
it to pour the water on the fool's head. Let me tell you
that. You're not smart enough...not for old Izzy. *(Card.)*

LEOPOLD: I wasn't going to throw water on you.

ISIDORE: You weren't? Hm...all right. Go on.

LEOPOLD: Don't imagine anything in particular. Don't imagine
orange groves or anything. Make your mind a blank. Just
imagine that you are in perfect harmony with everything
around you...

ISIDORE: Wait, I have to erase the orange grove.

LEOPOLD: Forget about the orange grove.

ISIDORE: I can't forget the orange grove. It's planted in my mind. I have to uproot it. You put things in my mind and then it's I who have to get rid of them. At least leave me in peace for a moment, while I do the work.

LEOPOLD: I didn't put anything in your mind.

ISIDORE: You said, "Don't think of an orange grove." You did, didn't you?

LEOPOLD: Yes...

ISIDORE: Well, the moment you said that, an orange grove popped into my head. Now give me time while I get rid of it.

(Isidore moves about the room as if he were picking up oranges and throwing them over a fence with his eyes closed. Leopold's impatience increases.)

ISIDORE: First I'll throw this orange over the fence. Then, this little orange. Then, this orange orange. Now this rotten orange. Now I pull this whole branch off the tree. Oh, oh, it's so hard. Now I pull this orange off the tree. Oh, oh, there are so many. There are thousands and thousands and I think millions and trillions. Oh, I'm tired. No, no, I must not rest. I can't take a moment's rest until I clear away all this mess of oranges. Thousands and thousands of acres, and then I have to clear the other side of the fence, and then the other, and then the other and then dismantle the fence, and then the other fence, and then...

(Leopold reaches for the pitcher of water and empties it on Isidore. They remain motionless for a moment. Isidore goes to his shrine and sits in his typical angry position. Leopold walks to the opposite end of the room and sits down.)

ISIDORE: I'll never trust you again.

(The lights fade. Isidore laughs out loud as the curtain falls.)

Scenes
for Two Females

. . .

Bad Girls

by Joyce Carol Oates

The Play: A look back at the teenage years of three sisters, Orchid (twenty years old as the narrator; fifteen in the past), Isabel ("Icy", sixteen years old), and Crystal (thirteen years old). The girls' mother, Marietta Murchison, is having a difficult life, what with suffering a head injury in an auto accident, attempting to find the right boyfriend, and trying to make "good" girls out of her "bad" girls.

Time and Place: The near-present. March. The Murchison living room in Yewville, a small city of thirty thousand in upstate western New York.

The Scene: *Orchid and her sister, Crystal, insist they have not been jealous of their mother's boyfriends.*

• • •

ORCHID: We *were not* jealous of Momma's boyfriends!
    (Crystal appears, sucking on a thumbnail.)
CRYSTAL: *(Vehemently.)* I sure wasn't.
ORCHID: *(Self-righteously.)* We just wanted Momma to be happy. A self-respecting and independent woman. To "date" men worthy of her. And of us.
CRYSTAL: *(Overlapping.)* —and of us.
ORCHID: *(Hooting laugh.)* Remember ol' "Open Wider, Please"?
CRYSTAL: *(Shuddery giggle.)* Oh! Dr. Prick—
ORCHID: -chard—
CRYSTAL: *(Trying to get it right.)* Dr. Pri-chard—
ORCHID: Prick-head—
CRYSTAL: Oh! was that one *gross!*
ORCHID: *(Incensed.)* Our own *dentist,* for God's sake. That asked Momma for a date right in the dentist *chair.*
CRYSTAL: —Having three wisdom teeth removed. Yuck!

ORCHID: The way ol' Prickhead would examine your teeth with this nasty little pick—"Open wider, please"—

CRYSTAL: "Open wider, please"—YUCK!

ORCHID: —and "rinse, please"—

CRYSTAL: —bloody spit—swirling around in the drain—

ORCHID: —and take hold of your tongue, your actual tongue in some kind of creepy-gauzy cloth—

CRYSTAL: *(Deeply revulsed, near-hysterical giggle.)* —And pull it—!

ORCHID: —and all sort of bump his potbelly against you—

CRYSTAL: DOUBLE YUCK!

ORCHID: *(Snapping her fingers, with satisfaction.)* At least—we don't go to the dentist anymore.

CRYSTAL: *(Snapping fingers.)* Anymore *ever.*

ORCHID: But a worser creep yet was John Calvin—

CRYSTAL: Potty!

ORCHID: Pot*ter.*

CRYSTAL: Momma's boss at Potty's Realtors—

ORCHID: *(Sarcastic.)* We gotta "be nice, be sweet" to this fat-ass—

CRYSTAL: —'cause Momma's working for him, she says it's the best job she's had in years—

ORCHID: —so this John Calvin Potter—

CRYSTAL: *(Overlapping.)* Pot*ty!*—

ORCHID: —he's paying Momma a "real generous" salary she says—

CRYSTAL: —except, is *he* gross! That whatdayacallit pretend-hair on his head—

ORCHID: *(A derisive tootling sound.)* TOO-PAY!

CRYSTAL: *(Loud giggling.)* TOO-PEE! TOO-PEE! POT*TY!*

ORCHID: His hands all over everything like a creepy-sticky *octopus*—

CRYSTAL: Calling Momma and us "gurls"—

ORCHID: *(Imitating.)* "Oh you GURLS are so pret-ty"—

CRYSTAL: Must've been fifty years old—some nasty old grand-pappy—

ORCHID: —trying to act like Burt Reynolds—

CRYSTAL: —trying to act like somebody'd want to kiss *him*— Yuck!

ORCHID: Just 'cause he had MONEY to spend—

CRYSTAL: Just 'cause he was Momma's BOSS—

ORCHID: Just 'cause he could FIRE her if he got pissed—

CRYSTAL: Nasty *cruel* ol' thing!

ORCHID: *(Shrugging.)* So?—Potty did fire Momma. One week's pay, and *out. (Gesturing with thumb.)*

CRYSTAL: That's O.K. We don't want our Momma who we love working for such a creep, do we?

ORCHID AND CRYSTAL: N-O. *NO.*

ORCHID: We *were not* jealous of Momma's "boyfriends"—we just wanted to protect her.

CRYSTAL: *I'm* not jealous of any Goddamn boyfriend. I hate men!

ORCHID: *I* hate men!—my father who left us fifteen years ago, and "Dad" Murchison who got drunk and knocked us all around—till Momma called the police.

CRYSTAL: Oh I'm just scared he's gonna come back—

ORCHID: Momma won't let him—she got a "court injunction."

CRYSTAL: I hate boys just as bad. Oh! they're nasty—

ORCHID: In school the guys try to pinch your breasts—if you have breasts.

CRYSTAL: *(Shielding breasts with arms.)* I don't! I don't have any! I never will.

ORCHID: If you don't have breasts, they bump into you anyway and laugh like hyenas, and it hurts—

CRYSTAL: —And you don't dare cry, 'cause—

ORCHID: —that's what they want: for you to cry. Like "Dad" Murchison spanking us harder and harder if we didn't cry—saying we were "bad girls" in need of "a little humility."

CRYSTAL: *(Passionately.)* I *am* a bad girl! You betcha.

The Ballad of Yachiyo
by Philip Kan Gotanda

The Play: Yachiyo, a poor peasant girl with not much hope of raising herself beyond working in the sugar fields of Hawaii, is sent by her father to live with a pottery artist, Hiro, and his wife, Okusan. Okusan hopes to teach Yachiyo proper Japanese language and customs, and before long Hiro finds new inspiration for his work through the girl. Eventually the young Yachiyo and Hiro develop a deep relationship that leads to a tragic outcome.

Time and Place: Kauai, Hawaiian Islands around 1919. It is night. Full moon.

The Scene: *Yachiyo and her friend Osugi (both mid-teens) are sitting high on a bluff overlooking the ocean; they pass a bottle of champagne back and forth. Osugi speaks with a pidgin accent.*

• • •

OSUGI: *(Looking out.)* That one's a pig! Okay, your turn—what's dat one?

YACHIYO: I can't tell, Osugi.

OSUGI: The cloud's changing, hurry up...

YACHIYO: *(Aside.)* Osugi is my best friend. She works at the McDonald house. I call her "head to mouth"—*atama kara kuchi e.* She thinks something, out it comes from her mouth. No in-between stops. I sometimes wish I could be more like her...

OSUGI: Hurry up!

YACHIYO: I don't know, what?

OSUGI: A horse, a horse, yeah?

YACHIYO: Oh yeah, yeah, a horse. *(Watching for a beat.)* And it's running, running—so fast its body is stretching out...

OSUGI: Getting long like an eel now.

YACHIYO: An eel, yeah. Umm, wouldn't you like some *unagi* right now. The way Tabuchi-san cooks it over the hibachi.

OSUGI: Umm, da best, with some hot rice. *(Noticing.)* Ooh look, look, dat's Mrs. McDonald's butt.

YACHIYO: Dat big. Your boss's *oshiri's* dat big?

OSUGI: Hey, if you never move, your butt get big, too. Just sit dere and do like this... *(Starts to point in several directions.)* Osugi get dis, Osugi get dat. Get dis, get dat, all the time. She do like dat.

YACHIYO: You gonna get into trouble taking the champagne?

OSUGI: *(Shaking her head.)* Good, huh? The bubbles make your nose tickle.

YACHIYO: This some new kinda work, huh. Just drink and fool around.

OSUGI: They all drunk and dancing back there. Da other girls take care of everything. Hey, I get you a job here. Da other girl, Shimokawa, getting big, starting to show, they fire her as soon as they know.

YACHIYO: My parents have other plans for me. I dunno yet.

OSUGI: When I get da job at McDonald's? Happiest day of my life. I don't have to work in the fields no more. And at night I get to see Pantat. Dat's it. Big smile on my face. I have everything. I can die now. *(Passing the bottle to Yachiyo.)* How 'bout you? What's your happiest day? *(Yachiyo thinks for a beat while she sips.)*

YACHIYO: When I took the picture of me...Dressed up in the kimono Mama had Papa's sisters send from Japan. Then, that day. 'Cause as we walk to Miyatake's photo shop, everybody stare. *"Bijin,"* they whisper, "Matsumoto-san's daughter is growing up to be a beauty." And when I look at Mama and Papa? They almost busting open they so proud.

OSUGI: Dat's it?

YACHIYO: *(Nodding.)* Un-huh.

OSUGI: Dat's your happiest day?

YACHIYO: *(Nodding.)* Un-huh.

OSUGI: *(Shaking her head.)* Un-uh, dat's not your happiest day. Dat's *their* happiest day. You still waiting, Yachiyo, you still waiting. *(She gets up and drags Yachiyo with her.)* Come on, come on, I show you how da rich *haoles* dance.

YACHIYO: You should get Pantat to dance with you.

OSUGI: Come on, don't be such an old fart.

(Music volume rises, an up-tempo song. It's a fun and lively rendition. Osugi and Yachiyo start to dance. Osugi has to guide Yachiyo, pushing her along. Soon, however, Yachiyo is enjoying herself.)

OSUGI: Drink break, drink break...

YACHIYO: No, no, come on Osugi, show me the slow one now. Show me the slow one...

(Osugi grabs the champagne bottle as Yachiyo pulls her back. Osugi pulls Yachiyo close. Music changes to a slow tempo.)

OSUGI: Like dis.

YACHIYO: Like dis?

OSUGI: *(Drinking from the bottle.)* Yeah. Just like dis.

YACHIYO: So close, yeah? The boy's body pushed up close like dis?

OSUGI: *Haoles* dance nasty, yeah. You can feel the boy's *chimpo* and everything if he gets excited.

YACHIYO: *(Stopping.)* That's enough.

OSUGI: What? You and Willie don't do this kind of thing?

YACHIYO: I'm thirsty. *(Yachiyo takes the bottle and takes a big gulp.)*

OSUGI: Pantat and me, all the time do this kind of thing. Not dancing, but you know.

YACHIYO: We don't do that kind of thing.

OSUGI: HOW come—Willie's cute, yeah?

YACHIYO: That kind of thing get you into trouble, Osugi.

OSUGI: You so old-fashioned Yachiyo. Everybody does it some.

YACHIYO: Do that kind of thing you end up bringing shame to

your family. Then you have nothing, no family, nothing. End up like that Shimokawa girl.

(During the following Yachiyo moves away to a watery pool of light.)

OSUGI: Shimokawa, she's a stupid girl, go too far. Go so far, cannot come back. And now, she don't even have no boyfriend to take care of the baby. I've got Pantat. He always take care of me. Just like Willie. He always take care you Yachiyo. He dance good, too. Hey, maybe we have a double wedding, yeah. You and Willie, me and Pantat, at the Japanese *Kaikan*—all our families dere. And lots and lottsa flowers—we'll have beautiful white blossoms falling down around us, we'll drown in a sea of white flowers!

(Yachiyo moves down by the water. She kneels and looks at her reflection in the moving watery lights. Osugi fades to black.)

YACHIYO: The water, it's like a mirror. *(She stares for a beat.)* My face. It's changing. Or maybe it's just the inside of me looking out that's changing. All I know is that sometimes I find myself staring at a stranger. Like when I look at my photograph. I don't recognize her. Who is she? *(She reaches out and touches the water's surface.)* She thinks things, wants to do things…I wonder what it's like to look at the world from the other side. Through her eyes.

Cleveland

by Mac Wellman

The Play: "A poem (or in this case a play) should not mean but be," to borrow from John Ciardi.

Time and Place: Cleveland during prom season and in the dreamtime of Joan; the present.

The Scene: *Joan (seventeen) is in the kitchen preparing an after-school snack; her mother is at the table reading a college catalogue. Mother is about to tell Joan who she really is. Note: Mirandan whispertalk only consists of consonants, except for an occasional ending. Mainly sibilants and fricatives. Vowels are open.* C *is pronounced like* ch *in* church.

• • •

JOAN: The prom's tomorrow.

MOTHER: You must be very excited.

JOAN: What's that?

MOTHER: Catalogue for Polytechnical College.

JOAN: *(Reading over her shoulder.)* "Human Body Fluid and Advanced Polymerization." Golly, Mom.

MOTHER: Just looking at what courses are available.

JOAN: Gee, when you said you wanted to go back to school I thought you meant something like Business I or Creative Writing.

MOTHER: How was cheerleader practice today?

JOAN: Fine. Learned some new tricks. *(Pause.)* Only. Mom.

MOTHER: Yes, dear.

JOAN: I had a kind of bad dream last night.

MOTHER: I shouldn't have told you. So explicitly.

JOAN: No, it wasn't about Dad. It was something else.

MOTHER: The sink is fixed again. There's fresh coffee.

JOAN: It was all kinda confused. All about Pope Joan and stuff.

MOTHER: I have to mend your dress for the prom. Why don't you try it on?

(She goes out for the dress.)

JOAN: *(Offstage.)* Mr. Delaplane said you know a lot about astronomy but that nobody knows the orbital eccentricity of Triton. It's too far away.

MOTHER: I knew it. I should never have told you the details. About your father's death.

JOAN: Was it ever fashionable to be a Trotskyite?

MOTHER: Yes, dear. Once it was very fashionable.

(She enters in a bright red prom dress. Her Mother sets about mending a hem. Pause.)

JOAN: How come you know so much about astronomy?

MOTHER: And we were personal acquaintances of the Mayor. If things had only worked out a little differently. We might still be fashionable.

JOAN: Mom, would you tell me something?

MOTHER: Our kitchen sink might not have been stopped up. Our front porch might not have. Fallen into the street. Poor dear, you know they haven't tcmbbd the body yet

JOAN: What? What did you say?

MOTHER: Slip of the tongue. They haven't identified his body yet. *(Pause.)*

JOAN: Have you seen that man? Again?

MOTHER: What man?

JOAN: The man that fixed the sink.

MOTHER: Once. Briefly. But it won't happen again. *(Pause. Mother finishes her mending.)*

JOAN: Did you sleep with him?

MOTHER: What do you want from me? Do I tell you how to live your life? No, damn it. Is that how they teach you to think at that fancy Catholic school? Just because we're Trotskyites and you feel socially embarrassed. Just because we were once fashionable but aren't anymore. Just because I want so desperately, once in my life, to do something, anything, original...

JOAN: Okay. Okay. Just curious.

(Pause.)

MOTHER: He's had an accident. Very serious one. He won't be back.

(Pause.)

JOAN: Mother, who are you?

MOTHER: Another cup of coffee?

JOAN: Really.

(Pause.)

MOTHER: Since you ask. My name is Bqbqpstu, Emissary of Larav, Empress of the Sshhs, who live on the world you call Miranda, a moon of Uranus. Very, very far away. I'm here on a secret mission. *(Her aspect becomes strange and unearthly.)* My world, Miranda, is in danger. Triton sleep-stickers and stickwalkers. Hammer-headed and creased foot splutch. The rain skies up and the suns dump on fells. That and the rats. They sqssqu and shake. Badass hocus pocus. Snsps. Pssps. Qvspt. Xxp. Tsspppcqtsm! Sks. Polymers. Xxxxxs. Plplp. Qsssp. Sskllpc. Hssssssp. O. Ppbb-ppsspc.

JOAN: I knew it, pure Whispertalk. You should know. I am immune to the subtle poison of Whispertalk.

MOTHER: What, who are you, to know our way?

JOAN: What did you do with father?

MOTHER: *(Holding up a clear glass vial.)* Only the purest spinal fluid for the wind machines of Larav. Empress Larav.

JOAN: Dad? And Mr. Barfly, too? You fiend.

MOTHER: Mr. Barfly. And the man who fixed the sink. And Mr. Delaplane next. And then the Mayor of Cleveland. And soon you, my dear. Qssssmssssssplxmnsxsxsxsssxku!

JOAN: *(Squaring off.)* Xtr. Tr. Rqnrhrdtt. C!

MOTHER: Tritonian? I suspected. Show your glide wave number and fight.

JOAN: I am Becky Brighteye, girl space-cop and I'm taking you back to Triton, world that you and your kind have despoiled. With your wind machines and inverted energy schemes. All of it Xxqmmmntnp, as you say it in your dialect.

MOTHER: Once I get your time feather, you're finished.

JOAN: Try and get it.

(They fight.)

JOAN: Qqkwvll. Llllgpppvmvptzc.

MOTHER: Hsstu. Psspmpsstmpt. Ptzc.

JOAN: Bhtsspssbh.

MOTHER: Filthy girl. I should've scwwpsst you in your sleep. Sleep hsp.

JOAN: Tsstssttp to you. What's your real name before I take your feather. *(She defeats her Mother.)*

MOTHER: Inglefinger. Fourth Dyad. Tenth moeity.

JOAN: One of the unclean ones? That's how desperate you are.

MOTHER: Wolfling, we'll destroy you yet.

JOAN: I've got a hot pllptpccclpu waiting for me. In a small apple grove in Indiana. Then it's clear sailing back home. With your time feather. You'll be out cold for a week.

MOTHER: No, no. *(Faints.)*

Darcy and Clara

by Daisy Foote

The Play: A family struggles to hold onto precious land and survive inner crisis. Both parents and children in the Chancy house face conflict and failure as they deal with a greedy world and crushed hopes and dreams.

Time and Place: The present. New Hampshire farm country.

The Scene: *Darcy Chancy (seventeen) is the fraternal twin of Clara who is in the hospital with kidney failure, a result of her severe diabetes. In this scene Clara plots with Darcy about a planned move to California, a move Clara hopes will be the promise of a new start for her complicated life.*

• • •

DARCY Clara, don't be so mean...

CLARA: Me...I'm being mean. She says these things...like saying them will make them true.

DARCY She's having a hard time, Clara.

CLARA: Aren't we all?

(Darcy looks at the sink overflowing with dirty dishes.)

DARCY I better do these dishes before Dad sees them...

(Darcy starts to do the dishes. Clara sits down and takes off her shoes and socks. It should be noted that taking off her right shoe and sock causes her some pain.)

CLARA: Ernie asked me to marry him last night.

DARCY What did you say?

CLARA: Nothing yet. He was so serious and into it. Telling me he loved me, wants to have a family with me...the whole nine yards. *(A beat.)* But I'll tell him tonight. I'm meeting him on the mountain...at Indian Look Out. A few beers...get him all lovey dovey and then I'll give him the bad news...

DARCY So you're going to say no?

CLARA: What do you think?

DARCY Well, I don't know...

CLARA: Well, you should know, seeing as you and I are getting out of this place together next year. Seeing as you and I are moving to California...to Los Angeles...and living on the beach. Remember?

DARCY Don't drink too much beer tonight, Clara.

CLARA: Shut up...

DARCY I mean it, Clara...your blood sugar has been going crazy lately...

CLARA: Should I tell him before or after we have sex...If I tell him before...he'll get all mad and won't want to have sex with me. But if I tell him after...he'll get even more mad cause he'll go all macho on me and think I was trying to pull a fast one on him. I'll just tell him. I'll tell him that we're too young for marriage. And that you and me are moving to California, and we're going to live on the beach. *(She takes a magazine out of her knapsack. She shows her sister the magazine.)* Look at this...*HOUSE BEAUTIFUL.*

DARCY Where did you get the money for that? You don't have any money.

CLARA: Will you just shut up and look at the picture. *(Showing her the magazine.)* This is exactly the house I want. All white with lots of windows and sitting right on the beach. Malibu, Darcy. That's us. *(Pointing to another picture.)* And look...they even have a pool...a pool right next to the ocean with a hot tub.

(Darcy turns back to continue with the dishes. Clara puts her arms around her sister.)

CLARA: You and me Darc...living on the beach...riding around in our convertible... *(She dances with her sister for a moment.)* We're going to get away from here, Darc...far, far away.

DARCY Your eyes look really bloodshot today, Clara.

CLARA: You'll lead me around, Darcy, you'll be my eyes in

California... *(She suddenly stops talking. She looks around the room. She starts to shout at the rocking chair.)* Hey! *(A beat.)* Old man... *(She goes over and kicks the chair.)*

DARCY Clara...stop it...

CLARA: What...he can't hurt you...he's just a lot of hot air now...he can't talk. *(A beat.)* Can't tell us that we're talking too much...or being disrespectful or... *(A beat.)* What else was he always yelling at us about, Darcy?

DARCY I'm doing the dishes, Clara.

CLARA: Oh right...not doing enough around the house... *(A beat.)* So what's it like being dead, old man? *(She runs over to the chair, sticks her rear in the middle of it and farts.)*

DARCY Clara!

(Clara starts to laugh uproariously at her joke.)

CLARA: Me and Darcy we're moving to California...leaving your tired old bones behind... *(She starts to laugh hysterically at her own joke. Clara suddenly starts to get very dizzy. She gets very red in the face, sweats, and shakes uncontrollably.)*

CLARA: Darcy...

(Darcy turns around. She goes to her sister and starts to help her over to the table.)

CLARA: Darc...Darc...Darc...

• • •

The Scene: *Darcy confesses to Clara her love for Tom, and her desire to stay and not move to California.*

• • •

DARCY Clara...

CLARA: Hey...

DARCY Couldn't you sleep?

CLARA: No. *(A beat.)* And I didn't want to wake you.

DARCY I wasn't sleeping...

CLARA: So we were both just lying there...pretending to be asleep...

(Darcy laughs.)

DARCY I guess so...

(Clara looks over at the rocking chair. Darcy watches her do this.)

DARCY You don't really see him, do you?

(Clara shrugs.)

CLARA: Don't you?

DARCY I don't know... *(A beat.)* I don't know if I see him because I'm so used to seeing him there or if he's really there...

CLARA: What's the difference? *(Clara watches the chair for a few more moment. Under her breath.)* Go to hell, old man...go to hell... *(A beat.)* Oh...that's so much fun doing that... *(To Darcy.)* You should try it, Darcy...

DARCY I'm sorry I didn't tell you about Tom.

CLARA: I'm sorry I got so mad. *(A beat.)* So...what's the story?

DARCY *(Blushing.)* I don't know...

CLARA: Oh...isn't that cute...Darcy has a little boyfriend...

(Darcy gets up.)

DARCY I'm going back to bed.

(Clara grabs her arm.)

CLARA: No...come on...I'm sorry. I'm sorry.

DARCY That's why I didn't say anything to you about it. I knew you'd just make fun...

CLARA: Well...Darcy...come on...what do you expect? Tom Clark...you went on a date with Tom Clark...

DARCY He's a nice guy, Clara. And he's really nice to me. Maybe he's doesn't drive a GTO, but I bet if I were sick, he'd call me... *(Darcy regrets what she has said.)* I'm sorry, Clara...

CLARA: Don't worry about it.

(Darcy touches her sister's arm. Clara jerks away.)

CLARA: I said...don't worry about it. *(A beat.)* Does Tom Clark know about our plans? Does he know you're moving with me to California after we graduate?

DARCY I don't want to move to California...

CLARA: What are you talking about?

DARCY It was always your idea. I never said I wanted to do it...

CLARA: You want to stay here...in Tremont?

DARCY Maybe.

CLARA: Marry Tom Clark...have kids...

DARCY I don't know... *(A beat.)* But I do want to get married, Clara. I'd like to have a family.

CLARA: How can you say that? After everything you know... everything you've seen in this house...

DARCY It doesn't have to be that way, Clara...

CLARA: Right...it's going to be different with you and Tom Clark. You're going to love each other forever. Blah... blah... blah... *(A beat.)* You have to come with me to California, Darcy. You have to come and live with me on the beach...

(Darcy says nothing.)

CLARA: I'm going, Darcy. With or without you...I'm going...

(Beats of silence.)

DARCY Clara, I want you to try and be nicer to Ma...

CLARA: Shut up...

DARCY You should know something, Clara. You should know that she stood up to Dad. She stood up to him. He doesn't want to sell, but it doesn't matter what he wants because it turns out Grandpa Joe left everything to Ma...the farm...the mill and the mountain. And Ma told Dad...she told him she was going to sell because she wants to help you...

CLARA: I keep thinking about when I first got sick, when we both had the chicken pox. *(A beat.)* We were on the mountain with Ma...having a picnic. She saw them on you first.

DARCY She thought I had jelly on my face but then she couldn't wipe it off...

CLARA: *(Making noise like a chicken.)* Bok...bok...bok...

DARCY I was so mad at you. I was all hot and itchy and you kept doing that...

CLARA: And then I started getting them that night.

DARCY But you never had them as bad as I did. My face was red with them I had so many.

CLARA: And Ma kept putting us in those stupid baking soda baths... *(Imitating her mother.)* You don't want to itch, girls. You don't want to scar.

DARCY Shake-and-bake pork chops, baked beans, and ice-cream...

CLARA: What?

DARCY That's all we would eat. Remember?

CLARA: No...

DARCY The whole time we were sick. She had to make that for us every day. And after the third day Dad and Grandpa Joe got so mad about it...they wouldn't eat it anymore. She had to make them something else for dinner.

CLARA: And then they kept sending me home from school.

DARCY You kept getting those fevers and you were tired...

CLARA: And thirsty...wicked...wicked thirsty...

DARCY We'd get home from school and you'd drink all the koolaid before I could even get one glass.

CLARA: And Ma kept saying, "What's wrong with you, Clara? You couldn't still have the chicken pox...people don't have the chicken pox for this long..." And when she finally took me to the doctor...all the way in the car there she kept saying how I had better really be sick. They couldn't afford to take me to the doctor for no reason. *(A beat.)* Then the next thing I know I was in the hospital. And Ma was whispering to Dad...that was one of the few times where I actually saw them with their heads together...talking to each other...asking each other questions. *(A beat.)* And I just wanted to know how come you couldn't come and visit me. I didn't think it was fair that I had to stay in the hospital and you didn't.

DARCY I don't know why you got it and I didn't. We both had the chicken pox.

CLARA: Ma asked the doctor once if it was the chicken pox, and he said it might have had something to do with it...or maybe it didn't. Something about there being no rhyme or reason for any of it...

DARCY No rhyme or reason.

(They sit in silence for a few beats.)

CLARA: I don't feel well, Darcy.

(Darcy puts her arm around Clara as the lights fade.)

CLARA: I don't feel well.

Early Dark

by Reynolds Price

The Play: Rosacoke Mustian and members of her family struggle with life in northeastern North Carolina, attempting to seek love and purpose amidst complex internal and external turmoil.

Time and Place: Summer, fall, and winter 1957. Warren County, North Carolina, and Mason's Lake, Virginia.

The Scene: *The dining room of the Mustian home. As Rosacoke and her mother, Emma, clear the table quietly, Emma probes for Rosacoke to confide in her the obvious trouble she sees in Rosacoke's spirit.*

• • •

EMMA: Whose car was that?

ROSACOKE: Macey Gupton's.

EMMA: Headed to church?

(Rosa nods. Emma glances to a clock on the mantel.)

EMMA: Lord, it's time for pageant practice and Macey's beating me.

ROSACOKE: Getting Marise there in plenty of time.

EMMA: Marise isn't Mary after all—didn't I tell you? She stopped me yesterday morning at the store and said she just felt too big now but that she knew Willie would gladly fill in. I knew it too but I waited as late as I could for you. Then when you didn't feel any better this morning, I tried to reach Willie. *(She has roused no sign of interest in Rosa but continues nervously.)* Her mother said Willie and Heywood had gone for a little ride—at nine in the morning—but that she knew Willie would be proud to serve. So Willie gets her chance after all these years—

maybe God will forgive me before I die! Frederick Gupton is Jesus and I hope he's tired enough to shut up tonight. *(The sound of another car. Rosa moves toward the window to see. Emma waits a moment, comes up behind her, reaches to touch her shoulder but doesn't.)*

EMMA: Rosacoke, you're my smartest child; and I've never claimed to understand you, but I know one thing—we're well into winter and you've barely laughed since summer ended. I know some reasons but I doubt I know all; and even if you are mine, I won't ask anything you don't need to tell. I just want to say, if you've got any kind of trouble needs telling—I'm your mother at least. Nobody else is. *(Rosa does not turn.)*

EMMA: If there's anybody you don't want to see at the pageant tonight, stay at home; I won't make you go. I understand. *(Rosa slowly shakes her head No.)*

EMMA: What does that mean?

ROSACOKE: *(Facing the road.)* That you don't understand.

EMMA: Tell me then. Now.

ROSACOKE: You said you wouldn't ask.

EMMA: I lied. I'm asking.

ROSACOKE: *(Turning, tired but calm.)* I'll tell you when I get home from work tomorrow.

EMMA: You don't know for sure?

ROSACOKE: I know, yes ma'am.

EMMA: Is there somebody you need to tell before me?

ROSACOKE: I halfway thought so. As usual he's absent.

EMMA: He's not. He's a half-mile away—a few bare trees.

ROSACOKE: That's the moon to me.

EMMA: Then you put him there. He's one local boy. Let me speak to him now; I'll see him at practice.

ROSACOKE: Do and I'll die. This is my thing, Mama.

EMMA: Yours and one other human's, if I understand.

ROSACOKE: You don't understand.

EMMA: It's not the first time. Will I tomorrow evening?

ROSACOKE: You'll know tomorrow evening.

EMMA: *(Stands a long moment, unable to touch her.)* I've got to go now. *(Moves to the door.)* Why don't you fix up and walk to Mr. Isaac's?—take him his Christmas candy early. You've carried candy to him every Christmas since your father died.

ROSACOKE: *(Nods Yes but speaks to the window.)* I know my duties.

EMMA: I'm praying you do.

(Leaves slowly, Rosa still at the window.)

Laura Dennis

by Horton Foote

The Play: Laura Dennis (seventeen) has lived with Lena Abernathy since the passing of her father. Laura has never been acquainted with her mother, as the mother abandoned the family when Laura was an infant and has since remarried and lives in South Dakota. As Laura faces the prospects of her adult life, she longs to understand the details that make up the history of her family, a history that ultimately unfolds with tragic consequences.

Time and Place: 1938. The fictitious small town of Harrison, Texas, on the Gulf Coast.

The Scene: *Laura's cousin Velma (late twenties) has recently moved back to Harrison from Houston, with her mother, Ethel, and Ethel's new fiancé, Seymour. A once beautiful girl, Velma has sunk to heavy drinking, emotional instability, and unkempt appearance. As Laura sits on the porch reading Velma wanders into the yard.*

• • •

(Laura is there reading. Velma comes in. She is very nervous and distraught, constantly humming half to herself a song like "Sunday." She wanders around the stage as she talks and hums.)

VELMA: Laura, honey, what day is it?

LAURA: Thursday.

(Velma continues to hum a song like "Sunday.")

VELMA: What time is it?

LAURA: Four-thirty.

(Velma continues to hum a song like "Sunday.")

VELMA: What are you doing?

LAURA: Studying for a history exam.

VELMA: I've slept around the clock every day since Mama has been gone. *(A pause.)* How long has she been gone?

LAURA: At least a week.

(Velma continues to hum a song like "Sunday.")

VELMA: Do you have any money?

LAURA: Two dollars.

VELMA: Two dollars? That won't do me any good. Mama gave me some money, but I can't find it. Is Lena home?

LAURA: No.

VELMA: Will she be back soon?

LAURA: In time to fix supper.

VELMA: Do you think she has any money?

LAURA: I don't know.

(Velma continues to hum a song like "Sunday.")

VELMA: You know what Mama did before she left on her honeymoon? She smashed all my records. Wasn't that mean? Do you remember my daddy?

LAURA: No.

VELMA: Too bad he had to be the one to die. When I cut off my curls he just cried like a baby. When I married Charlie Deveraux he said "what have you done marrying at fifteen." Did you know my husband Charlie Deveraux?

LAURA: No.

VELMA: The last time I saw him he was bald. What happened to your hair Charlie, I asked him, you're as bald as a billiard ball. I knew your mama, did you know that? I was younger than she was, but I knew her. *(She continues to hum a song like "Sunday.".)* How old would your mama be?

LAURA: I don't know.

VELMA: How old would your daddy be if he were living?

LAURA: I don't know that either. No one ever told me how old they were.

VELMA: Didn't you ever ask?

LAURA: No.

VELMA: Well, I'll ask Mama when she comes home. *(She continues to hum a song like "Sunday.")* She'll know. I remember the day your daddy killed our cousin, Harold Dennis. I was coming out of the drugstore and someone said, I forgot who now, "your cousin Roscoe has just shot and killed his cousin right in front of the Queen Theater." Papa was with me and he said, "My God, what's next." He made me go home and he went over to the Queen Theater to see what he could do. *(She continues to hum a song like "Sunday.")* What's your mama's name? I forgot.

LAURA: Cynthia Catherine.

VELMA: Cynthia Catherine. That's right. Where's she now? *(She continues to hum a song like "Sunday.")*

LAURA: South Dakota. *(She reaches in her pocket and takes out the snapshot.)* Here's a picture of my mother.
(Velma looks at it.)

VELMA: Is that your mother?

LAURA: Yes, don't you recognize her?

VELMA: No I don't. *(She continues to hum a song like "Sunday." She gives the picture back to Laura and she gets up.)* I don't think Lena's ever coming back. I've got to get some money. I'm going back to look for the money Mama left me.
(She leaves. Laura looks at her mother's picture, puts it back in the pocket.)

The Less Than Human Club
by Timothy Mason

The Play: A troubled young man recreates a turbulent year of his life (1968) with the hopes of finding answers for paths that have lead to today. The journey back replays the complexities of relationships, the crisis of sexual identity, the bonds of truthful friendship, and the search for purpose.

Time and Place: Fall of 1967; winter and spring of 1968. Minneapolis, Minnesota.

The Scene: *Julie (seventeen) and Kirsten (seventeen) are in the Girl's Bathroom at school, fixing their makeup while looking directly out into an imaginary mirror. The music from the Homecoming Dance can be heard in the distance.*

• • •

KIRSTEN: Okay. Okay. What has he said so far? God, he is just so cute. Julie?

JULIE: Wait a minute, willya, I got something in my eye.

KIRSTEN: He must be just so proud.

JULIE: Dammit, what is this thing?

KIRSTEN: And that suit! I thought it was so nice, the way he said hello to me.

JULIE: My eye is killing me.

KIRSTEN: So what has he said to you?

JULIE: When?

KIRSTEN: All night.

JULIE: Since he picked me up? You gotta be kidding.

KIRSTEN: Okay, just some of the things.

JULIE: I don't know, Kirsten, geez. Guys are pretty much the same. You just let 'em babble on. They're only looking at your breasts anyway.
(A moment's shock.)

KIRSTEN: Not Tommy Sanders. I thought he was such a gentleman, I mean, he didn't have to say anything to me, he's only the quarterback for goodness sake, but he did, he said he was enjoying the punch very much and he thought I looked wonderful and he wasn't looking at my chest at all and there I was, talking to the man of the hour!

JULIE: Kirsten. Didn't your mother ever, you know, teach you anything?

KIRSTEN: She died.

JULIE: Sorry.

KIRSTEN: Thank you.

JULIE: Anyway. You're nice, you should have a date.

KIRSTEN: Are you kidding, I am Chairman of the Food and Beverage Committee, I am practically run off my feet as it is!

JULIE: Can you see what this is? My eye is gonna go solid bloodshot.

(Kirsten examines Julie's eye.)

KIRSTEN: And I'm not the only one dancing alone, there's lots of us out there, I think that's almost more fun, did you see Debbie Meyers and me out there? We were cracking up!

JULIE: Ow! I'm tearing up, I'm gonna have to do my face all over again.

KIRSTEN: Tommy is definitely the most glamorous person here. He's a hero!

JULIE: Kirsten, we lost the game. We lost the Homecoming game.

KIRSTEN: That wasn't Tommy's fault! The other side just got too many points. And anyway, he scored that touchdown, I thought I was gonna die. The way he ran. Did you hear that crowd go wild or did you hear that crowd go wild?

JULIE: Well he's sure looking to score tonight.

KIRSTEN: What? You didn't say that. You didn't mean that. Do you mean that?

JULIE: Kirsten, please, we've only been in here for about five hours, would you please help me?

KIRSTEN: Wait a minute, I think I...Oh, yeah, there's something in there. Look up. You mean like, go all the way?

JULIE: I'm begging you.

KIRSTEN: Oh golly. Yeah. Just keep looking up, I think it's coming out. I think it's. It's an eyelash.

JULIE: Shit! Never ever ever get your makeup from Sears! *(Lights change.)*

Life Under Water
by Richard Greenberg

The Play: A biting yet amusing look at upper-middle-class values through the lives of two attractive college girlfriends, Amy-Beth and Amy-Joy, and Kip, the handsome preppie divorcé they encounter one summer. Set against this triangle is the young man's mother and her conceited married lover.

Time and Place: The present. Summer. Various locations on Long Island's Southern Fork.

The Scene: *As the play opens, Amy-Beth and Amy-Joy (both early twenties) are on the beach. Beth is eager to hear what Amy-Joy was up to the night before.*

• • •

BETH: So tell me.
JOY: You'll die. I'm bad, I'm so bad.
BETH: What did you do?
JOY: You will just die.
BETH: And what if I don't?
JOY: I'll be very disappointed. But it's not gonna happen, it's just not gon—...
BETH: So you went out to allay her fears...
JOY: I went out because the little one, the girl...
BETH: Yes, I know who you mean.
JOY: *Isolde?* Shit, what kind of people name the kids Tristan and Isolde and the dogs Brian and Susan? I mean...
BETH: Your uncle.
JOY: Uncle *Andre,* wouldja believe? Andre Vinegrad as in Abe Weingarten. I mean, the whole family.
BETH: And you went out to allay her fears.
JOY: 'Cause she thinks she sees a sea monster. I find out. I go there, I find it out. The other kid...

BETH: Tristan, this is.

JOY: Tristan—you believe that? A name like that he's gonna have serious trouble dating.

BETH: And then what happened?

JOY: And then what happened is like the other kid's a one-of-those-kids-he-swims-like-a-fish...water baby! Like this article in *People Magazine* and he's in it naked. So he's cool about the whole deal, he's working on her, saying there is no such thing as a sea monster, you know?

BETH: Mm-hm.

JOY: And he's got her just about I would say *half* convinced. And I'm watching and I'm thinking, well, nothing for me to do, a child is more likely to respond to a sibling any-way—I took this Family Planning course...

BETH: Things are going smoothly.

JOY: Things are going smoothly. And I think—I don't know what came over me—I see this little child, five years old—I see this kid, she looks so goddamn innocent, and I think—wouldn't it be kind of neat to scare her shitless?

BETH: You didn't.

JOY: I did.

BETH: Of course you did.

JOY: Who knows why?

BETH: Sea monsters exist.

JOY: In a big way.

BETH: Amy-Joy...

JOY: Shame on me, I know, I know. But you should see this kid. Too dumb for life. Her eyes look like...

BETH: A simile?

JOY: ...Big. Very big. The eyes are very big. 'Cause I tell her these sea monsters in the sea—and they eat anybody's ever been in the sea so too late now—and they especially eat little girls who someday intend to have expensive nose jobs—'cause already they're planning it, you can tell. And they especially *especially* eat little girls with stupid names. And they got these big, humongous—this is the best part—these big, humongous...

BETH: Jaws.

JOY: Jaws, you said it. 'Cause like she's got the lunch box? with the shark? with the mouth? with the kid? with the blood?

BETH: So right now she's...

JOY: Right now she's shitting her pants. But the beauty part is even if she never goes back in the water again, I fixed it so she's terrified. I traumatized her.

BETH: Why?

JOY: Why? Because. It was something to do. I was bored. Because her father's a fairy antiques dealer.

BETH: I wonder what she saw actually...

JOY: Probably Tristan's little zorch.

BETH: Would that have scared her?

JOY: It scares you, doesn't it?

BETH: I'm another story.

JOY: You're telling me...Hey.

BETH: *(Pause.)* Yes?

JOY: You're all right, aren't you? I mean...you're all right.

BETH: I'm all right.

JOY: Good. Let's do something tonight.

The Matsuyama Mirror

by Velina Hasu Houston

The Play: Adapted from an ancient Japanese fairy tale, this is a coming-of-age story of Aiko (twelve). Using traditional Japanese theater conventions, the play explores the cycle of life, from the mystery of developing sexuality to understanding the nature of death—life is reflected in the mirror.

Time and Place: The late 1600s. Matsuyama, Japan.

The Scene: *In Scene II, Aiko wakes from a restless sleep, curious to know more about the mystery of the "power" that is changing her body. Her older sister, Tooriko (sixteen) is preoccupied with anxiety over the return of their mother, Okaasan, who has gone in search of their father, Otoosan, in a snow storm. In due course, Otoosan returns with terrible news.*

• • •

TOORIKO: Go back to sleep.

AIKO: Oneesan?

TOORIKO: What now?

AIKO: …Tell me about the power.

TOORIKO: No. There is no power, only the suffering.

AIKO: I knew you were fibbing today!

TOORIKO: All right, you want to know about the power? Fine, I will tell you since you will probably never get a chance to use it on someone.
(*Aiko leans forward with anticipation.*)

TOORIKO: If you even hint at the fact that you are having your monthly bleeding, your husband will bring you sweets and have the maid cook your favorite foods.

AIKO: Truly?

TOORIKO: If you want time alone to dream, you hint again and he suddenly must leave the room. If you say that the bleeding is very heavy, he will not even want to sup with you or share the bed with you.

AIKO: Truly? Then I could play all night.

TOORIKO: Yes. I have never known such peace. *(Tooriko looks out of the window, nervously picks up her sewing, and starts to work on a piece of embroidery.)*

AIKO: Why must you sew at twilight?

TOORIKO: Because there is too much snow.

AIKO: Let it snow now that Father is home. Did he bring gifts? Did you see him before you fell asleep?

(Tooriko glances at her and then look away quickly.)

TOORIKO: Here. Sew to keep your mind off our troubles.

AIKO: What troubles?

TOORIKO: Nothing. There are no troubles.

AIKO: Father still has not returned home?

TOORIKO: You told Okaasan that rules sometimes have to be broken! She took the horse and rode into town to check on Father's traveling party.

AIKO: What? How long ago?

TOORIKO: Several hours.

AIKO: I shall go find her!

(Aiko tries to leave and Tooriko stops her.)

TOORIKO: A lady waits.

AIKO: I ride just as well as Father. Let me go!

TOORIKO: Not a man in Ehime prefecture will have you as a wife if you keep acting like this.

AIKO: Good riddance. I will wait for a man who will allow me to think.

TOORIKO: Then you will be waiting for a long, long time.

AIKO: Go to sleep, sister.

TOORIKO: No, Aiko, you cannot go.

(They struggle as sounds of horses are heard from offstage. Aiko tries to run out, but is stopped by Otoosan who enters covered with snow. He conceals grimness with a smile for his children. He carries a satchel filled to capacity.)

OTOOSAN: Good daughters. Hello.

TOORIKO: *(Bows low.)* Welcome home, Otoosan.

AIKO: Welcome, Father.

OTOOSAN: Where are you going in such a hurry, Aiko?

TOORIKO: She was going out in the snow to find you!

AIKO: Where is mother?

OTOOSAN: It is so cold.

AIKO: Otoosan, where is she? With the horses?

TOORIKO: Quiet, Aiko!

(He sits fighting emotion as Tooriko helps him off with his coat. He and Tooriko sit around the candle. Incredulous, Aiko puts on her father's coat and prepares to leave.)

OTOOSAN: Take off my coat and sit, Aiko.

AIKO: Tell me where she is, when she will be here.

OTOOSAN: Sit. *(Otoosan takes the coat off of her and forces her to sit by the candle.)* Children, your mother has...left us.

AIKO: What? Where has she gone?

OTOOSAN: ...there has been...an accident.

(The breath is knocked out of Aiko. She sits motionless. Tooriko is quiet with shock for a moment and then she weeps uncontrollably.)

AIKO: *(With an eerie calmness.)* You must tell me what has happened to my mother.

OTOOSAN: ...we will not see her again.

AIKO: What have you done to her?

TOORIKO: Aiko! Please. What has happened, Otoosan?

OTOOSAN: It is not for women to hear such things.

AIKO: I will hear everything if you say I shall never see my mother again. Tell me.

OTOOSAN: The snow. An accident with the horses. Her head struck a rock. When they found her, she was already—

TOORIKO: Say no more.

AIKO: Speak!

OTOOSAN: Too late, too late.

AIKO: Is that all you have to say?

TOORIKO: *Silence,* Aiko!

OTOOSAN: It is not for men to weep and curse fate.

AIKO: What then? To sit there like a piece of stone?

TOORIKO: Aiko!

OTOOSAN: Yes.

AIKO: How can you? What are you?

OTOOSAN: The bearer of our pain so that you can go on. *(Looks downward.)*

AIKO: *(Dazed.)* Was there a lot of blood?

OTOOSAN: *(Surprised by the question.)* Yes.

AIKO: *(Quietly.)* Women have lots of blood.

OTOOSAN: Yes.

AIKO: Were there horses trampling and high winds blowing?

OTOOSAN: *(Surprised again.)* Yes, Aiko.

TOORIKO: After she struck her head, perhaps there was no pain, just quiet…

OTOOSAN: …very quiet…

(The three sit quietly as Tooriko tries to suppress tears. Otoosan tries to suppress them as well. Aiko is surprised by this show of emotion; Tooriko is disturbed by it.)

TOORIKO: Oh, this family. Pull yourself together, Father.

OTOOSAN: Your mother drifts in the wind tonight, seeking her next existence. We must keep the sky clear; we must not weep.

AIKO: Bring her back. *(To the ether.)* Come back, Okaasan. Come back!

OTOOSAN: Enough, gentle Aiko-chan…we must go on as usual…

AIKO: How?

TOORIKO: Shall we sit around like fools and weep?

AIKO: You never loved her like I did.

TOORIKO: I am older and I have loved her longer. *(A beat.)* It is not our way to weep.

AIKO: Is it not equally as foolish to pretend that nothing has happened?

(Otoosan calms himself and reaches for the satchel. He takes out two packages.)

OTOOSAN: Here. Your gifts. Come. Let us be as curious and happy as we always are when I return from my journeys.

AIKO: I want no gift, only the return of my mother.

OTOOSAN: What do you think I brought you, Aiko-chan?

AIKO: Who will I ask for help when I am learning new embroidery?

TOORIKO: I will help you.

AIKO: You do not help. You order.

OTOOSAN: We will all help each other.

AIKO: Tooriko-san will only help herself and her husband.

TOORIKO: What is wrong with that? If you ever grow up, you will bring a husband to live here with you and Otoosan. You will know secrets that will make you selfish sometimes, too.

OTOOSAN: Yes, Aiko. I will find you a strong, patient man.

TOORIKO: In this case, perhaps a saint is required.

OTOOSAN: And Tooriko will always be near. Her husband plans to build their new house just on the other side of the village.

AIKO: It might as well be on the other side of the universe.

TOORIKO: Otoosan, she is topsy-turvy. I walk a straight and level path.

OTOOSAN: When I am gone, you two sisters will be all that is left of our family. Can you not be civil to one another? Come, Aiko-chan. Come sit by me.

AIKO: Who will cook tonight, Otoosan?

TOORIKO: I will cook.

AIKO: You? The taste will kill us all!

OTOOSAN: I have sent word to your aunt and she will come tomorrow to help us.

AIKO: Aunt Yukiko!

OTOOSAN: This is a time to find strength in family. Yukiko Obasan is good and kind.

AIKO: And as rough as a tree trunk.

TOORIKO: But as sturdy and lasting.

OTOOSAN: Are you not curious about your present, Aiko? Perhaps it will give you a little light in this darkness?

AIKO: *(She is.)* Not really. Not now.

OTOOSAN: Please, Aiko.

AIKO: Never mind.

OTOOSAN: Then if I have brought a new doll, must I find another little girl to give it to?

AIKO: Otoosan? What is death like? Could the gods have made a mistake? Can they be persuaded to give her back?

OTOOSAN: Open your present, dear child.

AIKO: She said she would be here.

TOORIKO: Stop it, Aiko-chan.

AIKO: How can I behold these gifts at such a time?

TOORIKO: Because we need to. If I stare at the tatami all night and cry, then I will not make it to morning.

OTOOSAN: Here, Tooriko-san.

(He hands her a gift. She opens it. It is a scarf.)

TOORIKO: Thank you, Otoosan. I shall save it.

OTOOSAN: Do not save it. Wear it. Make yourself look beautiful. Today. Now. And for you, Aiko-chan.

(He takes out a silver, sparkling box. Immediately, the Kuro-ko tinkles wind chimes and Aiko looks around, startled as if she hears something. Aiko holds the box and slowly opens it, scattering dust. She takes out a large silver and gold lacquered mirror with angel hair hanging in shreds from it. It leaves her in a state of awe. Tooriko is afraid of it.)

AIKO: What is it, Father?

OTOOSAN: It is called a mirror.

AIKO: ...mirror...

TOORIKO: I have never heard of such a thing. Does it belong in the house?

OTOOSAN: It is magic. Look in the glass.

(Aiko does and is startled.)

AIKO: There is a girl in the glass!

OTOOSAN: *(Laughs.)* And who does she look like?

(Aiko dares look again. She gasps. Tooriko is curious, but is controlled by her fear.)

AIKO: It is Mother, when she was a young girl!

(Tooriko screams in fright and Otoosan silences her with a gentle look.)

OTOOSAN: It is you, Aiko-chan.

AIKO: *(Looks again.)* She looks like Okaasan.

OTOOSAN: *(Sadly.)* Yes. A young lady.

AIKO: Her eyes are so black. Okaasan has become a child in this mirror. How can that be so? What have you done? Have you put mother in the mirror? Can I get her out?

TOORIKO: No! No! We will all be cursed.

OTOOSAN: Whenever you miss your mother, you must look in this mirror and you will find her looking back at you.

AIKO: ...magic...mother...

(A warm, loving woman's laughter is heard only by Aiko who jumps in surprise and fear.)

TOORIKO: *(Staring at her.)* You are possessed.

AIKO: That is not me in the mirror! It is a spirit.

OTOOSAN: It is you and you are the best memory of your mother. No one else in Matsuyama has such a mirror. You will be the talk of the town.

TOORIKO: And not just because of this mirror.

(Aiko brandishes the mirror toward her sister who jumps in fright.)

TOORIKO: Keep that thing away from me!

(Otoosan laughs, but Tooriko begins to cry again.)

AIKO: Come, look in the mirror, sister! It truly is Mother!

TOORIKO: No!

AIKO: See something above and beyond your straight and level path. Just this once.

TOORIKO: No! Please!

AIKO: Very well then. I shall keep the secrets of the mirror.

TOORIKO: Have them!

AIKO: The mirror will lead me to Okaasan.

TOORIKO: I will have nothing to do with such black magic.

OTOOSAN: It is healing magic.

TOORIKO: I will have tea instead.

OTOOSAN: I brought your mother a porcelain doll.

(He offers it to Tooriko, but she motions for him to offer it to Aiko. He hands it to Aiko. Her pleasure gives Tooriko pleasure.)

OTOOSAN: For you, Aiko-chan.

(Aiko takes it.)

AIKO: Thank you, Otoosan.

TOORIKO: Thank you.

OTOOSAN: I wish that I could have brought back more…I wish… *(He picks up his things and leaves. Tooriko tries to blow out the candle and Aiko stops her.)*

AIKO: Leave it be.

TOORIKO: But it is almost burned away. There is no use for it.

AIKO: Let it burn and, when it is gone, I want its scent to linger in my hair and kimono.

TOORIKO: *(Urging her.)* You must stop dreaming, little sister. Learn to be practical. As you can see, our parents are not immortal.

AIKO: But they are. Mother lives.

TOORIKO: Aiko-chan, childhood is a butterfly feeding on the dew of youth. And the dew disappears quickly. You *must* grow up.

AIKO: No. I must wait for mother.

TOORIKO: Oh, how can you behave so when she has died this night?

AIKO: She is only hiding.

TOORIKO: And you have been struck by the moon. Do you not see that the gods have punished her for riding out into the snow like a soldier?

AIKO: She *is* a soldier, a soldier of the soul, like me! I shall ride, too, and I will return in one piece with Mother at my side.

TOORIKO: Dear Aiko.

AIKO: She is somewhere and I shall find her.

TOORIKO: *(Sighs.)* Maybe in another life.

AIKO: No! In this one!

Only You

by Timothy Mason

The Play: Big-city life and complex labors of love find this group of young people trying to sort out each others problems—with little success. Eveyone's expectations are beyond any realistic reach, and the attempts are deliciously funny.

Time and Place: The present. A large metropolitan city.

The Scene: *Heather (twenties) and Miriam (twenties) meet in the coffee shop.*

• • •

MIRIAM: So. Here are his keys.

HEATHER: Miriam, what are you telling me?

MIRIAM: He won't see me, he won't speak to me, he wants his keys back. Would you take them to him? I just can't see doing it myself. I mean, I could do it myself. If you want me to do it myself I can do it myself.

HEATHER: Miriam, I'll do it.

MIRIAM: Do you think maybe we drink too much coffee? Sometimes I feel like I am spending whatever little remains to me of my youth in this coffee shop drinking coffee. Sometimes after one of our sessions I actually think my molecules have been rearranged. Unproductively. Like I've got a third arm or the brain of an antelope.

HEATHER: Waitress? Two more double espressos. Miriam the problem is clearly not the coffee, the problem is Leo.

MIRIAM: From Leo, Heather, I am free. Free at last, free at last, blow me down I'm free at last. I mean there are other things, for God's sake. Things worth thinking about, caring about.

HEATHER: Well of course there are.

MIRIAM: Chernobyl. You still seeing Eddie?

HEATHER: I try to make it every night. He's so considerate, he says "You don't have to come over every night if you don't want to" but I do so I do. I cook for him, he eats, it's a symbiosis something. But I think. maybe he's working too hard or worrying too much or something, he's getting these dark circles under his eyes and I don't like the look of that. Last week I told him he should get away for a while and he told me as a matter of fact he was going out of town very soon and I told him I had vacation days coming so I could go with him, but when I tracked him down at the airport his trip must have been canceled because he just turned around and went home. Did you know, he's fire captain for his whole building?

MIRIAM: Ah, you may have mentioned it, I don't really...

HEATHER: Last night, it was so strange, I couldn't find him anywhere in the apartment and then I saw this, like, rope of bedsheets tied together going out the bathroom window. He was halfway down the wall but when I hauled him up—yes, you guessed it—it was a fire drill. The man is so conscientious, it's incredible.

MIRIAM: You're very lucky.

HEATHER: That's just it, I should be counting my blessings, but, Miriam, it's not always easy relating to a man who is so nearly flawless.

MIRIAM: I wouldn't know.

HEATHER: It makes me sometimes think I'd feel more comfortable with him if he limped or stuttered or cross-dressed. *(Beat.)* You don't suppose he does?

MIRIAM: Cross-dresses? Eddie?

HEATHER: It would give me something to hang on to.

MIRIAM: Whatever happened to the Movement? Whatever happened to "I Am Woman"?

HEATHER: It'll turn up.

MIRIAM: At least Leo's stopped following me.

HEATHER: You miss him and you know it.

MIRIAM: Miss him? Miss him? Everything he did was wrong. He

was so utterly uncool. Everyone you meet is cool. Everybody wants their space, and you're expected to want your space, you meet someone new it's like, "Your space or mine?" With Leo there was no space, you were always tripping over his soul. Now at least when I look out the window, I know nobody's going to be there. Day or night, night or day, rain or shine. Standing, watching, waiting for a glimpse of me. There's no one there.

HEATHER: You're nuts about him and you've got to do something about it.

MIRIAM: I suppose I'll see him at Eddie's party.

HEATHER: See him? You go to that party and you drag him home by the hair if you have to!

MIRIAM: Heather, I am a control sort of person, what you are describing is inconceivable. You'll take him his keys? I mean I can do it if you can't do it so let me know if I should do it.

HEATHER: Miriam, I'll do it.

MIRIAM: Only Leo would have a key chain with a pocket thesaurus attached.

Sarita

by Marie Irene Fornes

The Play: Through a series of scenes spanning the years 1939 to 1947, this play with music explores the life of the title character, Sarita, a spirited young woman. In the course of the exploration, the nature of sexual passion and the often inharmonious states of desire are revealed with dreadful clarity.

Time and Place: Sarita's apartment in the South Bronx, New York; also the Empire State Building, a beach, and the waiting room of a mental hospital. 1939 to 1947.

The Scene: *In the first scene, "1939—Fortune Telling", Sarita's friend and neighbor, Yeye (also thirteen), is telling Sarita's fortune with a deck of cards.*

• • •

YEYE: 1-meringue. 2-big love. 3-rice pudding. 4-sticks. 5-butterfly. 6-everything. 7-beauty. 8-pork rind. 9-things. 10-string beans. 11-this is you. 12-cherries. 13-poppies. 14-candy. 15-hope. 16-you're welcome. 17-snails. 18-greens. 19-the same. 20-not enough. 21-saffron. 22-teenth which is teeth. 23-roses. 24-a denture. 25-you get nothing. 26-pink dress. 27-rice and beans. 28-something happens to you. 29-a tree. 30-red bird. 31-Rita. Who is Rita?

SARITA: I don't know.

YEYE: 32-no eight. Where is eight? Here. *(Turning the eighth card face down.)* No eight. Turn it down. 33-pan pan pan, like this, *(Tapping the card.)* pan pan pan. 34-we're almost finished. 35-this and 20 no. *(She turns 35 and 20 down.)* 36-sailors. 37-horse's head. 38-old woman. 39-nothing. 40-don't smoke. 41-here's the old man. 42-tea. To drink. 43-lantern. What is that? It's upside down. 44-toga. What

the Greek wears. 45-five. *(Looking back at 5.)* Five is butterfly. This is five. You understand?

SARITA: Hm.

YEYE: 46-onions. 47-you owe me three dollars. 48-many thongs
which is things. 49-naturally. What? 50-sickness. 51-nayts.
52-this is the last one. *(Looking back at cards 48, 49, 50,
51, 52.)* These came out upside down. This one is things. It
came out thongs. Naturally, which came out naturally.
Sickness. You know what that is. Nayts is nights. And the
last one is spike which is spoke. You understand?

(Sarita nods doubtfully.)

YEYE: What did you want to know?

SARITA: Whether he loves me or not.

YEYE: Give me three quarters.

(Sarita gets three quarters.)

YEYE: Put them here.

*(Sarita places them on the table. Yeye taps the coins as
she speaks.)*

YEYE: One, two, three. Quarter, quarter, quarter. He loves you.

SARITA: He does?

YEYE: See? This one is like this. This one's like this and this one
is like this. Don't you see? What else do you want to
know?

SARITA: If he loves me a lot.

YEYE: Give me three quarters.

(Sarita takes three quarters.)

YEYE: Put them down.

(She does.)

YEYE: One, two, three. Quarter, quarter, quarter. Yes, he loves
you a lot.

SARITA: What was he doing with her?

YEYE: Give me three quarters.

SARITA: I don't have no more quarters.

YEYE: What do you have?

SARITA: Pennies.

YEYE: Give me pennies.

(Sarita puts three pennies on the table.)

YEYE: One, two, three. Penny, penny, penny. He wasn't doing
    anything.

SARITA: I saw him do it.

YEYE: Do what?

SARITA: He was with her,

YEYE: He wasn't doing it.

SARITA: How do you know?

YEYE: It says so here.

SARITA: Where?

YEYE: I told you where.

SARITA: You didn't say anything.

YEYE: I told you plenty.

SARITA: You said nothing.

YEYE: What do you mean nothing?

SARITA: Nothing.

YEYE: Ungrateful! Say you're sorry to the cards.

SARITA: I'm sorry.

YEYE: What else do you want to know?

SARITA: If he loves me.

YEYE: I said he does.

SARITA: Where did you see it! Where? Show me! You didn't see
    it! You're just saying it! *(Reaching for the coins.)* Give me
    my money!

YEYE: Your fingers will rot.

    (Sarita pulls back. Yeye takes the coins.)

YEYE: What else do you want to know?

SARITA: You said he wasn't doing anything.

YEYE: He wasn't.

SARITA: Why was his thing standing up?

YEYE: What was?

SARITA: His thing.

YEYE: Was it?

SARITA: Would I lie to you? And he had his hand on it.

YEYE: He was scratching it. He had an itch.

SARITA: He didn't have an itch. He had something else. I know

what he had. I know when he's hot. He was hot. Son of a
bitch. I'm going to cut it off.

YEYE: No, you're not. He was just talking to her.

SARITA: Where is he! I'm going to cut it off!

YEYE: They'll put you in jail.

SARITA: Not me!

YEYE: Yes, they will!

SARITA: I'll tell them what he did!

YEYE: They won't care! They'll put you in jail!

SARITA: Let them! I'll kill them if they do!

YEYE: They'll burn you if you do.

SARITA: I'll kill him and her too!

YEYE: Who is she?

SARITA: It doesn't matter! (*She brushes some cards off the
table.*)

YEYE: Pick them up or you'll rot in hell...

SARITA: (*Picking up the cards.*) Do you think he cares! Do you
think he cares who she is! He doesn't care! He doesn't
care who it is! He doesn't care! Anyone! That's who it is.
Anyone! I'll kill him!

YEYE: (*Looks at a card.*) He was just talking to her.

SARITA: What about!

YEYE: Work.

SARITA: Whose work! He doesn't work.

YEYE: He was talking about work.

SARITA: And how come his thing was sticking up?

YEYE: He was thinking of you.

SARITA: You're lying.

YEYE: (*Pointing.*) Here it is.

SARITA: What is that?

YEYE: Sticks. (*She sings "He Was Thinking of You."*)
He was thinking of you,
that's what it means.
He was thinking of you,
not of her.
He called you.

You weren't home.
He walked up and down the block.
He called again,
you weren't there.
He turned the corner.
He paced up and down
and stopped a while.
She came along.
They started talking.
He was thinking of you,
that's what it means.
He was thinking of you,
not of her.
He didn't notice
he got aroused.
He was embarrassed
and covered himself
with his hand.

SARITA: He didn't notice. Don't tell me he didn't notice. He noticed! *(She sings "I'm Pudding.")*
I'm at school
I think of him and I
I get excited. I do.
I get excited. I do.
I think of him and I'm pudding.
I'm pudding...But I wait. Why can't he wait?

YEYE: Give me a dollar.

SARITA: I'm not giving you no "dollar."

YEYE: What is his name?

SARITA: You know his name.

YEYE: You have to say it so the cards hear it.

SARITA: Julio. *(In a softer tone.)* Julio...

YEYE: Boba.

SARITA: Boba tu.

YEYE: *(Holding Sarita's hands between hers in a position of prayer.)* Put your hands together.

SARITA AND YEYE: *(They sing "Holy Spirit, Good Morning.")*
> Holy spirit,
> bring your daughter,
> Sara Fernandez,
> what she wants
> and prays for.
> Holy spirit,
> don't forsake her,
> give your daughter
> all she prays
> and asks for.

YEYE: Holy spirit, good morning.

SARITA: Good morning.

YEYE: Holy spirit, good night.

SARITA: Good night.

YEYE: Holy spirit, good day.

SARITA: Good day.

YEYE: Holy spirit, good week.

SARITA: Good week.

YEYE: Holy spirit, good month.

SARITA: Good month.

YEYE: Holy spirit, good year.

SARITA: Good year. Yeye, I think I'm going to die. I think I'm going to die. I think I'm dying. Tell me I'm not dying. He takes my life with him when he leaves me.

YEYE: It's not so.

SARITA: It is. Look at me. I'm dead.

YEYE: You're not dead. *(Taking Sarita's hand and putting it over the cards.)* Put your hand here.

SARITA: I'm going to do what he does. I'm going out with every guy I meet. I am. I'm not going to sit here and wait for him.

YEYE: He loves you, Sari.

SARITA: Like hell he does.

YEYE: Ask the cards to make him be true.

(Sarita closes her eyes tight for a moment. Then, opens them.)

YEYE: Did you?

SARITA: Yes.

YEYE: *(Taking the cards.)* O.K. I'm going home now.

SARITA: Good-bye, Yeye, you're good.

YEYE: Good-bye, dummy. *(She drops a card. She starts to pick it up and stops. She looks at it.)*

SARITA: What is it?

YEYE: *(Picking it up.)* Nothing.

(Yeye exits. Lights fade to black. Music is heard.)

Scenes
for Two Males

• • •

Amulets Against the Dragon Forces

by Paul Zindel

The Play: A sensitive yet biting play that uncovers a complex story of a shy teenage boy forced to follow his mother, a practical nurse, from household to household as she nurses dying patients. Circumstances lead Chris (sixteen) and his mother to look after the dying mother of Floyd, a dockworker who drinks heavily and is a match for Chris's blunt and efficient overprotective mother.

Time and Place: 1995, Staten Island.

The Scene: *Floyd has been keeping a street kid, Harold (late teens), who befriends Chris. In this scene, early in the first act, Harold fills Chris in on the situation in the house.*

• • •

HAROLD: *(Calling.)* Hey, Chris! It's me. Okay to come in?

CHRIS: Sure.

(Harold opens the door and comes in, carrying sheets for the bed.)

HAROLD: I just wanted to make up the bed. Hey, what are you doing? You making a dollhouse?

CHRIS: No, I'm not making a dollhouse.

HAROLD: I didn't mean to offend you.

CHRIS: You didn't offend me.

HAROLD: There wouldn't be anything wrong if it was a dollhouse because a lot of people have dollhouses.

CHRIS: I once even met an undertaker who had a dollhouse.

HAROLD: You did?

CHRIS: Yeah, I had to go to his luxury apartment to pick up one of my mother's commissions. I didn't even know undertakers lived in luxury apartment houses. I thought they lived in their casket showrooms, or something, but right while I was in his apartment...I saw he had not one, but *three* dollhouses right smack in his living room, and I want to tell you these were also luxury dollhouses.

HAROLD: No kidding? You just wouldn't think an undertaker would have dollhouses...

CHRIS: He told me how he had built each one of them himself and how he had carved each little piece of furniture inside each of the dollhouses, and...when I looked closer I could see all three of them had tiny living rooms with tiny lamps and tiny kitchenette sets with tiny Mixmasters...

HAROLD: That's very unusual...

CHRIS: And in each dollhouse he had carved a little wooden mother and a little wooden father, and each dollhouse had stiff little wooden children and stiff wooden little cats—I mean, his dollhouses were filled with stiffs—and each dollhouse was sealed behind glass.

HAROLD: I never even met an undertaker.

(Harold begins making the bed. Chris helps.)

CHRIS: Well, it's very strange shaking hands with one because you never really know where their hand has been last.

HAROLD: I cleaned the place yesterday, but I had to do a wash at the laundromat. I almost choked to death up here from all the dust. It used to be Floyd's room when he was a kid, but he hasn't been in it in years. At least as long as I've known him.

CHRIS: Harold, do you mind cueing me in on why you're always doing culinary chores and working wonders with ammonia?

HAROLD: I like helping out. Floyd helped me when my father kicked me out.

CHRIS: Why'd he kick you out?

HAROLD: He wanted me to go to work, but I couldn't hold a job.

CHRIS: Couldn't you be a soda jerk or plumber's assistant?

HAROLD: I tried, but I couldn't concentrate with all that pressure. Besides, my mother wanted me out of the house, too, so she could spend all day setting the oven timer and wouldn't miss a single bus that went by. She waves to all the route #114 bus drivers. I think she puts out a lot.

CHRIS: There was a sensuous woman at the hotel like that who'd see her husband off and then sit around the lobby, but her husband finally caught her and tried to kill her by pressing a bottle of tarantulas on her neck. At least that was the rumor.

HAROLD: My father's got his own girlfriends.

CHRIS: My father has a girlfriend, too, in St. Augustine he really loves—Miss Getters—who can inhale cigarette smoke through her nostrils.

HAROLD: *(Putting the finishing touches on the bed.)* There. You ought to be able to sleep good.

CHRIS: *(Plopping down on the bed.)* Why doesn't Floyd ever come up here anymore?

HAROLD: He told me some bad things happened. At least they started here. He got caught doing something.

CHRIS: What?

HAROLD: Well, sometimes when he drinks too much he just starts talking about it. He doesn't always make sense— but his mother did something really horrible to him when he was a kid.

CHRIS: What did she do?

HAROLD: I think she caught him trying to do something with a girl up here—and his mother went berserk. He was just a kid fooling around with a girl...When Mrs. DiPardi caught him she dragged him downstairs, dragged him down to the oven, she said she was going to *burn* him—screaming that he was filthy and needed to be burned. She just kept screaming that at him. Filthy! Filthy! He says she just kept screaming that...

CHRIS: Burn him at the oven? Are you serious?

HAROLD: That's all he tells me when he's loaded...and I feel sorry for him, that he's been hurt. I know he's been very hurt.

CHRIS: He seems like a nice guy. A real drinker, but nice.

• • •

The Scene: *In this scene, Chris and Harold plot a way to run away together, Chris to flee his mother and Harold to get out of the clutches of Floyd.*

• • •

HAROLD: What happened?

CHRIS: She tried to bite *me* this time!

(Harold goes to Mrs. DiPardi's room, then Floyd's.)

HAROLD: What's she doing in Floyd's bed?

CHRIS: My mother put her there. Where were you? I was waiting for you.

HAROLD: Trying to borrow money at the Mayfair. Floyd caught up with me—and asked me to pick up his mother's funeral dress. *(He lays the dress across the pool table.)* A waitress at the Drop Inn hemmed and ironed it.

CHRIS: She asked if I was his dolly...

HAROLD: Yeah, she calls me that, too. She's always ready to drag somebody to the oven.

(Chris heads for the stairs but is stopped by Harold's voice.)

HAROLD: Floyd was downing boilermakers and saying he found out something about you.

CHRIS: He found out nothing about me.

HAROLD: He's drunk as hell, but says he's still checking. He kept falling off his stool.

CHRIS: Well, that really scares the hell out of me. A drunk shipyard worker's running a check on me while I'm stuck taking care of his cannibal mother! I've got to pack my stuff. *(Chris goes upstairs. Harold throws a few bottles of Floyd's liquor and some socks and underwear into a paper bag—which he sets next to his suitcase.)*

HAROLD: *(Calling up to Chris.)* Where's your mother?

CHRIS: *(Calling back.)* Out! We'll be gone before she gets back. I'll call her from the road.

HAROLD: Did you talk to your dad yet?

CHRIS: No. It'll be okay.

HAROLD: You really ought to talk to him.

CHRIS: He'll let us stay.

(Harold goes up to the attic, watches Chris put his figures back into their shoeboxes, and pack his other things.)

HAROLD: Floyd'll never make it back until after midnight. Sometimes he just sleeps it off in a bar booth...

CHRIS: You didn't tell him you were leaving, did you?

HAROLD: Hell, no. I asked him to lend me a few bucks, but he said no. I could only get eight bucks out of my brother Hank. He said if I was going on some kind of trip with Floyd, he'd crack Floyd's head open. Louie stopped by, too, but he was drunk. I borrowed twenty from the bartender. You know, I wasn't going to mention it to you, but Floyd says he found out something about you and some night watchman in the St. George Borough Hall clock tower. He was even bad-mouthing me in front of my brothers, and they didn't like that. They said they were going to fix him. One time, Louie got some guy to hit Floyd over the head with a beer bottle. He says you know the night watchman in the Borough Hall clock tower— and you know Chuck somebody.

(Chris freezes for a moment.)

HAROLD: Chuck works nights at the Ritz where you and your mother stay between cases.

CHRIS: I don't know any Chuck.

HAROLD: He's the son of some lady electrolysist...

CHRIS: I don't know...

HAROLD: This son of the lady electrolysist says he knows you. He came in for a beer with Floyd, and I heard it myself. The night watchman goes into the Mayfair, too, you know...Is that why you want to leave, Chris, because of something with these guys?

CHRIS: No…

HAROLD: I was just asking, because if that's what it is, then it might be the same anywhere you go. Did you ever think of that?

CHRIS: Nothing's going to be the same.

HAROLD: *(Sitting on the bed.)* You could have told me about it. You could have trusted me. I didn't keep anything back from you.

(Chris stops packing his figures.)

HAROLD: Did you finish your whole story?

CHRIS: I'm not finishing this one…

HAROLD: Don't they tell you the end?

CHRIS: No…

HAROLD: Why not?

CHRIS: Because they don't.

HAROLD: They don't tell you anything?

CHRIS: I didn't say they don't tell me anything.

HAROLD: Then why don't they tell you the end?

CHRIS: BECAUSE I HAVE TO LIVE THAT PART! AND I DON'T WANT TO! I'm getting out. Are you coming or not?

A Bird of Prey

by Jim Grimsley

The Play: A modern tragedy set in a large city in California where the young people face good and evil on their own terms, with calamitous consequences. When Monty's (seventeen) dysfunctional family moves to a complex urban environment from rural Louisiana, Monty attempts to find genuine faith, while at the same time struggling to shield his younger siblings from the temptation and danger they encounter everywhere.

Time and Place: The 1990s. An Unnamed City.

The Scene: *Thacker (seventeen), a complicated, dangerous, outsider has befriended Monty (himself an outsider) and encouraged a bond between them. In this scene, Thacker has encountered Monty and his brother Evan in a neighborhood park. After a blowup between Monty and Evan, Evan has run off in tears.*

• • •

THACKER: Tough for the little guy. Right? I mean, this whole moving to the city thing.

MONTY: Yes.

THACKER: Think we should follow him?

MONTY: I will. He's headed home.

THACKER: You sure about that?

(Monty nods.)

THACKER: Hey man, it's all right, you know? The kid will be all right.

MONTY: I know.

THACKER: You look like you need some relief.

MONTY: Some what?

THACKER: Relief. Like a tranquilizer. A nice hit of something. You ever do anything like that?

MONTY: No.

THACKER: You need some fun in your life, Starch. I mean, the Bible thing is great, but Jesus drank wine, you know?

MONTY: How do you know?

THACKER: I went to Sunday School, I know the score. Before my dad split, he took me. To church, too. I used to have a Bible, even.

MONTY: Your dad left your mom?

THACKER: Oh sure. Old story. We used to have this big house in Glendale. Now we live in this place off of San Miguel. Greasy neighborhood. My mom can't stand it but she doesn't have any money to move anywhere better. *(Shrugs.)* So what do you say, why don't you and me go find some fun.

MONTY: I need to get home, I guess.

THACKER: You guess?

MONTY: To help my mom. She's not feeling too good.

THACKER: You need to have some fun, that's what you need. You take it all too serious, Starch. You need to loosen up.

MONTY: Maybe I do.

(Thacker's beeper goes off.)

THACKER: Hey, all right. This is my man.

MONTY: Your man?

THACKER: *(More cautious, suddenly.)* A friend of mine. This old guy. He's really up to the minute, you know? He's loaded with money and he likes to throw it around. *(Pause; speaking with a strange air, as if compelled to make this offer, in spite of himself.)* I could take you to meet him, one of these days.

(Monty shrugs.)

THACKER: Sure you don't want to hang out?

MONTY: I need to go.

THACKER: *(Looking around for a telephone.)* All right. I need to get moving, call my man. Later.

MONTY: Did they ever find Corvette? *(Pause.)* I haven't heard anybody talk about him in a while.

THACKER: Why are you asking me?

MONTY: I was wondering. That's all.

THACKER: *(Beginning to exit.)* Who knows? Listen Starch, keep it in the street, all right? And think about that fun stuff. I'd like to take you places, you know? All right?

• • •

The Scene: *Thacker and Monty have just had a difficult encounter with some local girls. Thacker seizes this time alone with Monty to probe his background and feelings.*

• • •

THACKER: So. Do you like Donna?

MONTY: What? Oh. Yes, she's nice.

THACKER: She's got a good body.

MONTY: I guess so.

THACKER: Don't you think about things like that?

MONTY: Sure. I guess.

THACKER: I thought maybe the Bible kept you from thinking, like, impure thoughts, or something.

MONTY: No. *(Pause.)* At least she talks to me like I'm not some kind of a freak.

THACKER: I sure can't figure out why she hangs out with Tracey.

MONTY: She talked to me about you one day.

THACKER: Oh yeah?

MONTY: She told me I should stay away from you, she said you get people in trouble. (Pause.) She said you were dangerous.

THACKER: Did you believe her?

MONTY: *(Shrugs.)* I keep hanging around with you, so I guess I don't.

THACKER: I guess a lot of people think that about me.

(Silence.)

MONTY: Why do you hang around with me?

THACKER: *(Shrugs.)* Who knows?

MONTY: I'm serious. I want to know. Nobody else talks to me, they act like I'm a freak.

THACKER: Maybe that's the reason.

MONTY: What?

THACKER: Maybe I like you because everybody else acts like you're a freak. Maybe you remind me of me.

MONTY: You think you're a freak?

THACKER: Sometimes.

MONTY: I don't.

THACKER: *(Laughing.)* You don't know me very well. (Pause.) I don't think you're a freak, though. I think you're okay. But I wonder. *(Pause.)* I wonder if you're real.

MONTY: Real?

THACKER: Sure. I wonder if you're as good as you claim to be, or whether it's just fake.

MONTY: I don't claim to be good.

THACKER: *(Laughing.)* Sure you don't.

MONTY: I don't.

THACKER: Right. That's why you carry that Bible around all the time, that's why you're always praying.

MONTY: I'm not always praying.

THACKER: Come off it, man. I see you. You sit in class and you get this look on your face and you close your eyes, for just a second, and your lips move just a little, and I know what you've been doing. I know you've been praying. And I wonder if it's real, if there's anybody you're talking to up there. And I wonder if you're for real.

MONTY: But that doesn't make me good, to do that.

THACKER: What?

MONTY: It doesn't make you good. *(Pause.)* Maybe I am praying. Maybe. But I'm doing it because I'm afraid.

THACKER: What, you're afraid of going to hell or something?

MONTY: No. I'm afraid of this place. I'm afraid of people like Tracey. Like you, even.

THACKER: We're just normal people. Tracey's kind of strange, I guess. But people around here are just like people where you came from.

MONTY: I was afraid of them, too.

(Thacker laughs quietly.)

MONTY: I was. *(Pause.)* There's a meanness to it that I can't stand. To being alive, I mean. Do you ever think about that? *(Pause.)* It's why I pray. All the time. I ask for protection. I want somebody to protect me, and my mom, and my brother and sister. I want somebody to take care of us. Because I'm scared nobody's going to do that and we're all going to, I don't know. Get hurt.

THACKER: You don't pray for your dad.

MONTY: What?

THACKER: Your dad. You didn't say you pray for him to be protected.

MONTY: I pray for him sometimes.

THACKER: Do you think it works?

MONTY: I don't know. Sometimes it makes me feel better.

THACKER: I don't even know where my dad is, anymore. Did I ever tell you that?

MONTY: You told me he left you and your mom.

THACKER: That was a while back. I guess I was still in little kids' school. And for a long time we didn't have any money, my mom and me. It's just my mom and me. And we didn't have any money. Because he left us with this big house to pay for and these two cars. Mom still talks about that. *(Pause.)* I don't tell anybody about this stuff, much.

MONTY: It's all right.

THACKER: I guess.

MONTY: What did your mom do?

THACKER: First, she lost everything. The bank took the house and the cars, one at a time. Like torture, right? *(Pause.)* I was old enough to figure out what was going on. Old enough to look at Mom and know she was close to losing it. To going crazy, you know? Because she never handled money before, Dad did all that. She had a part-time job and she tried to go full-time but by the time she did we were living with my aunt, me and her in this bedroom with my aunt and uncle screaming at her to get her shit together. *(Pause.)* So I couldn't stand that and I started hanging out. You know. At the park, and other places. And I got into stuff. I learned how to make a little money in the park, and other places. *(Pause.)* Mom tried to stop me, to keep me at home, but I wouldn't do anything she said. It was like I hated her. I didn't. But it was like I did. So after a while she stopped, she let me do whatever I wanted. She acted like she didn't know I was staying out all night, or drunk, or whatever. *(Pause.)* We don't live with my aunt and uncle any more. We have this little apartment. I stay there most of the time. But sometimes I stay other places. *(Pause.)* I wish I could pray and feel better. I wish it could have helped me then.

A Fair Country
by Jon Robin Baitz

The Play: Spanning ten years, this hard-hitting story features a family compromised by greed and, finally, destroyed in the process. The Burgess family is living in Durban, South Africa, while the father (Harry) serves as a cultural attaché—bringing artists to South Africa to improve America's image. In an attempt to get the family out of Africa and secure a better position, Harry betrays his oldest son's (Alec) radical friends to the government. As events play through the next ten years, bitterness consumes the family, compounded by an emotionally overwrought mother, Patrice. The consequences are devastating.

Time and Place: 1977–1987. Southern Mexico; Durban, South Africa; and The Hague, Holland.

The Scene: *Gil (here in his late teens) is torn, through much of the play, between his parents and his brother, Allie (early twenties)—attempting to sort out all sides. Here Allie has returned home (Durban, South Africa) on the heels of a domestic racial incident. Allie attempts to extract the events of the incident.*

• • •

GIL: Allie, please don't make this into something it's not.

ALLIE: *(Exasperated.)* Then what is it?

GIL: You don't understand this country. Nothing is what it seems. You can't run around pretending to understand this place when you're just a visitor.

ALLIE: Maybe you would prefer it if there were no questions? If I just accepted... There's a woman sitting in the Durban jail.

GIL: Well, you're going to take her stuff to her. Ask her yourself. I'm sure she'll tell you what you want to hear.

ALLIE: I am just asking you to create a chronology. It's first year journalism, try and create a chronology of events—

GIL: *(Mock awe.)* Oh boy! A journalism *class!* I'm ever so grateful, do you think I could actually learn, Allie?

ALLIE: *(Laughing.)* Okay. I'm a pedant. Fine. I'm still interested in what happens when.

GIL: All right. Edna. Edna. She had worked here for five months. Very nice. No. Not very nice. Just a worker. Not— I would not say...happy or sad. Allie. I would say "working."

ALLIE: A blank.

GIL: *(Too quick to be trapped.)* No, not a blank. She was just another worker.

ALLIE: And you're saying she just suddenly blew up? Without any signs, without any provocation.

GIL: *(Dry.)* It's been known to happen. Here. In this country in case you hadn't noticed. There's a bit of anger. They get quite cross sometimes, or do you think it's all just smoke pot and play guitar on the beach?

ALLIE: Yeah. That's exactly why I came down here. For the...partying—

GIL: *(Cutting him off.)* Did you say anything to Edna?

ALLIE: Many things.

GIL: Well, what? For instance?

ALLIE: I tried to get to know her. I'm here for two weeks, please don't look at me like that. I wanted to make contact. Have a fucking conversation. Get to know her, her life...

GIL: Are you aware of what you do? You treat them like they're all girls that you want to date.

ALLIE: *(Scoffs.)* That is so completely disgusting, you're not even my brother.

GIL: I've always seen you do it: "Hullo. I'm cool. You're African. Let's be cool together..." *(Beat.)* But their lives don't get the least bit better from it. Their lives don't magically improve because you've befriended them on your little holiday. Charmed them. You're like Dad. You are. Exactly.

ALLIE: *(Exasperated.)* I don't understand. I talked to her. I didn't suggest she fly to Pretoria and bomb the Ministry of Bantu Affairs or try and beat the crap out of Mom. Look. Edna, she had, has, an enormously complicated life. Big problems. Huge.

GIL: Such as?

ALLIE: What do you mean, "Such as?"

GIL: No, I'm just curious.

ALLIE: But, you're not really. All that curious. I mean, if you had been, you'd have asked her.

GIL: And if I had, could I have been of any use? "Oh, a friendly ear?" Please. Allie. It does no good pretending these are your friends. Because they have to do certain things. For instance—get paid. They have these *jobs.* I have been here since I was thirteen. I know something about it.

ALLIE: I would say you know a great deal about it. But what you don't have. What you lack, Gil. Is—you don't have distance. *(Beat.)* Something has happened to you. Something—

GIL: *(Cuts him off. Quiet.)* Please don't tell me. Please don't come here and tell everybody where they don't measure up. Okay? Mother is terrified of you. You know that? Patrice is locked in her room. She's afraid you'll investigate her to death, and judge her and she's not up for it! Nobody wants your brilliant insight, Allie.

ALLIE: *(Backing off.)* Okay. You're right. It's unfair. I'm sorry. *(Pause.)*

GIL: *(Also regretful; conciliatory.)* It must be odd to visit like this. We must seem like foreigners to you.

ALLIE: *(Looks at his brother; he's pained.)* Gil. You just seem like my *brother* to me. My family.

GIL: *(After a moment.)* Did you have a nice trip up the coast? It's beautiful up there. The beach is amazing. I used to explore the tidal pools...Did you find your friends?

ALLIE: *(Beat. He thinks.)* I have this fairly fucked-up life back in New York. Dirt poor. They turned off the lights before I left. I'm cold. But what I have is...it's mine. *(Beat.)* I mean, maybe we could figure this out. You could come back with me. To New York. See how that works.

GIL: Come back to New York with you.

ALLIE: You could graduate high school in New York, you know, with the education you've had here, believe me, you're like practically a doctoral candidate by Manhattan standards. Fly back with me...

The Less Than Human Club

by Timothy Mason

The Play: A troubled young man recreates a turbulent year of his life (1968) with the hopes of finding answers for paths that have lead to today. The journey back replays the complexities of relationships, the crisis of sexual identity, the bonds of truthful friendship, and the search for purpose.

Time and Place: Fall of 1967; winter and spring of 1968. Minneapolis, Minnesota.

The Scene: *Night. A riverbank. Homecoming. Davis (seventeen), without a date for Homecoming, has joined Harley (seventeen), a troubled local boy who Davis is secretly in love with, for deep talk. It is clear that they have both been drinking for some time; Davis is the least experienced of the two.*

(Note: this should not be played as a drunk scene—the effect of the beer has only disarmed their otherwise private thoughts.)

• • •

DAVIS: It's hot.

> *(Harley doesn't respond.)*

DAVIS: Happy Homecoming. You drunk yet? Me neither. Maybe a little maybe. Little buzz. Is that a. That's a fire down there on shore, somebody's got a fire going. I think your mother likes me. She's nice, she's funny. I don't think my mom ever used a four-letter word in her life.

HARLEY: Not even, like, shit?

DAVIS: Especially not even like shit.

> *(Harley considers this.)*

HARLEY: What do you guys *talk* about?

DAVIS: I dunno. *(Pause.)* Dad's on the road a lot. She gets depressed. I dunno, if we talk it's. Stuff that's in the paper, what's on TV and why am I watching so much of it, things like that. She reads letters to me from the older kids. We go to Mass together. She doesn't really have any friends.

HARLEY: You were a mistake, right?

DAVIS: What? Oh. I never thought about it.

HARLEY: Get outta here. You're only about a zillion years younger than the other kids in your family and you never thought about it?

DAVIS: No.

HARLEY: I think about things like that a lot. You know, destiny? Like, your dad slipped and bingo! There you are.

DAVIS: Shut up. I don't. I don't think about them doing it.

HARLEY: Well, Davey, they did. Unless there's something about you you're not telling anybody. *(Pause.)*

DAVIS: I think I'm beginning to feel it.

HARLEY: You want another?

DAVIS: In a minute. God, it's hot.

HARLEY: If it weren't for my mom I'd be long gone. But she's just too all alone.

DAVIS: Where would you go?

HARLEY: Army, Air Force maybe.

DAVIS: You're out of your frigging mind. Vietnam?

HARLEY: Somebody's got to do it.

DAVIS: Why you?

HARLEY: Why not? Why not you? Forget it, you don't have to worry, you'll be tucked up in some college somewhere. *(They look out over the river.)*

HARLEY: Why do you hang out with me?

DAVIS: What? Why shouldn't I?

HARLEY: You got money, you don't get in trouble and your mother never says shit.

DAVIS: I don't have that much money.

HARLEY: Nobody in my family ever graduated from high school.

DAVIS: You're an only child.

HARLEY: My mom didn't, I don't know much about my dad, he

was just this thing on the couch, but he sure as hell didn't get through school, my cousins, uncles. If I graduate I'll be the first.

DAVIS: Of course you'll graduate.

HARLEY: How much money you got on you?

DAVIS: I dunno. You want another six-pack?

HARLEY: How much?

DAVIS: What is this? Two or three bucks.

HARLEY: I got fifteen cents in my pocket and that's it. In the whole world, that's all I got.

DAVIS: You wanna climb on down to the river?

HARLEY: You don't know who I am, you won't ever know how I feel.

DAVIS: Come on, screw you. Somebody's got a fire going down there, we could...Harley. We were having a good time here.

HARLEY: I think about her all the time.

DAVIS: This is who? Oh, Mandy, right.

HARLEY: Amanda.

DAVIS: Harley, she didn't go to Homecoming with anyone. She's just not into it.

HARLEY: I mean really all the time, if I'm brushing my teeth I wonder if she'd like how I do it. I try to brush better. I try to look, you know, more handsome while I'm brushing. It's like she can always see me, I carry her around in my head. It's hard having her watching me all the time, I can't ever relax, you know? I'm all alone and maybe I start to pick my nose or something and I stop myself, I pretend—I don't know—that I was just grabbing for a mosquito or something. And this is when I'm all alone, there's no one there except for this picture of her in my head, watching me. Davis, I don't hardly fart anymore if I can help it. But she doesn't really see me, not ever, I'm not even there. You like her?

DAVIS: I guess. Sure.

HARLEY: She likes you. She sees you.

DAVIS: Get outta here. Gimme another beer.

HARLEY: So I hang around you trying to figure out how you do all the things you do without even thinking about it.

DAVIS: You're kidding. You're crazy.

HARLEY: I know. Who'd want to act like a little wimp like you?

DAVIS: Screw you.

HARLEY: Pretty soon I'll be carrying my books like a girl.

(Davis jumps on Harley, they wrestle for just the moment it takes for Harley to pin Davis to the ground.)

HARLEY: Davis?

DAVIS: Yeah.

HARLEY: You might be an accident. Bur you're not a mistake.

(Suddenly Harley rolls off Davis, brushes himself off, and heads into the night.)

DAVIS: Where you going?

HARLEY: Down to the river. Gonna crash me a party.

DAVIS: God. It's kind of late. Harley! Wait up!

[(Davis turns to us. As he speaks, the table at Jake's Place fills up in the dim light. Only Davis does not sit.)]

DAVIS: We crashed the party on the shore. In my mind's eye these old guys down there, hunkered around the flickering bonfire, were, at the very least, murderers. I suppose now they were undergrads from the University. Anyway they were generous with their beer. When I finally crawled home, praying for a dark house, I saw instead lights on in every room. My mother said, "You have the opportunity to bring your friend up to your level; instead you sink to his." But I went to bed thinking, I'm not a mistake. Nobody had ever told me they loved me before. *(Davis is gone.)*

Marvin's Room
by Scott McPherson

The Play: Bessie has committed her life to caring for others, among them her invalid father and aunt. When she discovers that she has leukemia, she is forced to contact her long-estranged sister, Lee, about the possibility of a bone marrow transplant. Lee arrives with her two sons, Hank and Charlie, who have problems of their own, and a difficult reunion ensues. Throughout the play, Bessie meets the challenges of facing her own death, as she has always lived—by giving love to others.

Time and Place: The present. Various locations in Florida and a mental hospital in Ohio.

The Scene: *Hank (seventeen) and Charlie (twelve) are camping out while on a visit to Disney World with their aunt Bessie.*

• • •

HANK: Charlie? Charlie? (*Pause. Hank goes to Charlie, straddles him, and shines a penlight in his face.*) Charlie?
CHARLIE: What?
HANK: What are you doing?
CHARLIE: Sleeping. What are you doing?
HANK: Can't sleep.
CHARLIE: How come?
HANK: How come you do so bad in school?
CHARLIE: I don't know.
HANK: You gotta study more.
CHARLIE: Get off me.
HANK: This is cool. Your eyes shrink when I shine the light on them.
CHARLIE: I can't breathe.

HANK: And quit letting Mom buy all your clothes. You look like a geek.

CHARLIE: You're going to make me blind.

HANK: And pay more attention. Okay?

CHARLIE: Okay.

(Hank sits back down. Pause.)

CHARLIE: I don't think I look so bad.

HANK: Did you hear what I said?

CHARLIE: Yeah.

HANK: Okay. Charlie, how much money you got down here?

CHARLIE: I have fifteen dollars and thirty-six cents left.

HANK: Why'd you buy that stupid Goofy cap?

CHARLIE: I like it.

HANK: If I ever take anything from you, you know I'll find a way to pay you back.

(Pause.)

CHARLIE: Hank?

HANK: Go to sleep now.

(Blackout.)

Over the Tavern

by Tom Dudzick

The Play: A two-act play about a devotedly Catholic family, the Pazinski's—Chet and Eddie and their four children, Rudy (twelve), George (thirteen), Eddie (fifteen) and Annie (sixteen). The story unfolds with great humor and love of humanity, so, despite the tribulations of daily life, hope abounds.

Time and Place: The time is autumn, 1959. The Pazinski apartment above "Chet's Bar & Grill" in a city somewhere in the Northeastern United States.

The Scene: *Eddie runs into Rudy's bedroom and makes a beeline for the dresser in search of a catechism—he needs to know the difference between a venial and a mortal sin pronto. Note: Although little brother Georgie is present, his lines may be omitted for the purpose of scene work.*

• • •

EDDIE: *(Rudely enters.)* Where's your catechism? *(Plows through the mess in Rudy's dresser.)*

RUDY: *What are you doing?*

EDDIE: Where's your catechism?

RUDY: Get outa there!

EDDIE: I gotta look up something. *(Sees something on Rudy's desk.)* Hey! My good cartooning pen! I'll kill you, taking my stuff!

RUDY: I only borrowed it! It doesn't work anyway.

EDDIE: Moron, because it's not a regular pen. *(Gets Rudy in a headlock.)* You have to dip the point very carefully into a bottle of Higgins Black Waterproof India Ink, like the professional cartoonists!

RUDY: Which you'll never be!

(Eddie plants "nuggies" on Rudy's skull until he notices something.)

EDDIE: Wait a minute! Man, are you nuts? *(Re: nail in the wall.)* You can't be putting holes in the wall! Daddy's gonna kill you!

RUDY: They're small.

EDDIE: That's a railroad spike.

RUDY: *(Takes genuine article from desk top.)* That's a railroad spike.

EDDIE: You're gonna get creamed.

RUDY: *(Realizes Eddie's right.)* Aw, man.

EDDIE: Jeez, aren't things bad enough? You gotta *look* for things to put him in a bad mood?

RUDY: This stinks!

EDDIE: Where's the catechism? *(Picks it up, leafs through it.)* Is an impure thought a venial sin or a mortal sin?

RUDY: I guess I can forget about miniature golf tonight.

EDDIE: He wouldn't take you to a miniature car wash. Is an impure thought a venial sin or a mortal sin?

RUDY: Louie Kaminski is so lucky, man.

EDDIE: *Venial or mortal?*

RUDY: Is that all you care about? Louie will be playing miniature golf with his father tonight, and I'll be sitting home like a goofus!

EDDIE: Yeah, but at least the goofus doesn't get beat up after the game. Come on, impure thoughts! What's the official ruling?

RUDY: Beat up?

EDDIE: You heard me.

RUDY: Louie doesn't get beat up.

EDDIE: Are you moronic *and* blind? Didn't you ever see Louie with his shirt off? He didn't get those bruises from being clumsy.

RUDY: *(Throws pillow.)* You're lyin'!

EDDIE: *(Pins Rudy to the bed.)* Open your eyes, willya? I've seen Louie's father go after him with a belt. Normie Saluzo, too. And you're crying about miniature golf. Just be glad you've got a father who's only thing is he doesn't give an s-h-i-t about us.

RUDY: He's just busy. He cares.

EDDIE: He cares about two things: a neat garage, and being a perfect Catholic. Now shut up and tell me what you know about impure thoughts.

RUDY: We haven't gotten to impure thoughts yet. That's after Christmas vacation. *(Out of habit.)* Georgie, no thumb.

[GEORGIE: *(Ignores him.)* Nnn.]

EDDIE: *(Pages through book.)* You are totally useless… Georgie, no thumb.

[GEORGIE: Nnn.]

EDDIE: *(Finds something.)* Okay, here it is. "What are the three conditions that must be present in order for a sin to be considered mortal?"

RUDY: Oh, I hate this question!

EDDIE: "First, the action must be seriously wrong or considered seriously wrong. Second, the sinner must give sufficient reflection to the serious wrong. Third, the sinner must have full consent of the will."

RUDY: They really know how to take the fun out of sinning.

EDDIE: *(Slams book to floor.)* Why can't they say it in English?!

RUDY: Careful! *(Runs for book.)*

EDDIE: How am I supposed to know if it was seriously wrong? They think everything is serious. I got my ears pulled once for genuflecting on the wrong knee.

RUDY: Well, if you're so worried, go to confession.

EDDIE: I'm not telling this to a priest! *(Thinks hard.)* Except if I die with a mortal sin on my soul I go to hell. But if it was only venial, I just go to Purgatory. *(Grabs book from Rudy.)* Is there fire in Purgatory? *(Quickly finds something.)* Okay, there's fire. But it's not as hot as hell.

RUDY: Where does it say?

EDDIE: There's pictures. The flames are smaller.

RUDY: *(Looks.)* That's a drawing.

EDDIE: Whattaya think, they take cameras to hell?

RUDY: Well anyway, maybe there is no hell.

EDDIE: *(Stunned, he runs and shuts the door.)* Are you completely nuts?! Saying something like that out loud?!

RUDY: It was just an idea.

EDDIE: Public school kids have those ideas. That's why they're there. 'Cause they're gonna wind up in hell anyway!

RUDY: Aw, man! I'm gonna start my own religion. No uniforms, no catechism and no rules—except you have to eat spaghetti on Friday. Pazinski-ism!

EDDIE: *(Awed.)* Man, Satan's having your room painted right now!

RUDY: What was your impure thought about?

EDDIE: None of your bees wax!

RUDY: Just give me the subject matter.

EDDIE: Well...I guess that'd be alright. Okay, Vinny Carducci said—

RUDY: Who's Vinny Carducci?

EDDIE: Who cares? He's new, I haven't met him yet. So, Vinny Carducci told Iggy Sabadasz that there's this girl around here who leaves her shade up at night and gets *bare* in front of her window! *("Bare" is sotto voce.)*

RUDY: *Wow! Who is it?*

EDDIE: That's the thing, Carducci won't tell.

RUDY: Did you see her?

EDDIE: No, stupid, I'm telling you; I only had the impure thought! Now shut up, willya? This is Hell we're talking about! I gotta think! *(Racks his brain.)* ...Seriously wrong. ...Full consent of the will.

RUDY: Wait, that's it!

EDDIE: What?

RUDY: You didn't have full consent of the will! Vinny's description of the girl in the window was so good that you became, like...possessed by Satan!

EDDIE: Yeah! Yeah! Oh, that's so cool!

RUDY: *(Laughs.)* I can't believe they let you into high school with that brain!

EDDIE: *(Calmly.)* Y'know, you're right. I need to study more. *(Starts to rip page from book.)* Like this page right here...

RUDY: Hey, cut it out! I'll get killed for that!

EDDIE: Get away!

RUDY: I gotta take that to school, stop it!

EDDIE: Beat it!

RUDY: Stop it, willya?

(Eddie folds the page and pockets it; he tosses the book aside. Rudy picks up book and examines the damage, holding back tears.)

RUDY: Why'd you do that?

EDDIE: I felt like it.

RUDY: I was helping you.

EDDIE: So?

RUDY: You always do that. You pretend to be friends with me, then do something rotten.

EDDIE: So?

RUDY: I hate you!

EDDIE: Ooh, wow.

RUDY: *(Beats his pillow with his fist.)* I hate you, I hate you, I hate you, I hate you!

EDDIE: I'll live.

RUDY: Alright, then, here goes. I didn't want to tell you this, but you made me. *Daddy traded your good comic books to Green Teeth Malicki!*

EDDIE: Yeah, right.

RUDY: He did!

EDDIE: Nobody's that stupid. Nice try, though. *(Starts to leave.)*

RUDY: *(At a loss, he lashes out at Georgie.)* Georgie no thumb!

EDDIE: *(He plows into Rudy's room and shuts the door behind him.)* SISTER CLARISSA'S COMING!

RUDY: Sister Clarissa? From school?

EDDIE: No, from the Howdy Doody Show! Yes, from school! She's coming here! This minute, hobbling on her cane!

RUDY: How come?

EDDIE: Because of my dirty little mind, that's how come!

RUDY: What did you do?

EDDIE: I drew a picture on the wall by the church dumpster. A *dirty* picture, of course. What else would come out of my stupid brain?

RUDY: How do you know she's coming about the picture?

EDDIE: 'Cause Louie told me. He saw her looking at it real hard. Then she starts gimping down South Division. Alone! So he figures it's gotta be trouble, 'cause they always travel in pairs. Man, I can't believe that woman still gets to me. When will it end? I hear her clicker in my nightmares!

RUDY: You shouldn't have come *here.*

EDDIE: I had to; Butchie Travis was chasing me. There was nowhere else to go.

RUDY: Wait, I thought you could beat Butchie up.

EDDIE: *Will you forget Butchie?* What am I gonna say? She's gonna get Daddy upstairs and everything. Mom can't hide *this* one from him.

RUDY: What did you draw, anyway?

EDDIE: *(Groan.)* ...Me and the guys, see, we're always saying how Debbie Ronski is as flat as a board. Y'know, 'cause she is. She doesn't have anything up here yet. So I drew this long skinny board with Debbie Ronski's head on it.

RUDY: *(A pause.)* That's dirty?

EDDIE: *Sister Clarissa was gawking at it, so it must be!* Oh, I can't wait! Everybody staring at me, waiting for me to explain myself. Even Annie. Man, I don't want my own sister knowing I'm dirty-minded. What am I going to do?

RUDY: Well, if you want something to say, I'll give you something.

EDDIE: Anything!

RUDY: Say that you're sorry you drew on the church wall and that you'll gladly clean it off 'cause you meant no disrespect to the church or to Debbie Ronski.

EDDIE: *(Amazed.)* Beautiful!

RUDY: But that you want no more of being made to feel guilty and unclean just 'cause you have thoughts about sex, which at your age is natural.

EDDIE: *(A pause.) What?!*

RUDY: And that maybe this wouldn't be a problem if parents and teachers didn't treat sex like it was dirty. And that you'd actually like to discuss what's on your mind if everyone didn't get so nervous about it.

EDDIE: And then I'd like the Pope to get me a date with Kim Novak. Are you nuts?! Where the *H* did you get that?

RUDY: From the grown-up section of the library. There was this book called, *Telling Kids What They Want to Know.* They wouldn't let me take it out, so I'm going back there every day and read it.

EDDIE: Jeez, I'm not in enough trouble, you want me to say something crazy like that? I'm going to the bathroom. You're nuts.

RUDY: Wait. Did you get confirmed?

EDDIE: Of course.

RUDY: What's it like?

EDDIE: What's it like? It's lame. You answer a bunch of questions and the bishop slaps your face. *(Exits.)*

The Reincarnation of Jaime Brown
by Lynne Alvarez

The Play: The separate quests of a young New York street poet seeking fame and fortune, and a wealthy entrepreneur who will stop at nothing to find his son who committed suicide nineteen years ago, collide with astrological proportions, helped by a mystical and androgynous couple.

Time and Place: The present in New York City and the Hamptons.

The Scene: *Jaime (nineteen) has been staying at Wilson's estate lavishing in the high life. In the meantime Jimmy (nineteen) has been staying in Jaime's East Village studio apartment, when not visiting his new-found love, Boris (Wilson's butler.). In this scene, Jaime's one-time boyfriend, David (twenties), comes looking for her and is surprised to find Jimmy instead.*

• • •

JIMMY: *(Yelling.)* It's open! Just lift it. It's open.

DAVID: *(Climbs in.)* Well what do you know. Jimmy the juggler. How's tricks?

JIMMY: Wonderful. I'm in love.

DAVID: I see. Congratulations.

JIMMY: I highly recommend it.

DAVID: Is…ah…Jaime around?

JIMMY: Oh no, no, no, no, no.

DAVID: Don't worry, I'm here for a signature, not a seduction.

JIMMY: She's not here. She's living with a millionaire.

DAVID: Hold on. I thought you were in love?

JIMMY: Oh, you thought Jaime and I…? No. She's hit an incredible streak of luck. For that matter so have I. We have a truly karmic connection. Both Pisces. Born on the same day. She has a mansion. I have this apartment. She's got Daddy Bigbucks and I—have a brand new friend.

DAVID: What's she doing with this millionaire?

JIMMY: I don't know—what time is it? Just kidding.

DAVID: Let's go find out what she's up to. I assume you know where she is.

JIMMY: My my, aren't we headstrong. What's the hurry?

DAVID: Here's your hat. Let's go.

JIMMY: I don't need a hat. Actually I don't wear it any longer. It weakens my hair follicles. Does it look like I'm losing my hair? I'm only nineteen, but the brush looks full...

DAVID: You look great.

JIMMY: *(Puts on a shirt—rather Hawaiian.)* I'm wearing colors now. I always wore black. But I feel like a prism these days. Light passes right through me...ah love...Are you sure my hair doesn't look thinner? I can see the scalp.

DAVID: Is Jaime in love too? Seeing as you have such a karmic connection.

JIMMY: If I'm in love, she's in love.

DAVID: Are you ready?

JIMMY: Wait!

DAVID: Why?

JIMMY: Sorry.

DAVID: What?

JIMMY: Today's out of the question. Momentous decisions are pending. She can't be interrupted. No. No. Impossible. I'll tell her you called.

DAVID: I have to see her now.

JIMMY: Now? After you waited three weeks, it has to be now, right this minute no matter whom you inconvenience or—destroy?

DAVID: Right.

JIMMY: Well you're no Pisces!

DAVID: Not on your life.

JIMMY: Don't tell me, don't tell me. Let me guess... *(Walks around him.)* Reddish tinge, brash, headstrong. Headstrong.

You're an Aries, right? Aries rules the head. You're head-strong. Brash, romantic... If you want fireworks, take an Aries. Romeo was probably an Aries.

DAVID: So does that get me your recommendation?

JIMMY: No. Aries are romantic—but have no follow-through. Give me a Taurus. Steady. Built. I'm in love with a Taurus. I have the most beautiful, sweet, exotic big blond Russian Taurus you ever laid eyes on. Silver white hair, blue eyes, skin like a rosebud. And best of all—silent. One of those one-word Taurus wonders like Gary Cooper—the original "Yuuup" man. There was a Taurus. They're so terrific. Like stoked fire. Always burning and just stir them up a little...But oh, I do go on...

DAVID: Where do we have to go to find this millionaire?

JIMMY: So do you love her?

DAVID: I like her.

JIMMY: "Like"..."like"...how paltry. I don't even remember "like." I've never been in love like this before. It's a three-ring circus with four clowns and my head going 'round like a four-ball shower. *(He does a four-ball shower and tosses the balls into a canvas case.)*

DAVID: This has got nothing to do with love. We co-wrote a song together. A major label is making interested noises. I want to talk to her about rights and money.

JIMMY: Not love?

DAVID: Definitely not love.

JIMMY: Look, I know you're an Aries and it's hard, but think of someone besides yourself.

DAVID: Fuck you.

JIMMY: I shouldn't complicate things for her. Certainly not for "like." Now if you had been in love with her...

DAVID: I can say the word if that's what you want.

JIMMY: I'd do quite a lot for love. I understand passion, but business *(He shrugs.)* I mean this fellow is cultured, civilized, rich...

DAVID: And old. All that goes with old.

JIMMY: Seasoned. Well I won't take you. You'll queer the deal.

DAVID: I'm sure I'd have no effect on her. She's probably deeply in love with this man. Didn't you say you two were so cosmically attuned that if you're in love, her heart's going pitter-pat as well?

JIMMY: Actually, I know for a fact she's in love.

DAVID: Good for her.

JIMMY: Well, it may not be. But she has a mentor. Poets need mentors. Us jugglers, on the other hand, we're independent—there's the street, the circus, bar mitzvahs—n'est-ce pas? But a poet? What can a poor poet do? You don't have a lot to offer her.

DAVID: I have a voice that can kill a cow at a hundred yards. I have talent, management ability…

JIMMY: And money?

DAVID: I don't buy into a billboard mentality—money equals happiness—buy this, buy that, own it all and you'll turn into a cougar, jump on top of a billboard, screw the girl in the black velvet dress, and ride off into the sunset. However, if this deal goes through, they may offer me quite a bit of money.

JIMMY: But it won't help you. Sorry.

DAVID: *(Pushes Jimmy against the sill. He drops his juggling balls.)* Looking to get your balls busted, buster? Let's go.

JIMMY: All right. All right. I respond to passion as well as the next man. In fact I was going there anyway. Mercury goes direct today at noon. All this will be straightened out. No more Mercury retrograde. Thank God. *(He gets his things.)* I'm waiting until five past noon myself and then, I'll ask my Taurus to live with me. We'll walk by the ocean, hold hands, kiss, caress, embrace…My God, And I thought I'd die young, poor and alone. There's hope I tell you. There's always hope. Well follow me, what can you do with an Aries? *(David exits first.)* Typical Aries—always has to lead even if he doesn't know where he's going! *(He exits.)*

Slam

by Jane Nixon-Willis

The Play: Episode in the lives of two young "slam-dancers," Linc and Mel, who are on the brink of major changes in their lives.

Time and Place: A dirty, dark men's room in a Bowery punk club on a Tuesday night during the band's break, 1983.

The Scene: *Opening of the play, Linc staggers in, nose bleeding, cuts and scrapes on his arms. His T-shirt is torn, dirty, and sweaty. He wears jeans and cleat boots. As he searches for paper, Mel enters. Punk music plays offstage.*

• • •

LINC: What. No paper products? Great. Just great. What am I, gonna bleed to death here?
(Mel enters—he's dressed in similar garb—is equally sweaty, but his T-shirt has BILE or SCAB or INFECTION scrawled across the front.)
MEL: Here. Broke the dispenser in the girl's room.
(Pulls a couple of maxi-pads from his pockets—pulls the adhesive strip off them and tosses them to Linc—who glares at him.)
MEL: Well, it was the best I could do! That's the thanks I get! Bleed to death then.
(Goes over and dunks his head in a clogged sinkful of water while Linc takes a pad, pinches his nose and tips his head back.)
MEL: Whoo! *(Shakes his head—rejuvenated by the stagnant water.)* I got a headful of concrete on that last one. Whoo! All these memories from childhood welled up and flashed before my eyes! Even memories from the womb!

It was intense! *(Sticks his head under hand-dryer.)* Now *that's* what I call slammin'!

LINC: *(Taping pad wrong side to a cut on his arm.)* I don't know. Wasn't too much cooperation in that last one, thanks to you.

MEL: Yo, Nureyev. Takes more'n me to catch you. I figured you were doin' this ego thing so I didn't wanna interfere.

LINC: Well, you coulda broken my fall, man. A real friend woulda broken my fall.

MEL: You misjudged. Story is you're responsible for your own actions out there.

LINC: More like the story is you're shankin' to catch. It's a jungle out there, pal. Story is group cooperation. Why me? I got a wimp on my hands.

MEL: Who you callin' a wimp?

LINC: You saw me comin'. I hung in the goddam air for three or four seconds. Who was gonna catch me? The girls in the corner?

MEL: Tillie the Hun. She's good in a clutch.

LINC: Yeah, I know. She poked me in the eye with her mohawk.

MEL: I wasn't in a position to catch you. If I hadn't'a moved, my head woulda gotten nailed to the wall by them Florsheim boots of yours.

LINC: Oh, that's pussy.

MEL: Who's pussy? Who's cryin' and whimpering about a boo-boo on the nose?

LINC: Boo-boo? I broke it. I think my nose is broken.

MEL: But that's crucial! What are you complainin' about? A broken nose is crucial! That's like the Purple Heart Award—you'd have to go to Nam an' back to get the kind of respect you're gonna get when you go back out there...

LINC: Yeah. Right. *(Stands up and looks in the mirror.)*

MEL: *(Taking a sip from his paper cup.)* Gives you character.

LINC: Character. *(Guffaw.)* I got enough character to fill three people. *(Carefully wipes away some of the blood from his face—but leaves a little on for effect—then tears off two little pieces of cotton and sticks them up each nostril.)* Know something? It's true. These *are* more absorbent.

MEL: So. How about last week? When you tried to turn me into a permanent soprano? Remember? Think it felt good? But did I complain?

LINC: All right. All right.

MEL: All right then.

LINC: Yeah, yeah, yeah.

MEL: Okay then.

LINC: *(With decorum.)* It's a poor sport that holds a grudge. *(Music stops. Mel listens.)*

MEL: What are they, breakin' out there?

LINC: *(With a shrug.)* Them or me.

MEL: Used to be a time when they'd gig without stoppin' for anything.

LINC: Sign a old age, maybe. I think me an' slam dancing are goin' through a passing phrase. It's tough to set a trend and then try an' stick by it.

MEL: You graduatin' this year?

LINC: Got me. You?

MEL: Got me. You?

LINC: Got me.

MEL: You? Like it's no big deal. Longer I stay in school, the longer I stay away from my old man's shop. I don't wanna get locked into a future fulla numerical combinations just yet.

LINC: What's your old man? An accountant or something?

MEL: Nah. He's a locksmith.

LINC: Oh.

MEL: Yeah. Twenty-four-hour deal. Snap, snap, there goes my life.

LINC: Yeah, but you might meet a lot of people that way. Get a call from a good-lookin' chick who's just been robbed and plundered. Go over, install a Medico, maybe a window-gate. *(Lifts his eyebrows suggestively.)* With a coupla padlocks. Ke-e-eys for the padlocks. I imagine you could meet a lotta humanity that way.

MEL: Yeah. Well. It would still be easier to just not graduate.

LINC: Aw, don't say that.

MEL: I'm saying it. Why, I'm only a quarter of a way through *A Tale of Two Cities*—be a real shame to graduate and never find out if they catch that damn whale or not.

LINC: So who's stoppin' you from gettin' a li-berry card?

MEL: Nobody.

LINC: So get a li-berry card.

MEL: Nah.

LINC: Get a li-berry card.

MEL: Nah. *(Beat.)* So what are you doin' for summer vocation? Get it? *(Laughs.)* Summer? Season. Vocation? Job.

LINC: Yeah, yeah. Ha-ha, Einstein, I forgot to laugh. I've got a solid gold future ahead of me. I joined the Marines.

MEL: Yeah, yeah. Solid gold. You an' the Bee-gee's.

LINC: No joke. I really did.

MEL: The Marines! What the hell for?

LINC: "The Few, the Proud, the Brave"—the Marines.

MEL: What was wrong with being "The Many, the Silly, and the Scared?"

LINC: I need direction. I need a change.

MEL: But the Marines! Come on! That's like 1940 mentality, man. What're you doin' it for?

LINC: For me.

MEL: To meet girls? Is that how you think you're gonna meet girls? Nobody's gonna notice if you're wearin' a uniform. Certainly not girls.

LINC: I dunno. It's a great deal. I'll get to see the world, meet new an' interesting people, do some exercises, get some definition in my chest…

MEL: Yeah, but you got it all here! I mean you got your place in Flushing.

LINC: There's more to life than Flushing, Mel. *(Beat.)* What, do I gotta be bridge an' tunnel all my life?

MEL: I don't have a problem with that. You have a problem with that?

LINC: Yeah. I'm tired of takin' bridges an' tunnels to get places that I feel spectacular in. I wanna travel an' just be spectacular—I wanna be spectacular twenty-five hours a day.

MEL: What about Bunny?

LINC: What about her?

MEL: You think you're gonna do better than Bunny? Maybe some girl from Ipanema or something? I just don't get it.

LINC: Bunny doesn't know yet.

MEL: I hope at least you're gonna tell her. I know a million guys'd trade places with you.

LINC: I'll tell her.

MEL: Well, I hope so. Your bike. Your Harley. They gonna let you keep that in the barracks?

LINC: Nah.

MEL: Don't say you're gonna sell it.

LINC: I think I'll sell it.

MEL: I think you've fallen off your rocker. I think *(Taps his finger to his temple.)* the lights are on but nobody's home.

LINC: I dunno.

MEL: What do you mean you dunno?

LINC: I dunno.

MEL: What you mean you dunno?

LINC: I DUNNO! Want me to spell it for you?

MEL: You're sittin' here tellin' me that you're givin' up your apartment, your girl, selling your bike to go join a bunch of leathernecks. That would lead somebody to believe there's a screw or two loose somewhere. It's like you're leavin' without a trace. It's spooky as hell.

LINC: Maybe.

MEL: Well, then could I have your bike?

LINC: You got it. It's yours.

MEL: Thanks, buddy! My heartfelt thanks!

LINC: *(Shrugs.)* Sometimes you gotta lose a lot to get a little.

MEL: Sometimes you gotta lose a lot to get a little.

LINC: I can't find what I want around here. It doesn't interest me any more.

MEL: But this is the 1980s! There are alternatives!

LINC: Like what?

MEL: Like...like how the hell should I know? *(Beat.)* Do you have any idea what you're in for? Those dudes are brutal. We're talkin' basic training brutality. You gotta shave your head. Learn how to talk in a monotone. And those that can't cut it get strung up on the end of a bayonet.

LINC: Do the Marines use bayonets still? I thought they just diddled around with nuclear stuff.

MEL: I dunno. Do they?

LINC: Do they?

MEL: I don't know. But I can only say one thing. I hope to God you don't come back a weirdo. They have a hard time adjusting, you know. After being forced to eat milk-bones...

LINC: Least I won't have to worry about tartar buildup.

MEL: Trying to jerk off in the bunk without anybody hearing, an' pickin' lint off Mrs. Reagan's suits, they come back with a coupla problems.

LINC: Yeah, yeah, so what?

MEL: So what. I'll tell you what. I'd hate to see you come back like Son of Sam and all freaked out. I'd hate to see you a social misfit.

LINC: I won't come back a social misfit.

MEL: And what's more is you come back—decide you want your bike back—you can just forget it.

LINC: Great. Does that sound like something I'd do? Does that sound like me?

MEL: None of this sounds like you. This isn't like you at all.

LINC: How do you know what's like me?

Scenes
for Groups
· · ·

A Bird of Prey
by Jim Grimsley

The Play: A modern tragedy set in a large city in California where the young people face good and evil on their own terms, with calamitous consequences. When Monty's (seventeen) dysfunctional family moves to a complex urban environment from rural Louisiana, Monty attempts to find genuine faith, while at the same time struggling to shield his younger siblings from the temptation and danger they encounter everywhere.

Time and Place: The 1990s. An unnamed city.

The Scene: *A local boy, Corvette, has been missing for a few days. No one knows where he is or what happened, although speculation amongst his contemporaries is wild. Here, Tracy, Donna and Hilda (all seventeen), consider the rumors.*

• • •

TRACEY: He probably ran away. I mean, you said he hated his parents.

DONNA: But he didn't take any of his clothes.

TRACEY: This is so weird. I mean, I didn't even like the guy.

DONNA: I always thought he was cute.

TRACEY: Sure. But he was gay, wasn't he? And sort of, dumb. I always thought he was dumb.

DONNA: You always think everybody is dumb.

TRACEY: I'm not wrong, most of the time.

DONNA: This is so eerie. I was walking down the hall this afternoon and it was empty and I felt like somebody was watching me. I knew it was my imagination but I still felt like that.

TRACEY: You think somebody kidnapped him or killed him or something?

DONNA: I sure don't think he ran away. Not without any clothes or any of his things. His mom said he went out of the house to see a movie with a friend and he never came back. She woke up early in the morning and he wasn't in the house and his bed wasn't slept in and nothing was disturbed. That's what his mom said. And nobody saw him at the movie theatre. And the last time I talked to him, he was acting funny. He was talking funny. He scared me, a little.

(Silence. Enter Hilda.)

TRACEY: Oh please. This is just too serious. He's probably spaced out on drugs or something, wandering around the beach.

HILDA: You're talking about Corvette, aren't you?

DONNA: They'll find him dead. You watch. They'll find his body in some patch of woods somewhere, like they always do. We'll see it on the news one night, how they've matched this stinking corpse's jaw to Corvette's dental records or something gross like that. I hate this.

TRACEY: Are you going off the deep end or what?

DONNA: They'll come out of the woods with this scrap of rotten cloth that will look just like what Corvette had on when he disappeared. He was such a sweet guy.

HILDA: Oh please, Donna. He was not a sweet guy. He was a total asshole.

DONNA: My brother says this happened at another high school across town. This guy disappeared like this. And they never found him and they never heard from him. His parents even hired detectives.

TRACEY: Weird.

DONNA: Maybe it's a serial killer. You know?

(Tracey laughs.)

HILDA: Right.

Every Seventeen Minutes the Crowd Goes Crazy!
by Paul Zindel

The Play: The lives of the children in a large family turn complex when the parents abandon them in favor of traveling the country to the trotting races and Native American casinos. The absent parents (gone now for two months) have left no provisions and show no signs of return, communicating only by fax machine. As the children are divided about the pluses minuses of being parentless, the tensions mount.

Time and Place: The present, Staten Island.

The Scene: *Maureen (nineteen) has returned home to check in on her younger siblings. She has found the youngest (Ulie) behaving strangely. Here she confronts sisters Gabby (seventeen) and Wendy (sixteen), only to find equally disturbing circumstances.*

• • •

MAUREEN: *(Gives Gabby and Wendy a reprimanding glare.)* You weren't home over the weekend.

GABBY: *(Handing Wendy her backpack, who puts both in closet.)* How would you know?

MAUREEN: I called.

GABBY: *(Sits.)* We went to Olivia Schecter's Bat Mitzvah in Elmsford, but Dan called up with the news.

WENDY: *(Hovers above Gabby's chair.)* Warner Corbin, with the harelip, was going to rent a stretch limo...

GABBY: We all ended up in a Winebago...

WENDY: Nobody had to worry about a driver peering through a limo partition at us making out.

MAUREEN: *(Sits.)* I don't think you should have left Ulie alone.

GABBY: Don't make it sound like we deserted him. He likes to be left alone.

WENDY: We check in.

GABBY: How do you think he's taking the news?

MAUREEN: He says Peter and Jessica are in his room.

GABBY: I wish you'd stop referring to Mom and Dad as Peter and Jessica.

WENDY: *(Kneeling at coffee table, starting to take fishing sinkers out of her hair.)* It ticks me off, too.

MAUREEN: Wendy, are those fishing sinkers?

WENDY: Yeah.

MAUREEN: You're wearing fishing sinkers in your hair?

WENDY: Yeah, they make me weigh more. Olivia Schecter's mother is the school nurse...

GABBY: She catches Wendy trying to throw up all the time.

WENDY: She caught me with my finger down my throat in the lunch room last month.

MAUREEN: Wendy, if you have a problem...

GABBY: She says Wendy's bulimic anorexic.

WENDY: She weighs me whenever she sees me. Weighed me at a mall once.

GABBY: *(Picks up Maureen's bag of pretzels, opens it and starts to eat.)* She says if Wendy loses any more weight she's going to have to talk to the Department of Health...

WENDY: Or our parents...

GABBY: And we don't want that, now do we?

MAUREEN: I'm worried about you, Wendy...

(Gabby and Wendy exchange a look.)

WENDY: Well, we're worried about you.

GABBY: Yeah.

MAUREEN: Was it another fax?

WENDY: That's all they ever send.

GABBY: They can't even stand talking to us.

MAUREEN: Where from?

GABBY: Some trotting race track in Ohio. Northfield Park— They said it's beautiful. No racing December 24.

WENDY: They said it's really a great place and that every nine-teen minutes the place goes crazy.

GABBY: But they're leaving there. They heard there's a track in Virginia where the races are run within seventeen minutes.

WENDY: So like, every seventeen minutes now the crowd can go crazy.

GABBY: Yeah...

WENDY: And they heard somebody in California is building a new double track...

GABBY: Double stable, double starting gates, double wagering...

WENDY: So every *nine* minutes the place can go crazy.

GABBY: They can't wait until that track opens.

WENDY: Last week they were at trotters in Chicago.

GABBY: That was the week before—last week was St. Louis.

WENDY: They said when they're not at the trotters they're at a Native American casino.

GABBY: They look for new ones where most of the blackjack dealers don't quite know what they're doing yet.

WENDY: They're winning enough so they don't need to work anymore!

(All three become silent.)

GABBY: Did you know I've been seeing this guy *Max?*

MAUREEN: No.

GABBY: He's nice but a little strange in that he likes his parents.

WENDY: He's the son of a late marriage...

GABBY: It just happened that these old people gave birth to him...

MAUREEN: Are you in love with him?

WENDY: He's been asking her where Peter and Jessica are.

GABBY: Now you've got her doing it.

WENDY: What's she going to tell him?

GABBY: On a scale of one to ten I love him a three. *You can't meet my parents because they've run away from home and they're never coming back!*

WENDY: *They're just going to spend the rest of their lives going from one trotting race track and Native American casino to the next...*

GABBY: *For ever and ever...*

WENDY: *And they never want to see us again!*

MAUREEN: They said that?

GABBY: Read my lips—*"Never coming back!"*

WENDY: That's what they faxed us this time.

GABBY: It flipped me into a food binge at the Bat Mitzvah!

WENDY: *(Getting up to get water bottle from her backpack.)* You were disgusting.

GABBY: *(Snapping to Wendy.)* I know that. *(To Maureen.)* We got there and I knew I was emotionally vulnerable.

MAUREEN: Gabby, you know you have trouble with food.

WENDY: She asked if she could help put out the food platters.

GABBY: *(In defense to Wendy.)* I started with an Overeater's Anonymous abstinent meal.

WENDY: Pasta, tossed salad, sliced beef, and a slice of whole wheat bread.

GABBY: Like I was really in control...

WENDY: But she started to graze.

GABBY: I mixed with the normal kids and ate shrimp, egg rolls, baked ziti, designer pizza, baby quiches, salmon, whitefish, creamed herring, and humus dip.

WENDY: It was a great dip with just a touch of jalapenos.

MAUREEN: I don't need to know everything you ate!

GABBY: *(Moves to sit next to Maureen.)* Then I felt mentally strange.

MAUREEN: Mentally strange?

GABBY: *(Patting Maureen's shoulder.)* I mean, by *our* standards.

WENDY: She disappeared. I couldn't find her.

GABBY: *(Defying Maureen.)* I started fixing plates of baguettes, sliced Brie, curried buffalo wings, musaka, crab cakes, hot sausages, deviled eggs, caviar, linguini, and Clams Casino.

WENDY: This was like the *start.*

GABBY: *(Begins enacting the event.)* I was shoving the food into my mouth, hiding behind the band.

WENDY: Cute drummer. You were such a pig.

MAUREEN: Don't call your sister that.

WENDY: *(Rises, challenging.)* Don't tell me what I can say and can't say.

GABBY: *(Demanding attention.)* I waited until the games and free party Polaroid shot sessions...

WENDY: The ones framed with balloons. They also had *Make Your Own T-Shirt,* karaoke, and vogue dancers dressed like giant lobsters on stilts...

GABBY: Everyone else was away from the desserts...

WENDY: She laced into the cake.

GABBY: You didn't see me.

WENDY: You told me what you did.

GABBY: I started eating straight from the trays, pushing ladyfingers, strudels, chocolate-covered strawberries, cheese cake, vanilla mousse...

MAUREEN: That's sick.

WENDY: Petit fours, wildberry tarts, crème caramel, and a *Make Your Own Ice Cream Sundae* bar!

GABBY: My heart was pounding!

WENDY: She took a tray of food outside and hid on a dark terrace.

GABBY: *(On her knees behind coffee table.)* I went into a food trance. I had a large loaf of French bread, and I was smearing desserts onto the bread...

WENDY: Everything in the dark started to taste like sand.

GABBY: I'd been eating for over five hours...

WENDY: *(Hands over her ears.)* I have to cover my ears or I'll engage in reverse peristalsis!

GABBY: I was pressing the food into my mouth.

WENDY: She didn't know what anything was anymore...

GABBY: Grace Applebaum and her date...

WENDY: Last year's valedictorian...

GABBY: Came out onto the terrace...

WENDY: They almost caught her…

GABBY: I went back inside to the kitchen…

WENDY: I could upchuck right now.

GABBY: I looked down at the food tray in my hands. In the light I saw large red ants were crawling all over it—and I felt specks crawling around my lips…

WENDY: Ants!

GABBY: Bugs all over the food I was chewing…

MAUREEN: How disgusting.

WENDY: I told you. And she didn't spit anything out…

GABBY: I was so ashamed but then I did something so terrible, so *destructive*…

WENDY: She started poking the rest of the food on the tray…

GABBY: Looking for pieces of food the ants weren't on.

WENDY: She was out of her mind!

GABBY: I started to cry—and Mrs. Schecter came up to me and said, "Oh, Gabby, aren't you going to dance? Aren't you going to dance?" *(She bursts into tears.)*

MAUREEN: *(Going to her, but Gabby pushes her away.)* Oh, Gabby. *(Finally she offers Gabby some pretzels, which she accepts.)*

The Kentucky Cycle
by Robert Schenkkan

The Play: A series of nine short plays, this Pulitzer Prize–winning cycle of plays spans two centuries and seven generations of Kentuckians. The plays focus on the lives of the turbulent Rowen family as they evolve through the years, and probes the myths of American expansion and growth that have produced what we are today.

Time and Place: Summer. The Rowen homestead in eastern Kentucky. 1819.

The Scene: *In the opening of the fourth play in Part One,* The Tie That Binds, *Patrick and Rebecca Rowen's son, Zachariah (seventeen) playfully wrestles with Jessie Biggs (twenties), the African-American son of the Rowen's slave, Sallie. Zach's brother, Ezekiel (nineteen) sits nearby reading a Bible, attempting to ignore his younger brother's cries for help.*

• • •

ZACH: Three outta four!

JESSIE: Ain't gonna make no difference.

ZACH: Come on—three outta four! Or ain't you got the stomach fur it?!

JESSIE: Don't you be talking that way.

ZACH: Or what? Come on!

JESSIE: Shoot, you ain't won one yet.

ZACH: Hell...

ZEKE: Don't you curse, Zach.

ZACH: Mind your own business, Zeke.

JESSIE: Your daddy come back, find us wrestlin', he ain't gonna be too happy 'bout that.

ZEKE: Daddy's little darlin'...

ZACH: Come on, Jessie! I ain't hardly been tryin' yet. Just been
lettin' you win.

JESSIE: Oh, you been *lettin'* me win!

ZACH: Sure! I just been playin' with you so's you'd get to feelin'
confident. Get you all swole up like a lizard on a hot rock,
and then let your *guard down!*
*(He launches himself at Jessie. Jessie ducks and trips Zach,
who hits the ground hard.)*

JESSIE: Only thing I see down around here regular-like is you,
Zach.

ZACH: Hold on, I don't feel so good. Let me catch my breath a
minute, will ya? *(He tries to get up and can't.)*

JESSIE: You want me to getcha some water?

ZACH: Nah. Jist got the wind knocked outta me.

ZEKE: Don't know what you expect, wrestlin' on the Lord's day.

ZACH: Now, what's the Lord got against wrestlin'? Weren't you
just bendin' my ear the other day about a Jacob or somebody? Didn't he wrestle him an angel or somethin'?

ZEKE: He didn't wrestle him no field hand, and he sure didn't
wrestle him on the Sabbath!

ZACH: Ezekiel, that preacher may have saved your soul, but he
sure turned your brains to spoonbread.

JESSIE: Praise the Lord!

ZACH: Amen!

ZEKE: You boys laugh all you want now. Ain't gonna be no sin-
gin' where you headed—

ZACH: Oh, no!

JESSIE: Save me, Jesus!

ZEKE: —and you both gonna be a whole lot thirstier!

ZACH: Hold on there, I think mebbe I broke somethin'.

JESSIE: What?

ZACH: I don't know what! Somethin' inside. Oh shit, Jessie, I'm
spittin' blood.

ZEKE: You see!

ZACH: Shut up, Zeke.

JESSIE: I'll get your daddy.

ZACH: NO! Pa hears I hurt myself 'fore we get that second plantin' done, he'll nail my hide to the door. Gimme a hand— get me in the house and wrap this side of mine up.
(Jessie bends down to lift Zach up. Zach grabs him and flips him over, pinning him to the ground.)

ZACH: I told ya! I told you I'd git ya!

JESSIE: You sneaky piece of shit.

ZACH: I got you now, boy!

JESSIE: YOU got me, huh?

ZACH: Yessir!

JESSIE: You sure of that?

ZACH: Sure as my redeemer liveth!

JESSIE: All right, then. *(Jessie flips Zach over and pins him.)*

ZACH: Ahhh! You're chokin' me!

JESSIE: What?

ZACH: You're chokin' me!

JESSIE: Cain't hear you, Zach, you sound all choked up.

ZACH: Chkkkngmmmeee...

JESSIE: Did you say "uncle"?

ZACH: Uggghhhh...

JESSIE: Sound like "uncle" to you, Zeke?

ZEKE: Sounds like "more" to me.

JESSIE: You think so?

ZEKE: Well, give him a squeeze, let's find out.

ZACH: UNCLE!
(Jessie releases him.)

ZACH: Damn, Zeke! You just gonna sit there while somebody chokes the life outta your little brother? What the hell kinda family feelin' is that?!

ZEKE: I told you, Zach, you supposed to remember the Sabbath and keep it holy. It hurt me somethin' fierce to watch you suffer like that but I figure if it brings you closer to God, well, that's just the price I gotta pay.

ZACH: Shoot! You listen to that, Jessie? Man's just a natural-born coward, hidin' behind the Scriptures.

JESSIE: No sir, I think Mr. Zeke done got him the Spirit, all right. But it ain't Jesus got him by the short hairs.

ZACH: You ain't talkin' 'bout that mousy little thing live up on the Buckhorn, are ya?

JESSIE: Miss Joleen Johnston?

ZACH: That's the one!

ZEKE: That's enough of that.

ZACH: You pullin' my leg?

JESSIE: No sir! I hear that woman got your brother on a short rope.

ZACH: Well, I'll be! You mean all this prayin' and studyin'...

JESSIE: Them clean hands and shiny boots...

ZACH: That six-mile walk over and back to meetin's ever Sunday...

JESSIE: Yes sir.

ZACH: That all for some *woman?* That true, Ezekiel? Ol' Joleen got you towin' the line here and that's why you become this overnight holier-than-thou pain in the butt!

ZEKE: You keep your smart mouth offa Joleen!

JESSIE: Look out, kettle's boilin'!

ZACH: Well, I reckon I can keep my mouth offa her, but can anybody else?

ZEKE: You gonna eat them words!

JESSIE: Boilin' over!

ZACH: Way I heard it, 'fore she found Jesus, Joleen get down on her knees for just about anybody!

ZEKE: YOU SON OF A BITCH!

Life Under Water

by Richard Greenberg

The Play: A biting yet amusing look at upper-middle-class values through the lives of two attractive college girlfriends, Amy-Beth and Amy-Joy, and Kip, the handsome preppie divorcé they encounter one summer. Set against this triangle is the young man's mother and her conceited married lover.

Time and Place: The present. Summer. Various locations on Long Island's Southern Fork.

The Scene: *Amy-Beth and Amy-Joy are sunning on the beach, when Kip comes on, woozy from a night of drinking.*

• • •

JOY: Looking for somebody?
   (He collapses.)
JOY: God!
BETH: Who is that?
JOY: How do I know?
BETH: What are you doing, going to him? He could be dangerous.
JOY: I think I can handle myself. *(She kneels beside him, starts shaking him mildly, slapping his face.)* Hey. Hey! Are you all right? Hey! Wake up. Come on, wake up! Jesus, you must have had a night. Do you think he's cute?
BETH: Please.
JOY: Wake up.
   (Kip begins groggily to awaken.)
KIP: What's happening?
JOY: Who are you?
KIP: What...?
JOY: Your name.
KIP: Kip.

JOY: That's perfect…Are you sick?

KIP: I've been walking.

JOY: Walking where…?

KIP: All over. All night. I'm looking for…

JOY: What…?

KIP: Work.

JOY: Looking for work? All night? Very few people hire at 4:00 A.M.

KIP: No…I was…

JOY: What?

KIP: Running away.

JOY: Are you a fugitive?

KIP: In a manner of speaking.

JOY: What did you do?

KIP: Had a mother.

JOY: What? You're running away from home?

KIP: I guess so, yes.

JOY: Did you bring your skate key and a twinkie?

KIP: It may sound juvenile, but it's not.

JOY: No, I'm sure.

KIP: God, I must have walked twenty miles. I kept looking for a refuge. I recognized every house. Everybody in every house. They were all members of the club.

JOY: Which club?

KIP: Whichever. I don't know you.

JOY: I'm visiting.

KIP: Good. Nice…Oh God! I'm in no condition to face what I have to face.

JOY: What's that?

KIP: Poverty. I'm penniless. And I'm trying to make my way to the city. Do you have work?

JOY: …That depends.

KIP: I'll do anything. I'll mow your lawn.

JOY: There's no lawn. Why can't you just go home and get money?

KIP: Never. I can't even go in the vicinity of that place again.

I'm not very resourceful. This was a whim and I've got to stick to it or I'm dead. Dead. Finished. I just want to get to New York.

BETH: He's lying.

JOY: Hitch.

KIP: That's dangerous.

JOY: What about a ride from a friend?

KIP: I have no friends.

JOY: Oh.

KIP: Are you sure there's not something I can do?

JOY: …You can…hang out…

KIP: Excuse me?

JOY: Here.

BETH: Amy-Joy!

JOY: There are all these rooms and no people. Like you can stay here until you find a lawn to mow. You know? I mean—we got these two kids we gotta take care of—my cousins…You can help, we'll pay for that, I mean I will.

KIP: Is it legitimate work?

JOY: Wait till you meet them. They were raised by wolves.

KIP: I like children.

JOY: *Now* you say that.

BETH: Amy-Joy, this is ridiculous!

KIP: I don't know your name.

JOY: *(When Amy-Beth says nothing.)* Amy-Beth. She'll like you once she gets to know you.

BETH: That's never going to happen.

KIP: You really will, though. I'm very nice. I'm…harmless. I promise, I won't wear out my welcome.

BETH: You'll have to leave retroactively.

JOY: She doesn't mean it.

KIP: Look—I'm sorry—it's just that I can't go back there. Not if I want to be human. And I do. My mother's life is depraved. I like you two. Automatically. Instantaneously. You're not like the people I know. This gives me a lot of hope.

JOY: Why don't you go up to the house...

BETH: No!

JOY: ...To the house where people are allowed to stay only because I say so...and why don't you clean up? I'll be up in a minute and get you something for your hangover. Be careful of Tristan and Isolde. They're playing Apache.

KIP: Which house is it?

JOY: The big glass one at the edge of the hill.

KIP: Thank you. *(To Amy-Beth.)* We'll get along well. You'll see. *(He exits. Amy-Joy smiles. Amy-Beth glares at her. then looks away. They sit, not looking at each other.)*

BETH: Shit.

JOY: He'll give us something to do.

PERMISSION ACKNOWLEDGMENTS

253

254

Grateful thanks are given to Lynne Alvarez and Brad Slaight for contributing to the "Dramatic Études" section.

CRAIG SLAIGHT is the Director of the Young Conservatory at American Conservatory Theater. As both a director and an acting teacher, Craig has worked passionately to provide a creative and dynamic place for young people to learn and grow in theater arts. With a particular commitment to expanding the body of dramatic literature available to young people, Craig has published six acting anthologies, *Great Scenes for Young Actors from the Stage, Great Monologues for Young Actors Volume I* and *Volume II, Great Scenes and Monologues for Children, Multicultural Scenes for Young Actors, Multicultural Monologues for Young Actors,* and *Short Plays for Young Actors,* co-edited by A.C.T.'s Jack Sharrar. *Great Monologues for Young Actors, Multicultural Monologues for Young Actors,* and *Multicultural Scenes for Young Actors* were selected by the New York Public Library as Outstanding Books for the Teenage. Additionally, Craig began the New Plays Program at the Young Conservatory in 1989 with the mission to develop plays by professional playwrights that view the world through the eyes of the young. This past summer he directed the world-premiere of Lynne Alvarez's *Analiese* for the New Plays Program. The first nine New Plays are collected in publications by Smith and Kraus publishers, *New Plays from the A.C.T. Young Conservatory, Volume I* and *Volume II. Volume II* also received recognition from the New York Public Library as an Outstanding Book for the Teenage in 1997. Educated in Michigan in Theater and English, Craig taught at the junior and senior high school, college, and university levels, prior to moving to Los Angeles, where he spent ten years as a professional director (directing such notables as Julie Harris, Linda Purl, Betty Garrett, Harold Gould, Patrick Duffey, and Robert Foxworth). Since joining A.C.T., Craig has often served as Associate Director for main stage productions. Last season, he served as Associate Director for Carey Perloff's production of *The Rose Tattoo* by Tennessee Williams. In addition to the work at A.C.T., Craig is a consultant to the Educational Theater Association, the National Foundation for Advancement in the Arts, and is a frequent guest artist, speaker, workshop leader, and adjudicator for festivals and conferences throughout the country. In August of 1994, Slaight received the President's Award from The Educational Theater Association for outstanding contributions to youth theater.

JACK SHARRAR is Director of Academic Affairs for the American Conservatory Theater, where he serves on the MFA committee and teaches a variety of classes in the Young Conservatory. Dr. Sharrar is a graduate of the University of Michigan and holds a Ph.D. in theater history and dramatic literature from the University of Utah. His professional theater credits include roles at Michigan Repertory Theater, Mountainside Theater, the BoarsHead Theater, Theatre 40, Pioneer Theatre Company, and A.C.T. Studio. He has directed over 50 plays and musicals in secondary school, universities, and professional theaters, and is a member of Actors' Equity and the Screen Actor's Guild. He is author of *Avery Hopwood, His Life and Plays;* contributor to Oxford University Press's *The American National Biography;* and coeditor (with Craig Slaight) of *Great Scenes for Young Actors from the Stage, Great Monologues for Young Actors, Great Scenes and Monologues for Children, Multicultural Monologues for Young Actors, Multicultural Scenes for Young Actors,* and *Short Plays for Young Actors. Great Monologues for Young Actors, Multicultural Monologues for Young Actors,* and *Multicultural Scenes for Young Actors* were selected by the New York Public Library as Outstanding Books for the Teenage.